MOTORCYCLE TOURING

IN THE
PACIFIC NORTHWEST

The Region's Best Rides

CHRISTY KARRAS
STEPHEN ZUSY

gpp®

Guilford, Connecticut

To buy books in quantity for corporate use or incentives, call **(800) 962–0973** or e-mail **premiums@GlobePequot.com.**

Stephen Zusy photos: pages i, vi, xi, xxiii, 2, 4, 10, 19, 20, 21, 27, 29, 30, 31, 34, 39, 42, 43, 50, 52, 54, 60, 61, 63, 69, 72, 74, 79, 80, 82, 87, 89, 90, 93, 99, 101, 103, 108, 110, 112, 116, 118, 125, 126, 127, 133, 135, 140, 143, 144, 175, 176, 178, 182, 208, 213, 215, 233, 239, 242, 244, 249, 251, 252, 254, 259, 262, 263, 264, 268, 270, 272, 274, 276, 278, 292, 296, 297, 301, 303, 305, 308, 311, 312, 320, 321, 322, 326, 327, 329, 336, 339, 340

Christy Karras photos: pages xiv, xvi, xix, 8, 148, 151, 154, 155, 157, 158, 162, 164, 166, 167, 187, 190, 195, 197, 199, 201, 210, 220, 221, 223, 225, 227, 231, 235

Katrina Frank photo: page 191

P. M. Graham photos: pages 285, 287, 288

Text design by Sheryl P. Kober
Text layout by Melissa Evarts
Maps by Trailhead Graphics, Inc. © Morris Book Publishing, LLC

Library of Congress Cataloging-in-Publication Data is available on file.

ISBN 978-0-7627-5727-5

Printed in China
10 9 8 7 6 5 4 3 2 1

CONTENTS

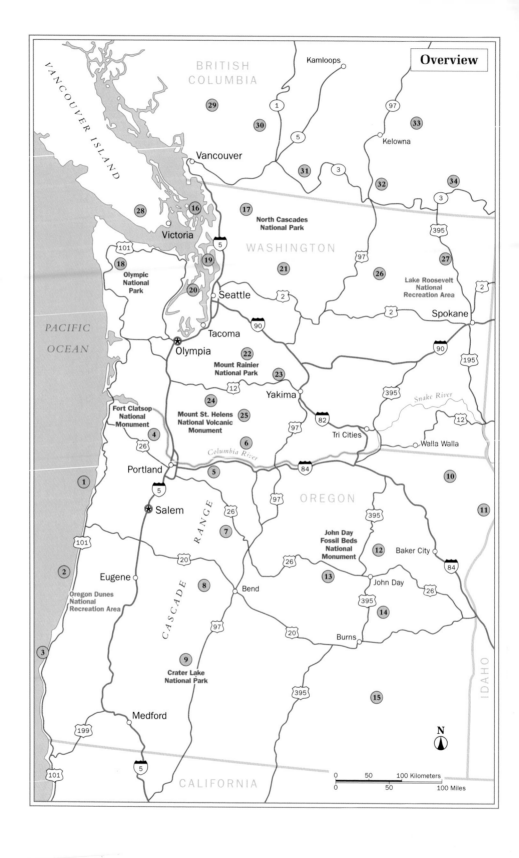

Fallen giants lie at the feet of the next generation on many of the Northwest's coastal beaches.

ACKNOWLEDGMENTS

We could never have written this book without the help of many people, so many that it's impossible to thank them all in this space.

We'd like to thank the rangers, tourist-information officers, innkeepers, restaurant owners, and fellow travelers who gave us advice and helped us plan our next steps. Thanks to our editors and everyone else at Globe Pequot who help make us look better in print than we do in person.

Our friends and family put up with a lot from us, including long absences while we were either on the road or huddled behind our computers. Your patience, understanding, and continued support are much appreciated.

Finally, thanks to every fellow biker who said hello at a rest stop or gas station, waved as you passed, or gave a tip on where to ride, eat, or drink—and better yet, where not to. It doesn't matter what you ride, where you're headed, or how far you plan to go, we all know that a bad day on two wheels is better than a good day on four.

Christy:
Thanks to the enthusiastic and welcoming riders of the Northwest, especially in the Puget Sound region, who welcomed me as a newcomer in their midst.

Thanks to Steve for being intrepid, unfaltering, and stubborn enough to make this thing work. Through the process of writing two books, I've come to know, in many ways, what it means to be a coauthor. And when the project in question is a book about motorcycle touring, it means a lot more. Steve has taken on much of the work of running this enterprise, and for that I'm more grateful than he would ever believe. It hasn't always been easy, but we have always made it work.

Finally, thanks to my fiancé, Bill, who joined me on an eighteen-month adventure that entailed writing three books on top of moving three times, remodeling a house, and taking on new responsibilities as we tried to figure out the next stage in our lives. You're the best sweetie a girl could ask for.

Steve:

A sincere and heartfelt thanks to my friends Andy and Dixie Noel and their son, Milo, for providing a much appreciated home-away-from-home in Portland. Milo, when you're old enough, if your mom allows it, I promise to give you a ride on the back of the bike . . . vroom, vroom!

A very special thank you to my friend Emy Noel for her constant support and encouragement during the research and writing of this book. Her belief in my ability to succeed surpasses that of anyone I've ever known, and her passion, drive, and talent continue to inspire me. She provided a sanctuary with hot meals and cold beer at the end of many a long day on the road, for which I can't thank her enough. Please don't let me forget I owe you a ride across the Southwest.

Thanks to Michelle McDonald for keeping an eye on my place and for watering my plants while I was on the road. My trust was well placed; as expected, all my plants were flourishing upon my return.

Thanks to Bruce Henriksen, a fellow biker I met in Detroit, Oregon, at the beginning of my journey and bumped into occasionally during my travels. He was a valuable source for "must do" rides, a few "secret" back roads, and hot springs in almost every corner of Oregon.

I would be remiss if I didn't thank Christy, who is perhaps the best proofreader, editor, and writing coach I know. She's been relentless in her effort to help improve my writing, and I hope she will agree that it has. I continue to put my faith and trust in her ability to critically edit and skillfully craft my rough drafts into more interesting and readable chapters, making the book far better than it would otherwise be.

INTRODUCTION

As anyone who rides a motorcycle knows, there's just nothing else like hitting the road on a bike. The scenery is more vivid when you have a nearly 360-degree view, and you feel the wind, the sun, and sometimes the rain—all of which makes you feel alive.

Being on a bike—away from the creature comforts and thick steel-and-glass shell of a car—gives us a rare combination of attention and meditation. It's the sort of sensation people work really hard to find: they do yoga, they do drugs, they seek religion, and they still might never achieve it. We find it through a good day on the road. And fortunately, motorcycle touring is both fun and legal.

In the Pacific Northwest, touring means scaling mountains, including the Cascade Range that forms the region's spine and features dozens of distinctive, snowcapped volcanic cones. It means knowing the vast Pacific Ocean is always somewhere off to the west, sometimes just a few feet from the road. It means following right alongside some of the thousands of rivers that carve out canyons, and curves for the many roads that parallel them. And it means exploring arid regions that most people don't even consider when they think of the Northwest, but which contain some of the best (and warmest) riding.

This book is for anyone seeking suggestions on where to tour in the Northwest. Obviously, any ride description will be most helpful for those new to the roads in question, though we hope to include tidbits to inform and entertain any reader.

This book is broken into rides of about a hundred to several hundred miles. Most of them represent a half to a full day of riding, though some are multiday rides.

We know we're leaving out some good rides. There are so many roads in the Northwest that covering them all would require writing a set of encyclopedias (and we are not going to sit behind a desk long enough to do that). This book is meant to give you some good options to explore the region, as well as useful tips and interesting background, and to encourage you to explore further. If you've got your map spread out and a road looks good, try it—with the caveat that roads that start in poor condition probably won't get better as they go along.

The Northwest's urban areas center around three major cities: Vancouver, British Columbia; Seattle, Washington; and Portland, Oregon. You may notice that we don't talk much about them. That's because for one thing, any one of them is worthy of its own travel guide, and those have already been written. For another, when we tour, we prefer to spend our time in smaller, less-expensive, more-navigable towns with more character.

The Northwest's big cities have a lot in common: great amenities, lots of history, and thriving culture—as well as aggravating roads with slow traffic, confusing layouts, and lots of pedestrians. We do advise you to explore them, and a fair number of the rides are written with one of them as a starting point. Because they're confusing, get a map before you try riding in them (especially if you ever want to leave). And remember that the pavement can be as bad in the city, if not worse, than on a mountain pass.

One of the best things about the Northwest has nothing to do with the roads or the scenery, and it's one of the best things about riding anywhere. No matter who you are, and, almost without exception, no matter what you ride, you're part of a sprawling fellowship of bikers—and that means immediate respect and friendship. Time and again in our travels, we've encountered all kinds of folks, on all kinds of bikes, who struck up conversations, offered help, and sometimes invited us to ride with them because we pulled up on a bike. There is a different sense of rules, biker to biker, a protocol that says you extend friendship first and ask questions later.

Within that fellowship of riders, those in the Northwest are some of the friendliest we've ever come across. Canadian riders are even more so. Motorcycle clubs get together and ride pretty much whenever the sun shines, usually without any membership

A rainbow breaks out above BC 3 as the road climbs into the hills above Rock Creek in British Columbia.

requirements besides a bike. It's a wonderful feeling to know that this network is out there, even if you're riding alone, and it will be there if you need it.

While everything you've heard about the Northwest's long winters and unpredictable weather is true, summer still follows winter, and foul weather eventually blows through. Don't let the prospect of riding in the rain prevent you from exploring this wonderfully diverse corner of the country. Fire up the engine, pull back on the throttle, and venture forth, seeking out new pavement, making new friends, and experiencing everything that makes the Northwest unique.

HELPFUL INFORMATION

Like any region, the Northwest presents its own set of challenges, some of which could potentially ruin a trip for even the most experienced biker. Here is some information to help you prepare for such eventualities and make the most of your trip.

WEATHER

Yes, the weather here is cool. West of the Cascades or in the mountains, temperatures even in summer will rarely rise above 80 degrees. The region's plentiful mountainous terrain means cool—even cold—days, and colder nights.

It's also notoriously unpredictable. Check the forecast before heading out, but know that it may change before you reach your destination. We've ridden in hail, rain at 50-degree temperatures, and 90-degree heat—and those extremes were all in June. In Oregon, when it's hot in the valleys between the coastal mountains

Steve: My first attempt to ride in Canada is a good illustration of the variable weather. When I left Portland, it was supposed to be clear for a week. I rode through 90-plus-degree heat, hit wild thunderstorms at the Canadian border, sat out a day of rain in a motel in Colville, and bailed out through central Washington with a bunch of other riders who were also trying to escape the storms. Washington east of the Cascades was about the only dry place in the region. I made my way back to Oregon, where it was raining in the Columbia Gorge and temperatures were in the 60s in Bend, with thunderstorms raging to the south and west.

I woke up to a frost-covered bike and frozen water bottles south of Bend in late August. It rained like hell on the Olympic Peninsula when it was supposed to be clear—I guess the storm moved in ahead of schedule. ●

Christy: No one ever knows what kind of summer it will be. In Seattle, things are supposed to be cool and rainy through the Fourth of July and sunny with temperatures in the 70s from mid-July through mid-September. But in the summer of 2009, Western Washington got hot in June and stayed that way through September, with nary a drop of rain and record-breaking temperatures soaring over 100 degrees. In the meantime, normally dry areas east of the Cascades were hit with late-season snow followed by rain and thunderstorms. In the Northwest, if it's sunny in the morning, it may stay that way until the end of the day. But that doesn't guarantee anything about tomorrow. ●

and the Cascades, it's cold and foggy on the coast. Rain can happen anytime. Bikers who live here just grab their bikes whenever the sun's out and hope for the best.

One of the great things about riding in the Northwest is that you can go from the mountains to the coast or the coast to the desert in a very short time, but that means you have to be prepared for just about any kind of weather. On the positive side, summers are usually pretty dry, and a few weeks of great riding weather in July, August, and September (plus parts of June and October, with luck) make storing a bike all winter worthwhile for the many locals who ride.

RIDING GEAR

Riding in the Northwest requires gear, gear, and more gear. If you've been looking for an excuse to buy some high-tech clothing, this is your chance. It's no wonder outdoor companies like REI are based here; they get plenty of practice testing water- and windproof items.

Those riding into the region from other parts of the country probably won't be prepared for the variability of local climates and regional weather patterns. The humidity west of the Cascades

Steve looks out on the sharp curve on US 20 far below the Washington Pass overlook near North Cascades National Park. Cool-weather gear is always a good idea through here.

means you'll need to dress warmer than you might expect, while the warm and dry conditions on the east side mean lighter-weight gear.

You'll need riding gear for the full range of temperatures and weather conditions—or be prepared to buy them once you get here. That includes gloves of various thicknesses and degrees of water resistance. Warm, sturdy, waterproof boots will prevent a lot of misery. Layers are always a good idea, since conditions can change with elevation, surroundings, and any fronts that blow in.

Effective rain gear is a must. If you don't spend the money for durable waterproof outerwear, you'll probably wish you had.

TRAFFIC LAWS

We've driven and ridden all over the country, and we have to agree with those who say traffic enforcement seems stricter in the Northwest than pretty much anywhere. Cops are plentiful, penalties are stiff, and warnings are few.

In Oregon in 2008, going even 1 mile over the speed limit could get you fined a minimum of $97. The basic fee for an 11-mph-over speeding ticket was $145. Any number of things, including speeding through a work zone or a "safety corridor," could add significantly to that.

In Washington, the maximum speed limit on most highways is 60 (bumped to 70 on some stretches of I-5), and even if traffic is light, you're likely to see cars puttering along at 50. In short, the Northwest's roads have many great things to offer, but speed is not often one of them.

Christy: When I lived in Portland, I heard jokes about speeding tickets making up for Oregon's lack of sales taxes. Now, living in Washington, I like to say folks here have never met a speed limit they felt like breaking.

Steve: I have firsthand experience dealing with inflexible cops. Returning to Portland on OR 6, I could see through the curve ahead, there was no traffic headed my direction, and a dashed yellow line made it legal to pass. Completely hidden by the big pickup I was passing and the fishing boat it towed was a state police officer on the side of the road. As soon as I returned to the eastbound lane, he flashed his lights and flagged me onto a tiny piece of asphalt. I had to brake suddenly with the truck and boat right on my tail. Apparently, I'd crossed a solid yellow line as I returned to the eastbound lane. I was cited for passing in a designated no-passing area even though the distance I traveled past where the dashes turned solid couldn't have been more than 100 feet.

I appealed the ticket, arguing that pulling me over with a big truck right behind me was more hazardous than the technical violation I had committed (it was eventually dismissed). I'm not the conspiracy-theory type, but since then I've paid attention to the length and placement of passing zones. I'm convinced that on many of the secondary roads in Oregon, especially those going to the coast, passing zones are too short to allow anyone traveling near the legal limit to pass and return to the original lane without crossing the solid yellow. ●

HELMET LAWS

Helmets are required for all riders and passengers in Washington, Oregon, and British Columbia. To see more about laws by state, go to the American Motorcyclist Association's Web site, www .amadirectlink.com/legisltn/laws.asp.

PUMPING FUEL IN OREGON

For a variety of reasons, it's illegal in Oregon for motorists to pump their own gas, and you could get slapped with a $500 fine for doing it. Motorcyclists can choose to have the attendant fill the tank or pump their own gas. Technically, the attendant is supposed to hand you the nozzle and allow you to fill your tank, and you're supposed to hand the nozzle back when you're done. In reality, most attendants will hand you the nozzle and walk away, allowing you to return it to the pump. In some cases, if attendants are very busy and you're paying with a credit card, they'll just tell you to go ahead and do it yourself.

FEE AREAS

Many state parks and all national parks require a day-use fee, which means you should pay the requested amount if you'll be parking there for more than a few minutes. The fees are usually low—and they're almost always lower for bikes than for cars—but they can be a hassle.

Your other option is to buy an annual pass. Some of these, including the National Parks annual pass, are the same price for

Mount Rainier's snowcapped peak is encircled by national park lands and twisty two-lane roads.

motorcycles and cars, making them less of a bargain (especially given the day-use discount for bikes). Still, they're a good deal if you plan to visit often. Passes are available at any U.S. Forest Service office or at the parks themselves.

A Northwest Forest Pass is required at many pullouts and trailheads in national forests. You can buy a motorcycle decal for $30, or it comes free with a national parks pass. Rangers have told us that most of the time, they give motorcycles the benefit of the doubt, given how vulnerable the removable decals are to theft. If you have questions, stop in at a forest service office and ask about the area's policies.

Many state parks are worth some time, and the state park passes are pretty reasonable. If you're riding the entire Oregon Coast, the Oregon Pacific Coast Passport, $10 for five days and more than fifteen coastal parks, is easily worth the money. For an easy-to-read summary of park passes, go to http://www.parks.wa.gov/fees or http://www.oregon.gov/OPRD/PARKS/recreational_pass.shtml.

Although we feel good about where the money goes (someone has to clean those pit toilets), we've never been hassled for not paying when we stopped briefly to look around in a park.

FERRIES

Most Washington State and oceangoing British Columbia ferries give bikes "first-on, first-off" status, no matter how many cars are waiting. Those arriving too late to get on the front of the ferry can hop on the back after cars have loaded. (The main exception is BC inland ferries, which are small enough that it doesn't make much difference.) On summer weekends, it's not uncommon for cars to wait two to four hours to make sure they get onto a ferry, so this can save lots of time and aggravation.

Some ferries, such as Port Townsend and Keystone, require reserving in advance to get priority loading. It's a good idea to know the procedures for any given route before you go. See "Motorcycle Loading Procedures" at www.wsdot.wa.gov/ferries/info_desk/faq/ and www.bcferries.com for up-to-date specifics.

The ferries also cost much less for riders—usually less than half the car fare. We like to think those in charge of the ferry system realize motorcycles pollute less and take up less space than cars do.

When you're on the ferry, park carefully and make sure everything's secure before you head for the passenger deck. Also note that there may be a bit of a jolt when the vessel bumps up against the dock, so be with your bike when that happens. Pedestrians and bicyclists will usually be allowed to leave the ferry just before you are, so fire up your engine when you see them departing.

We include information about specific ferries in chapters that incorporate them.

NATIVE AMERICANS AND FIRST NATIONS

Long before white explorers came to the region we now call the Northwest, it was filled with communities of people who had their own rich economies and cultures. Humans first came to this region as many as 14,000 years ago, across a land bridge that existed between North America and Asia. By 1500 B.C., people were scattered throughout the region, many living in pit houses near water.

The Northwest was spared some of the violence that swept over much of America as white settlers clashed with Native groups. Early explorers were most interested in trapping and harvesting other natural resources, not setting up full-time communities. By the time white settlers did arrive, Native populations had been decimated by the same diseases that killed many Native people across the continent.

Immigration exploded after the Oregon Trail and Gold Rush eras in the mid-nineteenth century. White Americans followed typical practices of the time, putting many Native groups onto reservations. Extensive dam-building for water and electricity projects destroyed villages and disrupted the salmon runs that were key to ancestral ways of life. Since the mid-twentieth century, state and federal governments have been trying to undo some of the damage, partly by returning fishing rights to tribe members. Many tribes have also built casinos to bring in revenue.

In Canada, indigenous people are called "First Nations" or "Aboriginal peoples" (they are technically divided into First Nations, the equivalent of Native Americans; Inuit, a group originating in the Arctic; and Métis, who have both white and Native ancestors). Canada's interactions with Native people have been less violent than in the United States, though not bloodshed-free. Today, First Nations are given wide latitude in how they run their own communities, called

Totem poles like these in Vancouver's Stanley Park symbolize Native peoples throughout the Northwest.

"reserves," even as they are well integrated in the general society. Unlike reservations in the United States, the reserves are usually in or near the bands' traditional homelands. Native traditions, culture, and arts are widely respected throughout the Northwest.

RIDING IN CANADA

Although it is an entirely separate country (as Canadians like to remind the rest of us), the cultures of Canada and the United States are very similar, and travel in Canada is relatively easy.

Immigration

In days gone by, American citizens only needed a valid driver's license to cross into Canada. Not anymore. As of June 2009, everyone needs a passport. (Washington residents may also get a special driver's license that doubles as a passport for entry into Canada.)

Steve: I was staying at a small motel in southeast Oregon when another guest approached me and struck up a conversation with questions about the Buell. The exchange flowed easily, and when it turned to our travels—where we'd been and where we were headed—I told him I was traveling around the Northwest and making my way to British Columbia.

He said he'd ridden all day from just south of the Canadian border on his way home to Arizona. He had planned to fulfill a lifelong dream by taking a trip into Alberta, the Yukon, and British Columbia. In preparation, he'd collected travel guides and brochures, calculated distances, and mapped out routes. I commented on what a great trip it must have been and asked if he had any recommendations.

That's when I learned he'd never made it into Canada. At the border crossing, his name came up on what he called "some sort of watch list." My curiosity piqued, I asked for details, wondering what I'd do if my name came up as well. That's when this polite middle-aged man surprised me by claiming to be a former Hells Angel, though he said he hadn't been a member for years.

I know enough about the Hells Angels to be a little wary of his story, but I heard him out as he continued. He said the Canadian authorities interrogated him for about four hours—digging for information on the leader of his former club—while his bike was "dismantled" and his belongings systematically searched. Obviously not convinced he'd made

Canadian officials will also deny anyone with a criminal record. That includes misdemeanors and any kind of drunk-driving offense. We've met some riders who made it all the way to the border crossing only to be turned away because of a violation they thought had been cleared up. Some of them didn't

a clean break from the club, the authorities escorted him to the border with a stern warning that if he ever tried to enter Canada again, he would be promptly detained.

The morning after we talked, as I left a cafe after an early breakfast, who should ride up but my friendly neighborhood former Hells Angel. He said he'd come by my room looking for me. My first thought was that I'd said or done something to offend him—but no. Since he couldn't get into Canada, he said, all those maps and brochures weren't any good to him. He thought perhaps I could use them, so he'd left them on the mat outside my room.

I was a little caught off guard by his unexpected act of generosity, and I fumbled through what I hope was a sincere thank-you. We wished each other safe travels and I returned to the motel where, sure enough, I found a thick stack of travel guides and maps. (I was also embarrassed to find that I had accidentally left the key to my room dangling in the lock—and relieved when I opened the door and found all of my belongings exactly as I'd left them.)

Happily, my name never came up on any watch lists, and I had no problems with Canadian immigration officials. In my experience, returning to the States is more of a hassle than entering Canada. The U.S. authorities ask questions about where I've been and whether I own the motorcycle and everything on it, and I've had to open my saddlebags several times. ●

even realize they were subjects of arrest warrants until Canadian border officers notified them! If you have any skeletons in your closet, make sure you get your record straight before you try to enter Canada.

Numbers

Like pretty much every country except the United States, Canada long ago adopted the metric system, which means all distances are in kilometers, all speed limit signs are in kilometers per hour, and all gas prices are in liters.

Conversions are easy: Multiply kilometers by 0.6 to convert to miles (100 kilometers converts to 60 miles, so 100 kph is 60 mph). To convert liters to gallons, multiply by 3.78. (Strangely enough, many Canadians still use feet and inches when discussing height and pounds when talking about weight. Also, English-speaking Canadians are more likely to use both metric and standard numbers, while French-speaking Canadians tend to stick to metric.)

Money

Canadians have their own currency. Conveniently, they're called dollars, and they're worth close to the same as U.S. dollars. Exchange rates are constantly changing. Many businesses in southern Canada, especially in tourist-oriented towns, will take U.S. cash as well.

Canadians don't have $1 bills; instead, they use gold-colored coins affectionately known as "loonies" because they depict a loon on one side (and an image of Queen Elizabeth II on the other; Canadians are proud members of the British Commonwealth, unlike Americans, who've never been forgiven for that revolution). They also have $2 coins nicknamed "toonies."

Parks and Fee Areas

Canada has its own network of national and provincial (regional) parks. Most of the parks within the scope of this book are British Columbia provincial parks (their Web site is www.env.gov.bc.ca/bcparks). Some of the parks require a $1 fee.

Laws and Police

Laws in Canada are enforced by the Royal Canadian Mounted Police (RCMP), also known as the Mounties (they haven't seemed to appreciate that nickname when we've met them in person).

East of the Cascades, much of the Northwest is farming territory, including these seemingly endless wheat fields.

Canada has lower speed limits and generally lower speeds than those found in the States. The upper limit on most highways is 100 km per hour, which is 62 mph, though it goes up to 110 in some places. While 100 is a nice, round number, it's not very fast. The limit drops to 60–70 kph (37–44 mph) on major suburban roads, and 30–50 kph in residential or downtown areas. Opinions vary as to how much the cops are sticklers on the speed limits, which some Canadians and many Americans find a little aggravating.

On the other hand, most of the roads we explore go through mountainous territory, include a fair number of curves, and may not be in pristine condition, so watching your speed is prudent whether you like the limits or not.

British Columbia is famous in some circles for the easy availability of, and tolerance for, marijuana. All we're going to say on this matter (aside from the information in ride 32) is that if you're looking for it, you'll probably have little trouble finding it.

In British Columbia, customers must either prepay for fuel or pay at the pump. This is called "Grant's Law," and is intended to protect employees from "gas-and-dash" crimes. The law is named in honor of Grant De Patie, who died while trying to prevent a "gas-and-dash" robbery where he worked.

Insurance

Call your insurance agent before you leave the States to make sure you have sufficient coverage in Canada and, when you go, bring proof that your insurance will cover you north of the border. You don't need it to cross, but you will need it if anything happens.

OREGON COAST

The Oregon Coast and U.S. Highway 101 are legendary, and rightfully so. For much of the ride, there's nothing between you and the Pacific—except rock formations, tide pools, beaches, and the occasional boardwalk. Much of the time, the road hugs steep mountainsides that fall (usually not literally) into the ocean.

The road's charms also lead to its disadvantages: Traffic can be frustrating at times, especially in summer. It doesn't help that much of it is composed of RVs and gawkers looking at the scenery. Weather can also be cloudy, foggy, or rainy almost any time of year. Fall is the best time to experience the coast. Over the summer, the waters of the Pacific Ocean (which are pretty cold here—swim if you dare) warm up, reaching their highest temperatures in about late August or early September. The waters warm the air over the land, which is also drier than in early summer. Many of the families in minivans and RV drivers have departed by late summer, too.

It would probably take weeks to see all those pullouts, most of which are spots to park and check out the scenery. We'll try to tell you about the ones we like; otherwise, just stop at any that appeal. Note that some are not paved, and rough pavement in others can make for a bumpy departure from the highway.

Also, keep a lookout for drivers who make last-minute decisions to turn in or pull out. We've encountered several accidents where a driver suddenly hit the brakes to turn into a viewpoint and got rear-ended. Worse yet are those who make sudden left-hand turns in front of oncoming traffic and get T-boned. Be on the lookout for these clueless rubberneckers: If they can't see other cars, they certainly won't see a motorcycle. ●

As a general rule—and US 101 is no exception—anywhere it's hilly and the pavement is within sight of the ocean, road conditions are not very good unless the pavement is fresh. You don't have to be an engineer to figure out that in a place with this much rain and where the hills or mountains descend right to the beach, the ground underneath is bound to be unstable and will eventually move—sometimes a significant distance.

All of Oregon's beaches are, by law, open to the public. This means that, theoretically, you could walk the entire 362 miles of coast and not have to so much as climb a fence (you would, of course, be blocked by the many cliffs and outcroppings along the way).

Innumerable pullouts and state parks grant easy access to everything from lakes to lighthouses, and, of course, beaches. Some have day-use fees; costs for bikes are often less than half those for cars. If you'll be spending a lot of time in Oregon parks,

Heceta Head Lighthouse, visible from US 101 north of Florence, is a beautiful building in a particularly lovely setting.

a five-day Oregon Pacific Coast Passport pass gets you into more than fifteen parks along the coast, and costs only $10. It's available at the parks in question, including Fort Stevens, Yaquina Head, and Cape Perpetua.

It's impossible to ride the whole coast in one day. We're splitting it into three, which gives you plenty of time to see the sights and enjoy some leisurely seafood lunches. Two days is doable if you don't find yourself wandering into museums or spending too much time relaxing at brew pubs.

We'll start at the northern top of the coast and work our way southward. Obviously, you can ride the coast in either direction (this way, of course, puts you in the oceanside lane, which also makes it easier to pull off at viewpoints or seaside towns).

Because rooms and campsites can get booked up quickly in summertime, you may want to make reservations. Most towns of any size have a lot of motel-style accommodations. We tend to like smaller towns with a welcoming vibe.

On the north coast, we like the Manzanita area. Lincoln City is not our favorite, but it is a natural stopping point and has a lot of amenities, including lodging and a casino.

Newport is another good option, with plentiful inexpensive motels and lots to do nearby. The Waldport area, at the end of the fun ride to the coast along Oregon Highway 34, is smaller but nice.

Florence feels a little sterile to us, but it's in a great mid-coast location and has a ton of motels. Coos Bay is big enough to offer all amenities, but it doesn't feel much like a vacation spot. Gold Beach is in the middle of a very scenic stretch of US 101 (not to mention the middle of the relatively warm "Banana Belt"), and recreation options—including jet-boat rides on the Rogue River—abound.

At the Banana Belt's south end, Brookings is warm and welcoming. Finally, if you're coming up the California coast, Crescent City is a good place to stay before you hit the Oregon Coast.

You have to get to the coast somehow, and some options are faster or more scenic than others. Our thoughts:

From Portland, you could take US 30 to Astoria (we explore one slower but more-scenic alternative in ride 4, Escape to the Beach).

If you can leave before rush hour, US 26 to Cannon Beach is a fast road that starts as a four-lane artery to Portland's northwest suburbs. During busy times, though, traffic can be slow or completely stopped. This is especially true on Friday afternoons, when it seems as if half the population is making a beeline to the coast. US 26 becomes the Sunset Highway State Scenic Corridor, passing through farm- and pastureland before rising into forested mountains around Manning.

OR 6 veers off from US 26 about 5 miles west of North Plains. The road is in great shape with nice hills and wide curves. It's similar to US 26 but slower and more remote, with fewer businesses and tourist traps along the way. It gets less weekend traffic since Tillamook isn't really a beach destination.

OR 18 is perhaps the worst road for getting to the coast on a bike. It runs through suburban sprawl that spreads almost to the heart of wine country. It's flat and straight and boring until the last few miles before it hits the coast at Lincoln City (at least you'll ride right past the *Spruce Goose,* housed at the impressive Evergreen Aviation & Space Museum in McMinnville).

US 20: This is a good route to the central coast from either Portland

The coast south of Port Orford features rocky outcroppings, sandy beaches, and warmer weather.

(take I-5 south to Albany) or from eastern Oregon via Bend. It takes you through Corvallis, an attractive college town, and fairly quickly rises into the hills, passing a couple hamlets along the way. There's a short stretch of curves before you make the last descent into Newport.

OR 34: One of the best routes to the coast, it splits from US 20 in Philomath and heads southwest, tracing the course of the Alsea River from the town of Alsea all the way into Waldport. For the most part, the pavement is good, and once the curves begin, they flow one after the other. It also passes through national forest land, giving it a wilderness feel.

OR 126 from Eugene to Florence: This road is not the most fun, but it's in good condition, and frequent passing lanes make it fairly quick. Leaving the depressing suburbs of Eugene, it heads through fields and rolling hills with some 35- or 40-mph curves in the Coast Range; otherwise, it's mostly 50 mph. Mapleton is a cute little town along the way. OR 36, a winding road often used by recreationists, branches north of Mapleton and ends just north of Eugene.

OR 38 from Eugene to Reedsport: Also known as the Umpqua River Scenic Byway, it's one of the most scenic options for travel to and from the coast. It's nice pavement, mostly 55 mph, with a few curves. A mix of evergreen and deciduous trees along the road makes this a lovely ride in the fall. OR 38 east of Elkton is fast, with well-banked big curves, but the scenery—heavily logged low hills and the aptly named sad town of Drain—aren't appealing. Take OR 138 northwest from I-5 at Sutherlin and connect to OR 38 in Elkton if you can.

Despite its name, Elkton is known mostly for fishing. It also boasts a "butterfly pavilion," two wineries, Arlene's and Becky's cafes, and Tomaselli's Pastry Mill & Cafe, whose menu admits "We specialize in Great Food, Good Coffee & Questionable Humor." West of Elkton, the road follows the Umpqua River's big bends past tiny settlements nestled into lush forest. As it descends toward the coast, it's occasionally patched or scored. This is prime elk territory, and you'll notice elk-viewing platforms along the river bottom. Better there than on the road, we say.

Pretty much the only option to get to the south coast from I-5 is OR 42 from Roseburg. If we were riding north up I-5, we'd prefer to take US 199 southwest to Smith River from Grants Pass and pick up US 101 in California. If we were coming from the north, we'd head to the coast long before we got to Roseburg. ●

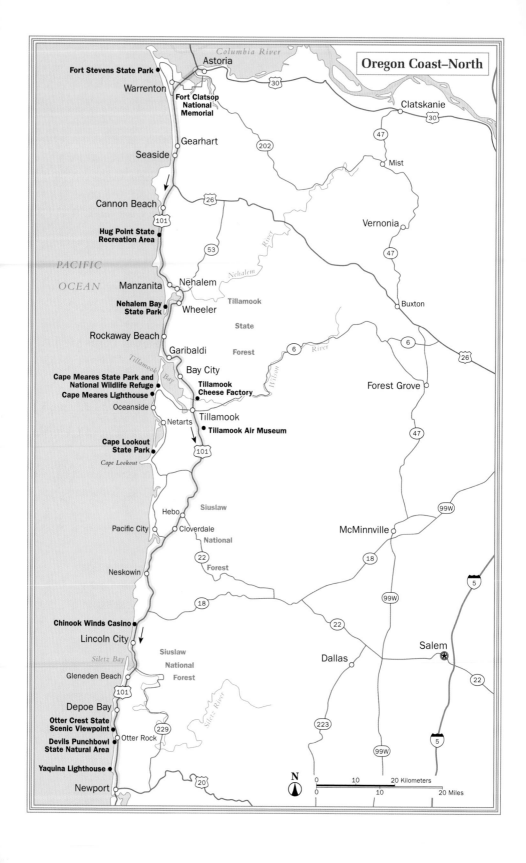

Oregon Coast—North

Directions:
south on US 101 from Astoria to Newport

Distance:
from Astoria to Newport: 133 miles (add 40 miles for Three Capes Scenic Loop)

Time:
half a day to a full day, depending on stops

Services:
in most towns

Best Time of Year:
late spring through late fall

Highlights:
Oregon's historic northwest corner; tourist-oriented towns with nice beaches; farmland, fish, and cheese

Much of the northern Oregon coast is rough and hilly right down to the water. That means sometimes the road skirts the rocky coastline, while other times steep coastal bluffs or deep bays force it inland, where it rolls through forests and farmland until it reconnects with the coast. Some sections are rough or slow going; others are straight and flat and boring. But scenic viewpoints reward you with some of the best seascapes on the coast. Portland's proximity makes for all kinds of amenities along the way, since city dwellers hitting the coast for a weekend want relatively upscale shopping and dining when they arrive.

Astoria is the biggest city on the coast's north end (it's actually a bit inland, on the wide mouth of the Columbia). It works hard to make itself a prime tourist destination, but it still retains its blue-collar feel. The main drag is lined with all kinds of small businesses of the non-chichi kind. If you want a workingman's bar or a tattoo, this is a good place to find it, though the town also caters to cruise-ship crowds.

On the way to the coast, U.S. Highway 101 passes Fort Stevens State Park, on a peninsula at the end of 10 miles of ordinary two-lane road. At the very tip of the peninsula, the wreck of the *Peter Iredale* is partly buried on a forbidding, windswept strip of sand. The four-masted sailing vessel ran aground in dense fog in 1906 and has been there ever since (if you don't mind dealing

Tourists can walk right up to the wreck of the *Peter Iredale,* still partly buried in the sandy beach at Fort Stevens State Park.

with sand, you can walk right up to it at low tide). The steel skeleton is a spooky reminder of why this part of the coast is called the "Graveyard of the Pacific."

Away from the beach, the park is full of maze-like roads past lots of RV and camping spots; maps at the park entrance can help you navigate.

Between Astoria and Cannon Beach, US 101 runs inland, with the occasional short road out to the beach. The highway itself is straight and flat and punctuated by small businesses and restaurants.

Seaside is touristy in the old-fashioned sense, which is appropriate given that people have been vacationing here for more than 100 years. Some things haven't changed much. The 2-mile-long beachside boardwalk, "the Promenade," is lined with shops, eateries, and amusements including a carousel (Seaside has been called Oregon's version of Coney Island, for better or worse). Although some find it tacky, the Promenade offers easy access to a wide, flat, sandy beach. To get there, turn right off US 101 when you see signs for the town center and the aquarium.

The next easily accessible ocean views are at Cannon Beach. While most of the Oregon Coast's towns are unpretentious and laid-back, Cannon Beach is a notable exception. Its boutiques, bakeries, ice-cream shops, and better-than-average restaurants cater to Portlanders making a quick getaway to the coast (U.S. Highway 26 hits the coast just north of here), which means summer and weekend traffic can be heavy and parking hard to find. On a particularly hot weekend, we've seen it a mess all the way to downtown Portland.

Below the town's main drag, the beach is wide, flat, and often filled with tourists. It's also home to Haystack Rock, a 235-foot monolith rising from the sand. The third-largest single rock of its type, it's one of the coast's most photographed icons.

South of Cannon Beach, the coast is finally visible from US 101. State parks—usually some combination of picnic tables, trails, points of interest, and beach access—pop up around almost every turn. The road curls around hillsides, through luscious forests, and past miles and miles of beaches. In short, this is the Oregon Coast you've been waiting for.

Hug Point, about 3 miles south of Cannon Beach, is an easy-access beach that's not as crowded as Seaside or Cannon Beach. It has a paved, then pebbled path you can walk on in your riding boots all the way to the beach.

Manzanita, Nehalem, Wheeler, and Brighton circle Nehalem Bay, one of several good Dungeness crabbing bays along the coast; others include Tillamook, Yaquina, and Alsea. You can rent crab-bing boats and traps and have the crabs you've caught cooked on the spot. (If you don't want to do the crab-catching yourself, you can also buy freshly caught crab on the dock.)

After skirting Nehalem Bay, US 101 returns to the coast and through Rockaway Beach before heading inland again to round Tillamook Bay. On the bay's southeastern side, Tillamook is well known for its cheese; if you're a dairy lover, stop at the visitor center 2 miles north of Tillamook on US 101. It's open 8 a.m. to 8 p.m. mid-June through Labor Day, and 8 a.m. to 6 p.m. the rest of the year. And yes, you do get free samples. The ice cream may be even better than the cheese!

Bays along the Oregon coast are full of crabs like these tiny ones. You can rent traps to catch larger ones at Nehalem Bay and have them cooked up for you on the spot.

Two miles south of Tillamook is the Tillamook Air Museum, which has a collection of about thirty combat aircraft.

US 101 remains inland, while the slower, less-traveled Three Capes Scenic Loop cuts out to the coast, then reconnects with US 101 in Pacific City to the south. The loop meanders past a lighthouse, beaches, parks, rocky outcroppings, tiny towns, and wildlife areas. Whether you take the fast road or the slow road depends on your schedule and how dedicated you are to seeing as much of the coast as possible. You can either do the whole loop or make a smaller one on the north end, returning on Oregon Highway 131.

Get to the scenic loop by taking 3rd Street / OR 131 west from downtown Tillamook. OR 131 intersects with Bayocean Road about 2 miles west of downtown. Hugging the south shore of Tillamook Bay on its way to Cape Meares, Bayocean Road is rough in places, with lots of shifts, humps, and heaves. The closer you get to the lighthouse, the hillier the terrain gets and the worse the road becomes. You'll hate it if you're riding two up and don't have solid suspension.

The Cape Meares Lighthouse is the shortest on the coast; sitting on a 200-foot-high outcropping, it doesn't need to be tall. After it was decommissioned in 1963, but before its absorption into the Oregon State Park system, vandals severely damaged the keeper's quarters and stole the four "bull's-eyes" (sections of the lens that magnify light) from the lighthouse's Fresnel lens.

Remarkably, three of the four bull's-eyes have been found. One was recovered in a drug raid, another one was returned to a nearby museum, and one was anonymously deposited on a park employee's front porch. The lighthouse is open from 11 a.m. to 4 p.m., April through October, and accessible via a paved trail, so you can climb its few steps and see where the bull's-eyes used to be. ●

The road from the lighthouse through Oceanside and Netarts is in good shape, with nice hills and curves. Pick up OR 131 again in Netarts to avoid the loop's less-rewarding southern section, which wanders along the edge of Netarts Bay to Cape Lookout and into Pacific City. This section—which is not a great ride or a great road—cuts away from the coast through the hills north of Pacific City, then drops to flat coastal marshland. The asphalt through the hills is chewed up, with lots of slumps and heaves.

If you stick to US 101, you'll ride short stretches of 50- to 55-mph road between smooth 30- to 40-mph curves through dairy country where farms spread out on both sides of the road.

Pacific City is a cool little beach town with its own haystack rock. It also has hills to climb and a long, wide beach accessible from a parking lot in the heart of town. On warm summer days, lots of people surf, swim, or play volleyball just off the deck of the Pelican Brew Pub. South of Pacific City, at Neskowin, the road travels inland and doesn't hit the coast again until near Lincoln City.

Many of the rest stops along US 101 have circular wayfinders with displays and kiosks to help you figure out where you are and what the area offers. Winema Wayfinding Point north of Lincoln City is a good example. It has information on camping and day-use areas, nearby communities, activities, bridges, lighthouses, and wildlife viewing.

Riding along Lincoln City's main drag, you would hardly know there's an ocean just on the other side of those bluffs to the west. It feels like a long strip of suburbia with all the resulting ills (including an outlet mall) as well as its benefits (you can buy just about anything you need). Part of its growth can be attributed to the Chinook Winds Casino and Convention Center, whose parking lot must have some of the best views of any casino anywhere.

South of Lincoln City, the road curves around Siletz Bay. Although the businesses and homes feel like part of Lincoln City's sprawl, they're actually a series of small towns, including Glendenen Beach and Lincoln Beach. Amenities are plentiful.

Information panels at Siletz Bay tell you a little about this place's long history with tsunamis, or tidal waves. Pieced-together records and geological studies show a major disaster hit on January 26, 1700. During an earthquake measuring an estimated 9.0 or more, the ocean floor heaved 20 to 30 feet along a zone from the northern California coast to British Columbia. Siletz Bay got hit with a 30- to 50-foot tidal wave about twenty minutes later, and Native villages were wiped out.

In 1964, a magnitude-9.2 earthquake off the Alaska coast created a tsunami that washed over parts of the Oregon Coast, killing more than 100 people. Earthquakes with magnitudes over 9.0 are very rare, but smaller quakes can also cause tsunamis. Since the Oregon Coast, like the rest of the West Coast, is prone to frequent (usually small) earthquakes, you never know when another one could strike. These days, an emergency warning system evacuates low-lying coastal zones, and signs are posted at entrances and exits to these zones. Needless to say, if you feel the earth shaking or hear a siren blast, head for higher ground. ●

Depoe Bay is a sweet place to stop for a rest. It's also the "whale-watching capital of Oregon," and while that may seem like a big claim for such a small place, we have seen whales here several times. A roadside kiosk gives you a nice (indoor) vantage point from which to scan the ocean, with telescopes for better views. You'll know immediately if whales are out there, because excited fellow visitors will point them out.

A walkway along the road lets you imagine navigating a boat through the tight, rocky mouth of the world's smallest harbor. At high tide, water sometimes crashes against the seawall and over the road. Watching unsuspecting tourists get drenched is entertaining—from a distance.

State-park pullouts just south of Depoe Bay are good for watching booming high-tide waves or checking out tide pools. From the Otter Crest viewpoint, you can see the beach and rocky shoreline 500 feet below, as well as Cape Foulweather to the south.

Restaurants

Cannon Beach
Bill's Tavern & Brewhouse
188 N. Hemlock St.
(503) 436-2202
Burgers and brews

The Bistro
263 N. Hemlock St.
(503) 436-2661
Smaller, pricier, a bit more gourmet

The Driftwood Inn
179 N. Hemlock St.
(503) 436-2439
Substantial portions of steak and seafood; famous
Bloody Marys

Nehalem
Wanda's
12870 H St.
(503) 368-8100
Tasty homemade breakfasts

Pacific City
Pelican Pub Restaurant Brewery
33180 Cape Kiwanda Dr.
(503) 965-7007

RIDE

2

Oregon Coast—Central

Directions:
south on US 101 from Newport to North Bend

Distance:
total distance from Newport to North Bend: 95 miles

Time:
half a day to a full day, depending on stops

Services:
Newport, Waldport, Yachats, Florence, and Reedsport have all services

Best Time of Year:
late spring through late fall

Highlights:
some of the world's most gorgeous coastline; quaint, friendly towns; appealing and accessible recreation

The stretch of coast from Newport to Florence is one of the world's most picturesque and relaxing. This is what people think of when they think "Oregon Coast." Tiny to midsize towns, each with its own character, dot the coastline.

Newport is one of the coast's most welcoming towns. It's big enough (about 10,000 people) to support a thriving tourist

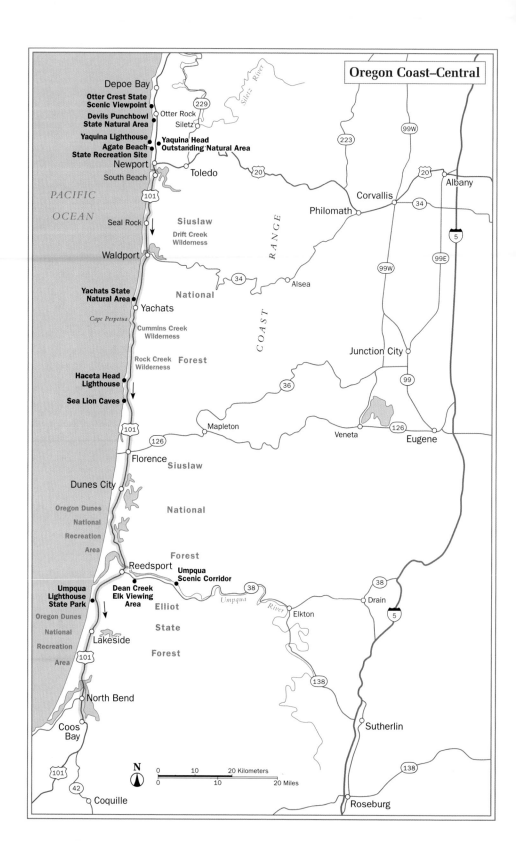

industry and has the attractions (lighthouses, a quirky waterfront district, and a very nice aquarium) to back that up. Since its economy is more diversified than most, tourists are a small-enough piece of the pie that you won't get gouged for being one. Cheap hotels are plentiful.

Entering Newport from the north, stop at Yaquina Head Lighthouse (the turnoff is technically in the hamlet of Agate Beach). A short, paved road runs along the edge of a slender basalt promontory called Yaquina Head to the lighthouse, at 93 feet the tallest on the Oregon coast. The paved area around it is a nice spot to watch for whales and other wildlife. The light's 1,000-watt globe is still active, and you can climb 110 of the steep 114 steps to the top (it's open from 10 a.m. to 4 p.m., but the park is open dawn until dusk). There's a $3 per bike fee to enter ($7 for cars).

The beach at Agate Beach, by the way, is reached by a tunnel originally built by cattlemen who wanted to let their cows stroll to the beach (the cows were less interested in sand castles than they were in licking salt off the rocks).

Oregon's largest commercial fishing fleet processes some of the catch right along Newport's picturesque waterfront. It has a laid-back, blue-collar feel despite all the art galleries and restaurants. Follow signs for the waterfront (also called "Bayfront") from U.S. Highway 101 in the center of town. Though it can get congested, it's walkable, and there's plenty of parking.

Christy: Newport has about eighty restaurants, including Rogue Brewing, a favorite of mine. You can get Rogue beer all over the Northwest, but like any beer, buying a bottle is just not the same as drinking it at the Bayfront brew pub. You might even meet John Maier, the wonderfully obsessive-compulsive brewmaster, as you sample beers alongside fishermen on Newport's historic bay. Just make sure you have an alternate way back to your hotel or plan to spend some time walking off a significant buzz. •

At Newport's south end, US 101 crosses the lovely Yaquina Bay Bridge, built in 1936 to replace a ferry system that hauled cars from one side of the bay to the other. If you happen to be there on a rainy day or just love sea creatures, visit the Oregon Coast Aquarium, where animals including sea otters, sea lions, and a giant Pacific octopus live in roomy, attractive habitats. The aquarium was also once home to Keiko, the rescued killer whale who played the title role in *Free Willy*.

South of Newport, US 101 undulates atop low bluffs next to ocean beaches. There are not many towns for the next few miles, so the scenery is the only distraction.

Alsea Bay is wide but shallow, and clamdiggers flock to its mouth at low tide, when it becomes mostly sandbar. Waldport's small downtown is just south of the Alsea Bay Bridge. Note that the speed limit is 25 mph through town, and cops will be happy to nab you for speeding. Whether you're coming from the north after crossing the relatively high-speed bridge, or from the south, where the road winds in following a gentle curve, the lower limit may surprise you.

After Waldport, US 101 narrows and the landscape returns to sandy beaches topped by grassy bluffs. The road curves inland just a bit and enters forest; then things open up at the charming town of Yachats, which offers several food options. The Blue Whale is a diner with giant breakfast biscuits and no-nonsense waitresses who won't kiss up to customers but can take as good as they dish.

From Yachats to Florence, much of the land on both sides of US 101 is protected as part of the Siuslaw National Forest. The landscape changes: once again, the road hugs a section of rocky coastline, curving around an inlet and rising to skirt the steep headlands of Cape Perpetua. This is one of the most beautiful points on the coast.

As you might expect by now, the dramatic scenery also heralds a different road surface. Conditions south of Yachats are typical of roads along steep rock cliffs that drop sharply to meet ocean below, with uneven pavement that sometimes seems about to slump off down the hillside.

Cape Perpetua Scenic Area is worth some time. Short trails (many at least partly paved) lead uphill to panoramic views; inland to old-growth rain forest; and down to rocky outcroppings, churning water, and dramatic spouting water horns created when waves hit rock. Adventurous types hike up the 800-foot promontory, where on a clear day, you can see for 70 miles in either direction. We prefer to take the steep and switchback-filled but paved road to the top. Stop in at the on-site visitor center for more information.

One of the highest points along the coast, rocky Cape Perpetua offers hiking trails, tide pools, and ocean vistas.

For the next few miles, US 101 rolls through a series of nice curves around ridges jutting into the ocean. Massive sand dunes and beaches are laid out in front of you like a string of bunkers on a golf course. Coming around one of those curves, you'll see signs for Heceta Head Lighthouse. It's a lovely building in an extraordinarily beautiful spot. A steep gravel trail leads from the parking lot past the keeper's house (now a bed-and-breakfast) to the light.

South of Heceta Head, the road is nice and straight. Once it hits the north end of Oregon Dunes National Recreation Area near Florence, you lose sight of the coast for a while. Florence is a midsize town that caters to the throngs who recreate here. That means plenty of restaurants, inexpensive hotels, and stores. The historic waterfront district along the Siuslaw River is an agreeable place to stretch your legs and get some ice cream or a beer.

The Sea Lion Caves, which bills itself as the "world's largest sea cave," is carved out of a bluff between Yachats and Florence. Visitors to this privately owned tourist trap take an elevator into the cave, a gathering spot for sea lions. Locals look on it with disdain and point out that you can watch sea lions for free at the docks in Newport (a visit to the Sea Lion Caves costs $12). If you're lucky, the creatures will be sunning themselves on rocks or the beach along this part of the coast.

Although California sea lions are plentiful along the Oregon coast and its bays, Steller sea lions are more rare. They can top 2,500 pounds (California sea lions are no slouches themselves, reaching 1,000 pounds) and use their flippers to "walk" on land. Highly social animals, they congregate in large groups and don't usually hang out in harbors, as California lions sometimes do.

Seals are also common along the coast. They're smaller than sea lions, weighing in at a mere 300 pounds. Both seals and sea lions are intelligent animals; two of the California sea lions at the Oregon Coast Aquarium have been taught to paint and even had their work published (proceeds went to aquarium programs). ●

A raft of sea lions congregates on the beach south of Heceta Head.

South of Florence, and especially south of Reedsport, US 101 tracks inland and rarely edges the ocean until about Port Orford, making this one of US 101's least-interesting sections. But many

What's west of the highway here? Sand, and lots of it. For almost 50 miles along this coast, the Oregon Dunes National Recreation Area encompasses dunes that rise up to 500 feet above sea level. It's full of hiking trails, lakes, and off-road-vehicle areas. In some places, forests come all the way into the dunes (or, more accurately, the dunes are coming into the forest—winds blow the sand from west to east).

The dunes' sand was originally mountain rock. Streams washed it into the ocean, tumbling it into smaller and smaller stones along the way. The ocean picked up the pebbles, beat them even smaller, and then threw them onto the beach. Without a steep coastal mountain barrier, winds blew the sand inland. The process that began millions of years ago continues now in a panoramic demonstration of nature in action.

The best views require taking off your boots and doing some walking, though there are some viewpoints right off US 101. There is quicksand in the dunes, but mostly in winter and only in wet, low-lying areas. (No one has ever been lost in the sands of the Oregon dunes.) ●

Miles of dunes lie along the coast south of Florence.

access roads connect US 101 to state parks on the coast with often-empty beaches.

Just south of Reedsport—a tiny town with a series of historic bridges—and surrounded by dunes, Umpqua Lighthouse State Park has a small lake with its own sandy beach, yurts, cabins, and tent and RV sites. The Umpqua Lighthouse in the park is open for tours during the summer. The coast's first lighthouse was built on the banks of the Umpqua River in 1857, but it was undercut by water and fell into the river a few years later. This lighthouse, its 1894 replacement, is one of the most accessible on the coast. (If it looks familiar, it's because it was built from the same plans as Heceta Head.) The original two-ton Fresnel lens is still working and sends out the only red light on the Oregon Coast. A museum is housed in a former Coast Guard building nearby.

Restaurants

Newport
Rogue Ales Public House
748 SW Bay Blvd.
(541) 265-3188

Yachats
LeRoy's Blue Whale
580 US 101
(541) 547-3399

RIDE

3

Oregon Coast—South

Directions:
south on US 101 from North Bend to the California border

Distance:
total distance from North Bend to border: 115 miles (add 30 miles, round-trip, for the Cape Arago Highway)

Time:
half a day to a full day, depending on stops

Services:
North Bend, Coos Bay, Coquille, Bandon, Port Orford, Gold Beach, and Brookings

Best Time of Year:
late spring through late fall

Highlights:
miles of stunning coastline; historic towns with lots of amenities; the welcome warmth of Oregon's "Banana Belt"

Oregon's south coast departs from the dunes, but more sandy beaches await—as does the state's own "Banana Belt." We pick up this ride in Coos Bay, a good place to equip yourself with whatever you need before you head off in pursuit of more beauty.

North Bend and Coos Bay together make up the Oregon Coast's most populated area. Unlike other coast towns, they're

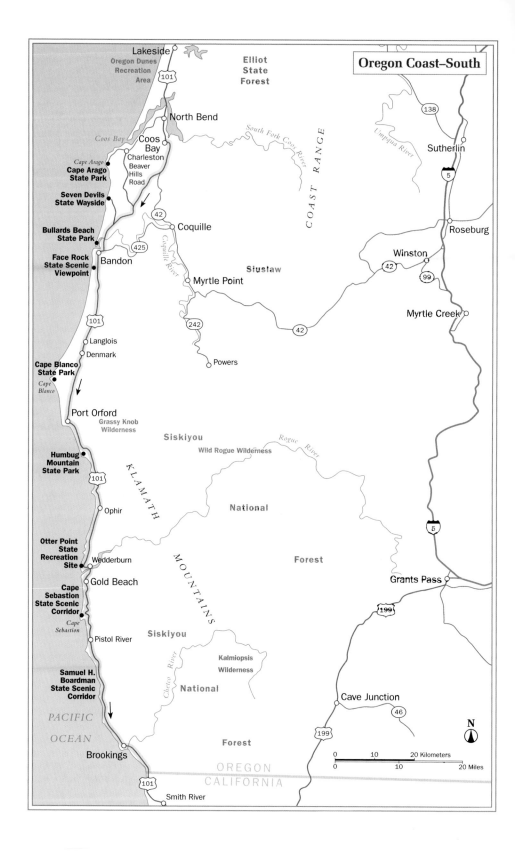

Lakeside

Oregon Dunes
Recreation
Area

101

Elliot
State
Forest

138

Sutherlin

North Bend

Coos Bay

Coos
Bay

South Fork Coos River

Umpqua River

Charleston
Beaver
Hills
Road

Cape Arago
Cape Arago
State Park

Seven Devils
State Wayside

Bullards Beach
State Park

425

Bandon

Face Rock
State Scenic
Viewpoint

Coos
Bay

42

Coquille

Roseburg

Winston

42

99

Coquille River

Siuslaw

Myrtle Point

Myrtle Creek

101

Langlois

Denmark

242

Powers

Cape Blanco
State Park

Cape
Blanco

Port Orford

Grassy Knob
Wilderness

42

COAST RANGE

5

Siskiyou

Rogue River

Wild Rogue Wilderness

Humbug
Mountain
State Park

101

KLAMATH

National

Ophir

Otter Point
State
Recreation
Site

Wedderburn

Forest

5

MOUNTAINS

Cape
Sebastian
State Scenic
Corridor

Gold Beach

Grants Pass

Cape
Sebastian

Pistol River

199

Siskiyou

Chetco River

Kalmiopsis

Wilderness

Samuel H.
Boardman
State Scenic
Corridor

PACIFIC

National

OCEAN

Cave Junction

46

Forest

199

Brookings

OREGON
CALIFORNIA

101

Smith River

N

0   10   20 Kilometers
0   10   20 Miles

Oregon Coast–South

not all that picturesque. Coos Bay, the largest natural harbor between Seattle and San Francisco, boasts a major fishing port. Its proximity to Oregon forests destined it to be a lumber shipping center, reputed to be the world's largest until recent declines in the timber industry.

Those diminished fortunes took away some of the money that might have gone toward restoring the towns' aging historic centers. Definitely workingman's cities, they can seem either charmingly old-fashioned or depressingly dilapidated. At any rate, they have character. You'll find plenty of restaurants and some intriguing buildings, including the beautifully restored Egyptian Theatre, right on U.S. Highway 101 as it becomes the old-fashioned main thoroughfare.

US 101 doesn't run right next to the ocean here. Cape Arago is one option to get to the beach, though it's a bit out of the way. This prominent hilly headland with a sandy beach and lots of hiking trails is 15 miles southwest of Coos Bay at the end of the narrow Cape Arago Highway.

To get to the cape from downtown North Bend or Coos Bay, follow signs for Charleston and ocean beaches (the turnoffs end up in the same place). Signage isn't great, so keep your eyes peeled. Charleston's motto is "Oregon's Bay Area Playground," but in reality, it's a tiny fishing village where the smell of shellfish and salt water invades your nasal cavities as you cross the bridge into the heart of town.

Situated on a little island just off the cape, the Cape Arago Lighthouse has always been one of the most difficult to reach. For many years, it was only accessible by boat (the keeper once got blown off course en route to the light and, carried by currents, finally landed 90 miles north of here), and the rickety bridge that crosses to it now is closed to the public.

One return option from the cape is Beaver Hills Road, which runs south from Charleston to US 101. It's a twisty, narrow strand through a mix of houses and trailers. At one point, the forest opens enough to show you that you're riding along a ridge with 360-degree views of surrounding valleys and ridges.

You'll see the name "Seven Devils" in several places around here. Any traveler on the Oregon Coast (or anywhere in Oregon) can't help but notice the proliferation of diabolical names—Devil's Punchbowl, Devil's Churn, Devil's Kitchen, and, of course, Hells Canyon on the state's east side (names concerning angels are a lot less prevalent, for some reason). There's a Devils Gulch on Mount Misery. Some of them don't seem to make much sense—Devil's Garden is on Paradise Mountain, for example, and Idiotville is near Gods Valley.

It's hard to say exactly where all the hellish names come from, especially when they refer to beautiful places. Many of Oregon's names were coined by pioneers who left more-civilized places and experienced hardships here. No matter their origins, the names are memorable. ●

Don't worry if you don't make it to Cape Arago; more beautiful (and easily accessible) beaches are just a few miles south on US 101.

Founded by Irish immigrants who named it after their hometown, Bandon is a longtime tourist destination and a cranberry capital. With many travelers wanting to make a stop here, hotels are relatively expensive and may fill up entirely, so plan ahead.

For a long time, many of Bandon's shops and other businesses were built on wooden pilings over the swampy edges of the Coquille River. They (and much of the rest of the town) burned down in 1936 and were never rebuilt, but informational signs on the present-day waterfront tell their story. Maybe because of the posh Bandon Dunes Golf Resort nearby, Bandon has more than its fair share of pricey but good restaurants, if you feel like splurging. Otherwise, head down near the docks to a number of seaside restaurants or the casual Tony's Crabshack / Port O' Call—or, if it's lunchtime, Bandon Baking Co. and Deli.

Just south of downtown, easy paths lead from high bluffs

to gorgeous beaches and tide pools. Follow signs for Face Rock State Scenic Viewpoint to Beach Road, a short loop right along the beachside bluffs. Some of the coast's most craggy and dramatic rock formations, especially beautiful in early morning or late evening, are right below the road. Wooden steps take you to the beach itself, so you can pause without taking off your boots.

While the term "Oregon's Banana Belt" might seem an exaggeration, the weather here is downright tropical compared to the rest of the Oregon Coast. The difference in temperature is astonishing, especially in midwinter when this area can hit 70 degrees. Cool air over relatively broad, high mountains to the east flows downhill to the west. Since air warms as it falls, by the time it gets to the coast, it might be 20 degrees warmer than it was in the mountains. Citrus trees and all kinds of flowers grow here.

US 101 runs along the coast through much of Oregon's Banana Belt. Many overlooks give you chances to stop for views of Southern Oregon's craggy coastline and deep blue waters.

From Port Orford south, things just get warmer until the California border. This makes the south coast a beloved riding spot in the Northwest's cooler months (though rain, unfortunately, still falls frequently). We have some friends who trailer their bikes from up north just to ride around the Banana Belt in winter. ●

US 101 south of Bandon is in good shape but not all that scenic as it jogs away from the coast. It's mostly a straight ride in and out of forest interspersed with what appear to be old farms and homesteads. The road returns to the coast at Port Orford, the oldest townsite on the Oregon Coast. It's also the northern end of Oregon's "Banana Belt," so called because the weather from Port Orford south is noticeably warmer than the weather to the north—or for a long way south, for that matter.

Just north of Port Orford, Cape Blanco is a beautiful bluff with a big, sandy beach. It's the westernmost point in Oregon. The lighthouse, the southernmost on the coast, has continually operated longer than any other lighthouse on the coast (since 1870). It's also at the highest elevation above the ocean (245 feet) and had the coast's first female keeper. You can tour it and the historic Victorian Hughes House, where keepers lived, from 10 a.m. to 3:30 p.m., April through October. Reach it via the Cape Blanco Highway, 4 miles each way from US 101.

At the open-water port of Port Orford, crab boats are launched using a crane. Battle Rock, the town's other landmark, is named for the skirmish that occurred when white sailors first landed there in 1851 and clashed with Native people.

South of Port Orford, US 101 hangs on a thin strip of land between the cliffs above and the ocean below. It's very rare not to see the ocean from the bike, since the road rarely leaves the coast. When it does, it's to cut behind the likes of Humbug Mountain, a massive piece of land that juts out into the Pacific.

South of Humbug Mountain, the coast takes on that quintessential weathered look, with cliffs and huge offshore rocks that look as if they were left behind by a giant playing in the surf. With a few exceptions, the road follows the contours of the terrain, climbing, dipping, and twisting south through a craggy coastline where the mountains to the east meet the Pacific to the west. Keep in mind that the features creating stunning scenery make the pavement quality unpredictable.

The Isaac Lee Patterson Bridge connects Wedderburn, just barely recognizable as a town on the north bank of the famous

The rain forest near Humbug Mountain inspired one amateur artist to create Prehistoric Gardens' life-size dinosaur sculptures.

On the backside of Humbug Mountain, between Port Orford and Gold Beach, US 101 passes the Prehistoric Gardens in Oregon's rain forest, a roadside distraction with an enormous Tyrannosaurus rex out front. This "world-famous exhibit," the creation of sculptor E. V. Nelson, opened in 1953. The swampy rain forest in this valley made him think of prehistoric times and inspired him to spend forty years creating vibrantly colored, life-size dinosaur sculptures RoadsideAmerica.com described as "pop-art refugees from the Land that Earth Tones Forgot." For a small fee, you can wander among the statues. Plaques give details about the dinos, including how to pronounce their names. ●

Rogue River, with the bigger burg of Gold Beach on the south side. The little harbor that greets you at Gold Beach, one of the sunniest spots anywhere on the Northwestern coast, looks like a refurbished fishing village or a polished version of San

The sad remains of the *Mary D. Hume* lie in a few feet of water at the mouth of the Rogue River. You can get a gander from a viewpoint on the south side of the port. While it doesn't look like much now, this was once one of the most productive working boats ever built.

With a strong keel made from a single spruce tree, the vessel was launched by R. D. Hume in 1881 and named for his wife. The 98-foot steamer hauled goods along the northern Pacific coast, then worked as a whaling ship until the whaling industry took a dive. She was a tugboat until 1978, making her the longest-used boat in Pacific Coast history.

When it came time to retire her, she chugged back here, where the Curry County Historical Society planned to refurbish her. She waited while a sling was built to lift her out of the water for repairs, but when the lift started hauling her up, she came apart. Impossible to move without being destroyed, she's been left here to slowly drift away, piece by piece. It's a sad ending for a vessel with such a long life of service. ●

You can view the remains of the *Mary D. Hume,* once a hardworking whaling and shipping vessel.

Located about 6 miles north of the Oregon-California border on Highway 199, O'brien is a great place to fuel up and grab a snack.

Francisco's Fisherman's Wharf. The main attraction here isn't sourdough bread, chocolate, and chowder, though, but jet-boat river excursions.

From just south of Pistol River until just north of Brookings, you'll cruise through the Samuel H. Boardman State Scenic Corridor, a 12-mile stretch of US 101 through 300-year-old trees along a steep coastline. It's named for Oregon's first state parks superintendent, who wanted this beautiful expanse to remain in public hands. The corridor has so many overlooks and viewpoints it's impossible to stop at all of them. Some—including Arch Rock and Natural Bridges, where water has eroded openings in the rocks—are so impressive that you might find yourself circling back to have a look.

Brookings and Harbor, separated by the mouth of the Chetco River, are the last towns on Oregon's southern coast. This is the end of the Banana Belt; just south of here, the cool coastal breeze could have you zipping your jacket even before you cross the California border.

US 101 crosses into California and leaves the coast. One way to loop back into Oregon is to take U.S. Highway 197, which peels off from US 101 just south of Smith River, California. It connects to U.S. Highway 199, which stretches northeast for about 80 miles into Grants Pass, Oregon (this is also a good route from Interstate 5 to the Oregon Coast if you want to ride it south to north). On the Rogue, Grants Pass is a casual recreation-oriented town with all amenities.

The best part of US 199 is the Smith River Scenic Byway in California, a mix of tight 30-mph turns with a few short sections of four-lane divided highway that allow faster vehicles to pass the slower ones that have been holding up traffic for miles. In some areas, the turns are so tight, it feels as if the outside-lane handlebar hangs off a cliff over the boulder-strewn Smith River below, while in the other lane, sheer cliffs rise straight up from the pavement.

Restaurants

Bandon
Bandon Baking Co. and Deli
160 2nd St. SE
(541) 347-9440
Open for breakfast and lunch, with yummy baked goods and sandwiches

Tony's Crab Shack
155 First St.
(541) 347-2875
Fresh seafood—or they'll help you catch your own off the dock

PORTLAND AREA

With a thriving cultural scene, a laid-back social vibe, and easy access to mountains, rivers, ocean beaches, and forests, Portland is consistently named one of America's most livable cities. It's easy to remember that designation as long as you're not, say, trying to get out of town via the interstate or riding during rush hour on one of the many thoroughfares that get clogged with traffic even when the weather is good. Friday nights during the summer are especially bad, and rain always makes things worse. And, like the Northwest's other big cities, Portland's city center can be a nightmare to navigate if you're not familiar with it.

Aside from those negatives (which apply to any major city in the Northwest), Portland isn't a bad place to be. Smaller than Seattle or Vancouver, and just a tad warmer, it feels more welcoming and is easier to navigate. If you're prepared for the weather, you can ride almost year-round. Because Portland works hard at being bicycle-friendly and many people commute by bicycle, motorists are more likely to be on the lookout for all kinds of two-wheeled vehicles.

Once you do get out of the city, great day rides and weekend trips are less than a couple hours away. Mount Hood rises to the east, the Pacific Ocean is just over the Coast Range to the west, and farmland and wine-growing country spread out to the south. The Columbia River Gorge is, well, gorgeous. Roads run in or above the chasm on both sides, starting just east of town, with picturesque views around every bend. The mountains in northeastern Oregon and the southwest corner of Washington make for good day rides or multiday trips. And the Cascades' many campgrounds and recreation-oriented towns (that's code for "they have good beer") are practically just down the road—albeit long and winding ones. Come to think of it, that's just the kind we like.

The Astoria Column recounts events in the town's history. Climb to the top for great views of Astoria, the Columbia River, and surrounding mountains.

RIDE

4

Escape to the Beach

Directions:
northwest on US 30 from Portland to Scappoose
west on Scappoose-Vernonia Highway to Nehalem Highway
/ OR 47
north on Nehalem Highway / OR 47 to Mist
north and west on Nehalem Highway (becomes OR 202)
northwest on OR 202 to Astoria
north on US 101 over Astoria Bridge to Ilwaco, WA
north on OR 103 to the end of Long Beach Peninsula
south on OR 103 to US 101
north on US 101 to WA 4
east on WA 4 to WA 432 and WA 433, across the Lewis
and Clark Bridge
east on US 30 to Portland

Distance:
total distance: 295 miles

Time:
a full day; two days with stops in Astoria and the Long
Beach Peninsula

Best Time of Year:
late spring through fall

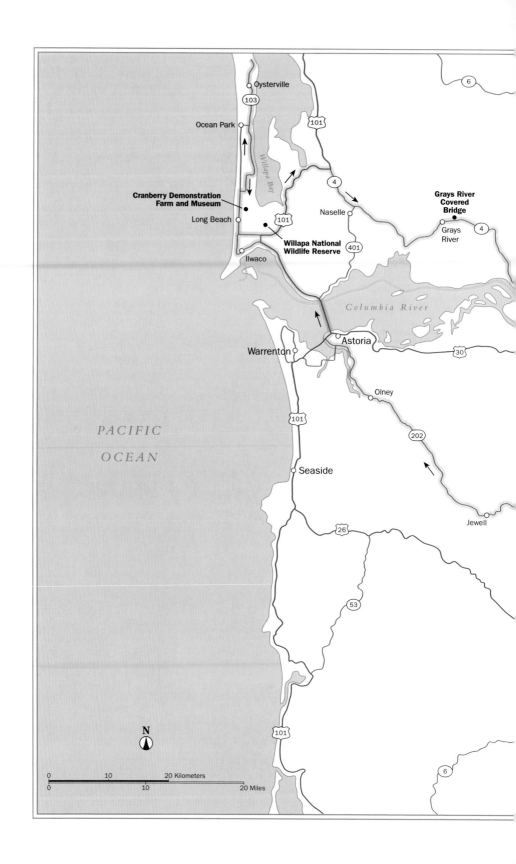

Escape to the Beach

Highlights:
rural, winding, forested back roads; quaint little towns, the
slightly tattered charm of Astoria, restored Victorian town of
Oysterville, the touristy attractions of the "World's Longest
Beach"

This ride is a nice escape from Portland's urban hustle and bus-
tle. If all you want to do is get out of town and ride without
stopping at tourist attractions, it can be a long but relaxing day
ride. If you prefer to take in the sights and sounds of places along
the way, give yourself two days and plan to stay overnight in
Astoria or one of the small towns on the Washington side of the
Astoria Bridge.

Your first instinct will probably be to take U.S. Highway 30
from Portland to Astoria. After all, it follows the course of the
Columbia River, one of the mightiest in the Northwest. How
could this not be a beautiful ride? It's not a bad ride, but a series
of little-known back roads will make your trip much more pleasant and prevent having to deal with US 30's stoplights and resulting traffic.

You can't completely avoid starting out on US 30; pick it up
as it leaves the northwest corner of Portland and travel about 20
miles to the little town of Scappoose. Look for signs for Vernonia
and Pittsburg. The turn for them, a left about a mile past the center of town, will put you on Scappoose-Vernonia Highway. The
route leaves the wide roads and traffic lights behind until Astoria,
some 76 miles up the road.

These back roads do have some shortcomings. For starters,
the quality of the pavement is inconsistent, with almost track-
smooth stretches interspersed with others that have any or all
of the following: grooves created by logging trucks, debris from
logging trucks, the logging trucks themselves, humps, heaves,
gravel, rocks, potholes, patches, and the occasional tree leaning
from the hillside into your lane.

The upside is that some of the curves are so well banked that you'll feel the bike compress under you as you lean into and power through the turns. In our opinion, it's worth dealing with those shortcomings to avoid US 30.

The road crosses Scappoose Creek, then Alder Creek, then gently climbs into forested hills as it follows North Scappoose Creek. The road will wind its way over ridges and hills and through a series of valleys containing all manner of farms and ranches. The surrounding hills show a history of logging, not surprising for this part of the country.

About 20 miles from Scappoose, the road intersects with the Nehalem Highway, another name for Oregon Highway 47. Go right on OR 47 toward Mist. Big Eddy County Park is about ten minutes down the road. A full-service park with camping, it fills up on weekends during the summer but is a nice place to take a break.

The terrain and scenery remain constant as OR 47 follows the Nehalem River, crossing it what seems like dozens of times. As you pass through Natal, consider stopping and taking a peek at the historic Natal schoolhouse and grange, built in 1908.

It would be easy to zip right past the well-preserved Natal schoolhouse, built in 1908, which sits quietly near OR 202.

From Mist, OR 47 heads north to US 30. You've chosen this route to avoid US 30, so go straight, following signs for Oregon Highway 202.

Birkenfeld is the next town of any size. Its historic store and cafe are inviting, and we've always seen at least one bike parked out front. About 12 miles farther, you'll enter Jewell and the Jewell Meadows Wildlife Area, which provides winter habitat for a herd of about 200 Roosevelt elk. These are massive animals with some adult bulls sporting impressive antlers and tipping the scales at 1,200 pounds. The Oregon Department of Fish and Wildlife provides food for the herd from December to February. We've slowed to look, but we've never seen them.

The 20 miles of asphalt from Jewell to Olney can have any of the shortcomings typical of these roads, so ride with care. Short stretches twist and climb through the forested hillside, bursting out of the trees into sections of clear-cut. As shocking a sight as that may be, keep your eyes on the road. Astoria is just twenty minutes or less from here.

This route brings you into Astoria from the back side. Astoria feels a little worn and tattered, like an old Persian rug. It retains much of its charm in Victorian and Art Deco architecture, and seems to be doing its best to hold on to its past while moving with the tide into the future. Downtown is quaint with a mix of shops and restaurants that cater to locals and tourists alike. There are plenty of motels, but the town plays host to summer crowds, so lodging on the weekends can sell out. From pleasant little bakery cafes to brew pubs and high-end steak houses, there are many restaurants to choose from.

One of the town's highlights, standing proudly on its highest hill, is the Astoria Column (photo page 34). Built in 1926, the column commemorates important events that contributed to Astoria's role in history. To get to the tower from OR 202, take a right on Williamsport Road and stay to the left when the road becomes a Y. Follow Williamsport through a 90-degree left to 15th Street and take a right. Take your first right on Madison Avenue, which becomes Coxcomb Drive, and a series of low-speed switchbacks leading to the column.

Your view from the column will depend on the time of day and time of year. If the weather is clear, it will treat you to views of the city, the surrounding rivers and mountains, and the Pacific Ocean. If you feel up to it, climb the 164 steps to the top for even more impressive views.

The Columbia River Maritime Museum is well worth the time and $10 admission. You may also tour the Flavel House Museum or the Fort Clatsop National Memorial. Stop in at the visitor center at the Astoria Column for a simple map and directions to any of the above. Go to www.oldoregon.com, Astoria's official Web site, for more information.

To get to the north side of the Columbia River and the Long Beach Peninsula, take US 101 north up and over the Astoria Bridge. The surface is concrete, so there's no need to worry about rubber tires on a steel grid.

Over the bridge, follow signs for US 101 north to Long Beach and Ilwaco. Ilwaco is a picturesque, artsy town with well-maintained clapboard houses and a couple decent restaurants (including the Sea Breeze Café, which serves all-you-can-eat fish and chips). From here, Cape Disappointment is an easy jaunt. Though it's named for the killer waters at the mouth of the Columbia River—which led many a fisherman to his doom—it could also apply to the Cape Disappointment Lighthouse, which is hard to find. Step into the Lewis and Clark interpretive center and look at displays to get information about how to explore

Steve: The Astoria Bridge is 4.1 miles long and two lanes wide—one for each direction of traffic. I mention this only because the first time I crossed the bridge, I was surprised to see a dashed yellow line painted on the pavement. If I recall correctly from driver education classes, this allows traffic in either direction to pass if it is safe to do so. I'm not sure it's ever safe to pass on a two-lane bridge 200 feet above a river; I've never seen anyone do it and I hope I never do. ●

the park's maze of roads, paths, and boardwalks. Artwork found along the trails is part of the Confluence Project, a collaboration between artist Maya Lin (of Vietnam Memorial fame) and non-profit groups.

Just north of the cape, North Head Lighthouse is welcoming and easily accessible. The road to it is a little uneven but short.

There is plenty to do and see on the Long Beach peninsula, which according to signs here is the world's longest (a claim that is, sadly, not true. It is one of the longest in America, if that's a consolation). Any list of attractions would be woefully incomplete, but here are a few: lighthouses, two state parks, miles and miles of beach, oyster fisheries, and nicely restored old buildings, including a historic church and school in Oysterville. (To plan a trip to the peninsula, go to www.funbeach.com.)

The town of Long Beach is the largest and most developed on the peninsula. It's a classic beachside tourist trap with all of the requisite attractions—including T-shirt shops, go-cart tracks, and curio shops—to keep the kids occupied for a day. If you enjoy an occasional oddity, head for Marsh's Free Museum, home to Jake the Alligator Man, supposedly half man, half alligator. Walking into Marsh's is like walking into the pages of a supermarket tabloid.

Long Beach is not really the world's longest, but don't tell the locals.

Piles of oyster shells line the banks of the harbor in Nahcotta, Washington. This area is all about the oysters.

If you prefer to avoid the town of Long Beach but still want to explore the peninsula, here's the locals' secret: Just south of Seaview, watch for Sandridge Road. It cuts off US 101 at about a 45-degree angle to the right. Sandridge runs up the east side of the peninsula unimpeded by the traffic, crowds, and chaos of Long Beach. If you pass the turn onto Sandridge and end up in Seaview, look for the Long Beach Peninsula Visitors Bureau. Stop in, pick up a map of the area, then head east on 40th Street, following signs for US 101. You'll come to the Sandridge Road intersection in about 0.5 mile.

Ride north on Sandridge toward Oysterville, where the entire town is on the Register of National Historic Districts and many of the buildings, including the church and school, are nicely restored. From Sandridge Road, only a couple roads connect to the peninsula's west side. If you're interested in learning more than you need to know about cranberries, take one of them, Pioneer Road, to the Cranberry Demonstration Farm and Museum.

When you want to return to parts south, there's no need to head back over the Astoria Bridge. Instead, follow the signs for

US 101 out of Seaview. US 101 wraps around the southern edge of Willapa Bay and past the Willapa National Wildlife Refuge, crossing the mouth of the Naselle River before connecting with Washington Highway 4.

WA 4 is a pleasant ride along the north side of the Columbia River, passing through a series of small fishing villages and resort towns. You'll be riding in the trees most of the time with only the occasional glimpse of the Columbia.

About 20 miles past the point where US 101 and WA 4 meet, you'll enter the little town of Grays River, home to the Grays River Covered Bridge, the only covered bridge still in use in Washington. Turn onto Loop Road at either the west or east end of town. The bridge is 2 miles from the turn at the west end of town, 0.2 mile from the turn at the east end.

WA 4 eventually intersects with Interstate 5, but by now you've spent too much time on back roads to finish the ride racing toward Portland on the interstate. So here's a shortcut: As you approach Longview, watch for signs for Washington Highway 432 / Truck Route. Take a right and head through residential development to your left and an ugly industrial part of town on your right. After about 4 miles, WA 432 intersects with Washington Highway 433, where you'll take a right. WA 433 crosses the Lewis and Clark Bridge and intersects with US 30 back to Portland.

RIDE 5

Hood Winks

Directions:
(from Portland):
east on I-84 to exit 17, Troutdale
east on Historic Columbia River Highway to I-84
east on I-84 to exit 63, Hood River City Center
east on State Street / US 30 to US 35
south on US 35 to US 26
north on Timberline Road to Timberline Lodge
west on US 26 to Portland

Total Distance:
about 160 miles
Portland to Troutdale: 16 miles
Troutdale to Dodson (junction with I-84): 23 miles
Dodson to Hood River: 29 miles
Hood River to Mount Hood / Parkdale: 15 miles
Mount Hood / Parkdale to Government Camp: 28 miles
Government Camp to Portland: 48 miles

Time:
half a day

Services:
Portland and suburbs, Troutdale, Hood River, Parkdale,
Camp Creek, Government Camp

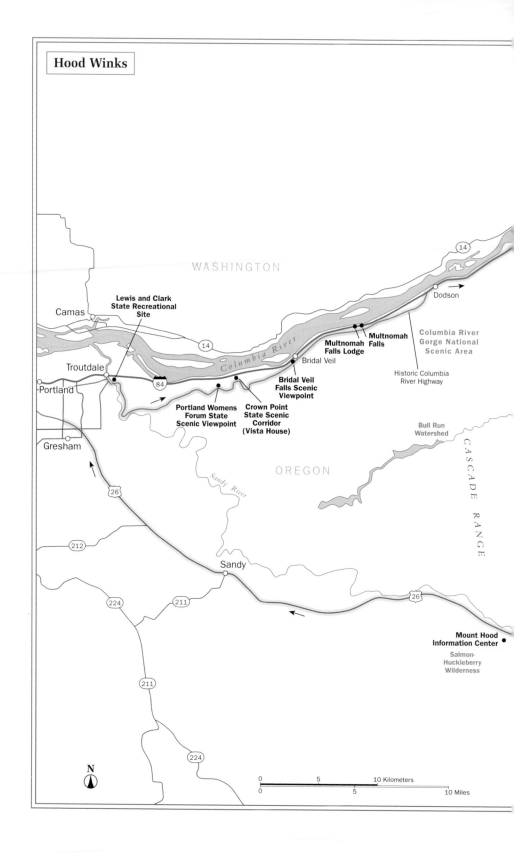

Hood Winks

Lewis and Clark State Recreational Site

WASHINGTON

Camas

Dodson

Columbia River Gorge National Scenic Area

Troutdale

Multnomah Falls

Multnomah Falls Lodge

Bridal Veil

Portland

Bridal Veil Falls Scenic Viewpoint

Historic Columbia River Highway

Portland Womens Forum State Scenic Viewpoint

Crown Point State Scenic Corridor (Vista House)

Gresham

Bull Run Watershed

CASCADE RANGE

OREGON

Sandy River

Sandy

Mount Hood Information Center

Salmon-Huckleberry Wilderness

N

0   5   10 Kilometers
0   5   10 Miles

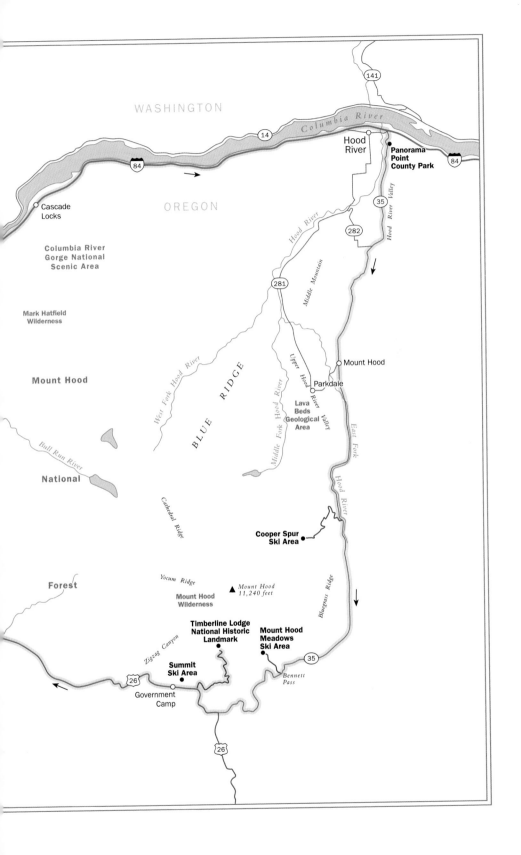

Best Time of Year:
late spring to fall

Highlights:
friendly small towns; an old-fashioned historic highway;
miles of orchards and vineyards; getting close to Mount
Hood's pointy peak

The loop around Mount Hood is an understandably well-loved day ride. It's a mix of old and new, modern and historic, with some big-mountain riding around Mount Hood, northwest Oregon's iconic anchor. Leaving Portland's urban center, it travels back in time along the Historic Columbia River Highway, granting expansive Columbia River Gorge vistas and access to waterfalls that pour from basalt cliffs carved by the mighty river. From Hood River—an outdoor recreation hub surrounded by the orchards that first put it on the map—the route winds around the base of Mount Hood, then climbs as close as bikes can get to the volcano's glacier-capped cone.

We prefer riding the loop's Columbia Gorge section first, since the winds that make for optimal windsurfing and kite-boarding conditions tend to pick up velocity as the day goes on, and battling 35-mph headwinds at the end of a ride is exhausting.

This journey really begins about 15 minutes east of Portland. From Interstate 84, take exit 17 for Troutdale, make a right at the end of the off ramp, go about 0.25 mile, and make a left on Historic Columbia River Highway. You'll be on the western fringe of downtown Troutdale. Although it's just a few blocks from an interstate and its neighbors are an outlet mall and suburban sprawl, Troutdale's historic district has a quaint, small-town feel.

From the east end of town, the road bends to the right, then to the left, and crosses the Sandy River. The official start of the Historic Columbia River Highway is at the west end of the bridge; take a right at the T just beyond it. Lewis and Clark State Park is on the left as the road runs parallel to the river. The Sandy River runs clear now, but when Lewis and Clark camped on its banks in 1805, it was still gray and gritty with ash from the 1802 eruption of Mount Hood.

After about 4 miles, the river swings away toward its origins on the southwest flank of Mount Hood, and the road climbs past the small farms and orchards surrounding Springdale and Corbett. A few miles past Corbett, check out panoramic vistas of the Columbia River and the Columbia River Gorge from Portland Women's Forum State Park. It also offers a peek at Crown Point Vista House.

Winding gracefully toward the river through a series of zig-zags and losing about 600 feet of elevation, the road enters rich woods where moss dangles from a canopy of trees and white wooden guardrails impart a nostalgic, early-twentieth-century look to the narrow lane. As the twists follow the contours of the land, the road passes a series of seven waterfalls that emerge from the cliffs on both sides of the road. Some are tucked in tight little coves within feet of the road while others are more major attractions. Bridal Veil Falls, for example, is an easy twenty-minute hike from a roadside parking area.

Multnomah Falls is Oregon's most-visited natural attraction, and it's easy to see why. Originating at an underground spring on

Perched atop Crown Point, a rocky promontory 733 feet above the Columbia River, Crown Point Vista House is one of the most recognizable and photographed sites in the gorge. With its awe-inspiring multidirectional views, it's a common stop on the historic highway. The octagonal stone structure was built in 1916 as an observatory, pioneer memorial, and "comfort station"—code for "bathroom." With its brass fixtures and marble interior, some mocked it as "The $100,000 Outhouse," but it's undeniably the most magnificent rest stop we've ever seen. ●

Right off the historic highway, Multnomah Falls is understandably one of Oregon's most-visited tourist attractions.

Larch Mountain, water pours through a narrow gap in the rock, cascading a total of 620 feet in two stages. A paved trail from Multnomah Falls Lodge to the top ascends 600 feet or so in 1.2 miles. It's steep and fairly strenuous, so you may not want to go all the way up in riding boots. Requiring significantly less effort and easily done in riding gear, the Benson Bridge segment takes you onto a span that crosses the falls between the upper and lower cataracts.

On almost any weekend—especially if the weather is clear—both sides of the road close to Multnomah Falls are lined with cars that didn't fit in the parking lot near the falls' base. Chances are, a bunch of bikes will be grouped together at one end of the main lot; unless you're with a big group, you should be able to squeeze in somewhere.

This section of the historic highway ends at Dodson, and I-84 whisks us east to Hood River and the junction with U.S. Highway 35.

In 1855, the first fruit trees were planted in what is now downtown Hood River. Those apples, pears, peaches, plums, and apricots were the beginning of a long and bountiful history of fruit-growing in this valley. By the end of the nineteenth century, apples were Hood River's major crop. Sadly, December temperatures in 1919 changed that when they plummeted to almost 30 degrees below zero. Many apple trees suffered damage, and some entire orchards were wiped out. Growers replaced apples with winter pears, which can better withstand freezing temperatures; pears took over as the top crop and have remained number one since.

Though orchards still dominate its landscape, Hood River is an energetic little community changing with the times. It's home to notable microbreweries and outdoor-sports businesses as well as vineyards and wineries. This part of the gorge boasts some of the region's best kayaking, mountain-biking, and hiking, and the winds funneled between the gorge's cliffs make this the unofficial windsurfing capital of the world.

Having spent some time looking from afar at Mount Hood's distinctive cone, it's time to strike out for the top of it—or at least as close as pavement will take us. Turn south onto US 35 when U.S. Highway 30 intersects with it a few blocks east of downtown Hood River, near where US 35 connects with I-84.

US 35 cruises south through more orchards and ridges, then slides into the hamlet of Mount Hood. Aside from a small market, it's just a wide spot in the road. Parkdale—about 3 miles to the west on Oregon Highway 281—has more services, including fuel, which is nonexistent for about the next 30 miles to Government Camp.

Charging at the base of Mount Hood, US 35 makes a huge sweeping turn to the right and another to the left as it enters national forest. The changing geography makes a noticeable difference in the mood of the ride. The valley narrows, and mountain slopes converge on the road from both sides as it ascends with every mile. Everything seems bigger and is more rugged as the highway twines up the mountain's lower reaches. The exposed, boulder-strewn bed of the East Fork of the Hood River parallels the road for a time, intermittently visible as the sweeping curves gain energy and elevation.

As the highway bends to the west, the river disappears and the incline grows more noticeable, especially as the road clambers over 4,650-foot Bennett Pass before dropping in to the White River Canyon. The pavement through White River Canyon has a long history of washouts, which have forced twenty closures since 1907. Five of those have come since September 1998. Its

Consider making a short and worthwhile detour from US 35 to Panorama Point County Park, just outside Hood River. The turnoff is on the left, less than a mile south of where US 30 and 35 intersect. It isn't well marked (the road sign may read East Side Road), and there isn't a turn lane. The road climbs over a forested ridge and cruises past rows of fruit trees to Panorama Point, which overlooks a vast expanse of orchards, vineyards, and rolling hills, with Mount Hood's glacier-capped peak towering in the distance.

South of Panorama Point, East Side Road wends through orchard-covered inclines and curves, each giving a slightly different perspective. Short spur roads cut east into the hills above or dive back to US 35. About 4 miles south of Panorama Point, East Side Road comes to a T intersection with Fir Mountain Road; make a right turn and soon Fir Mountain Road brings you back to US 35. Turn left and redirect the front wheel toward Mount Hood. ●

The detour to Panorama Point County Park is worth making for these views of Hood River Valley and Mount Hood.

immense debris field is an unmistakable reminder of the unpredictable and awesome forces at work in the mountains.

Be especially cautious here: the canyon's new pavement is in excellent condition, inviting you to pull back a little on the throttle and power through the curves, but windblown sand accumulates in the bends and fine dust kicked up by other vehicles can cling to windshields, face shields, and goggles. (Use an aerosol dust remover before wiping this surprisingly scratchy dust off anything made of plastic.)

Having hooked to the peak's south side, US 35 ends when it merges with U.S. Highway 26, which sweeps in climbing and twisting and overlooking the valleys below. On its approach to the mountain, US 26 swings through an entertaining sequence of enormous switchbacks. As it rounds the top of a curve, the mountain's 11,237-foot volcanic cone comes into view, looming over

Christy: With its close proximity to civilization, steep slopes, and deep crevasses, Mount Hood sees its share of serious climbing, hiking, and skiing accidents.

In 2002, nine climbers fell into a 40-foot crevasse; three died immediately. The Air Force helicopter sent to rescue the others crashed into the mountain and tumbled down the slope, rolling right over one rescuer (he survived). In 2009, another of those rescuers had an accident of his own, falling 200 feet and breaking both legs. About 10,000 people attempt the summit each year, and more than 130 have died in the effort.

Although experienced climbers suffer spectacular mishaps, many other accidents involve people completely unprepared for its challenges. Some are hikers who decide on a whim to explore new territory, only to find themselves going off the edge of a cliff. Needless to say, emergency-response teams here get a lot of practice with mountain rescues. ●

Summer visitors to Timberline Lodge play on remaining snowpack that descends to the parking lot.

the tree line ahead. The highway dives into a bend at the base of the trees, and the peak disappears—until the road rounds the top of the next bend, where it looms even larger. This happens several times, and before you know it, you've passed the turn for Timberline Lodge and are cruising into Government Camp.

Since it's not really a resort town or a classic mountain town, Government Camp's business district and small ski resort act as a gateway to the larger, busier Timberline Lodge and Mount Hood Skibowl resorts. In the summer, it feels a bit like a staging area for all the outdoors enthusiasts flooding the mountain and the surrounding national forest.

The well-marked turn for Timberline Lodge is a short backtrack from Government Camp. The road—a steep coil that gives you the occasional chance to peer down on the road you just rode—brings you as close as possible to the volcano you've been circling for half the day. The lodge itself, built in 1937 as a Works Progress Administration (WPA) project, is worth at least peering into. Its massive timbers and slabs of native stone give it a rustic and, some would say, romantic quality.

The area around the lodge is an entertaining place to explore and people-watch. Remaining snowpack descends to the edge of the parking lot, encouraging T-shirt-clad visitors to unwisely engage the more heavily dressed members of their party in snowball fights. Adventure travelers cross the parking lot toting backpacks full of gear for long treks in the backcountry, while day-hikers don smaller packs for jaunts up the exposed ridgelines. Relax and enjoy the wildflowers blooming in fields below a chairlift; chances are, wherever you're headed from here is no more than an hour or two away.

The road west of Government Camp descends fast and furiously through a couple of buttonhook-shaped curves that gradually evolve to big sweeping bends, losing elevation in the process. The road passes through a string of small villages between the wilderness around Mount Hood and the eastern suburbs of Portland. US 26 eventually enters those suburbs in Sandy, passing through Gresham and becoming Powell Boulevard, one of Portland's main arteries.

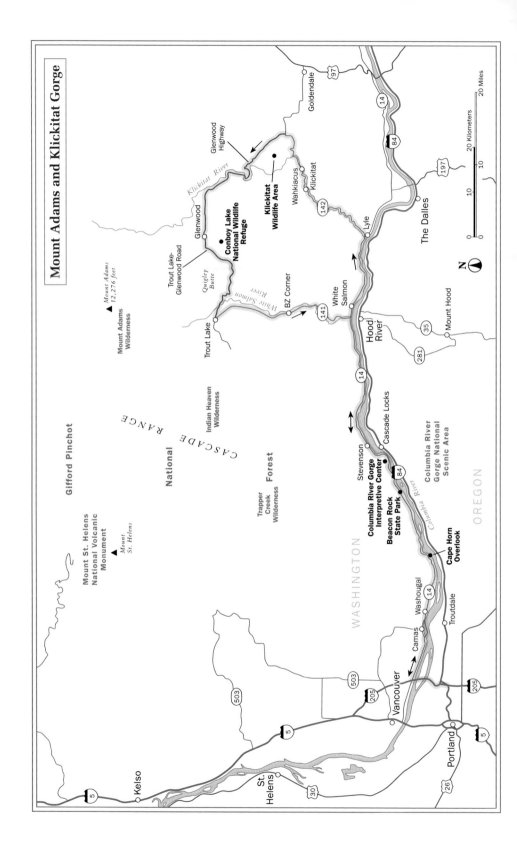

Mount Adams and Klickitat Gorge

RIDE

6

Mount Adams and Klickitat Gorge

Directions:
north on I-205 from Portland to WA 14 exit
east on WA 14 to WA 142
north on WA 142 to Glenwood Highway
northwest on Glenwood Highway to Glenwood
west on Trout Lake-Glenwood Road to Trout Lake
south on WA 141 to WA 14
west on WA 14 back to Portland

Distance:
total mileage for the loop: 206 miles
Portland to Stevenson: 46 miles
Stevenson to Lyle (intersection with WA 142): 34 miles
Lyle to Glenwood: 25 miles
Glenwood to Trout Lake: 16 miles
Trout Lake to Underwood (intersection of WA 141 and WA 14): 20 miles
Underwood to Portland: 65 miles

Time:
the better part of a day, depending on speed and stops

Services:
in Oregon: Portland
in Washington: Vancouver, Camas, Stevenson, Glenwood, BZ Corner

Best Time of Year:
late spring to fall

Highlights:
pleasant roads leading to magnificent rivers and the
gorges they cut; huckleberries (if they're in season); Mount
Adams's volcanic peak

This ride mixes beautiful scenery and roads that allow for a relaxed pace. Toss in the twists and turns through Klickitat Gorge, and you've got a better-than-average day ride. The stretch through Klickitat Gorge will make you work a little, but this is nice work if you can get it.

In Portland, pick up Interstate 205 northbound and cross the Columbia River into Washington. Take Washington Highway 14, the first exit on the Washington side, and ride east toward Camas. As WA 14 enters Washougal, the number of lanes diminishes as the road narrows, eventually paring itself down to just two. Just past Washougal, the highway leaves suburban Vancouver and climbs into the bluffs overlooking the Columbia River.

Steve: I often wonder how many people living in or near Portland or Vancouver take for granted this magnificent river that is the Columbia. I never tire of the spectacular scenery and the endless views of the gorge it has carved on its way to the Pacific Ocean. Atop the bluffs a few miles east of Washougal, you round a bend and come upon a pullout for the Cape Horn overlook, which gives a rare top-down direct view of the gorge's cliffs. Well-marked and large, it offers plenty of reasons to stop, look, listen, ponder, and appreciate the power and influence the mighty river has had on this region for thousands of years. ●

Once you've had your fill of the Cape Horn overlook at the top of the bluff, get back on the bike and roll into Stevenson, just a few miles downhill. On the way, you'll pass Beacon Rock State Park; this 850-foot basalt volcano remnant is supposedly the second-largest single rock in the world, but Gibraltar and Ayers Rock might have something to say about that. (Still, it's impressive.) If you left Portland before breakfast and have built up an appetite, Stevenson features plenty of places to eat right on its main drag.

Stevenson is also home to the Columbia River Gorge Interpretive Center, a great place to learn about the natural history of the gorge and the competing cultural and economic interests of Native peoples and European settlers. It can also be a stop on a return trip to Portland.

The turn for Washington Highway 141 Alt is about 20 miles past Stevenson, at the confluence of the Columbia and White Salmon Rivers. The mouth of the White Salmon is a very popular fishing spot, so watch for campers, trucks with trailers, and folks crossing the road to launch all manner of boats and rafts from which to wet a line.

You may be inclined to take the turn onto WA 141, but we have a better idea. Continue on WA 14 for another 13 miles until the turn for Washington Highway 142 and the confluence of the Columbia and Klickitat Rivers. This stretch of road, from Lyle to the top of the gorge and the little town of Glenwood, is great fun for bikers of every style. Some sections can get congested with automobile traffic on weekends, especially during the summer.

The Klickitat River can be calm in mid- to late summer, but it's also powerful, especially in the lower section below the town of Klickitat. Over the eons it's carved through hundreds of feet of cement-hard basalt on its way to the Columbia. As the temperature rises, people take to the river in rafts, inner tubes, dories, and pretty much anything that floats (fishermen call this the "rubber hatch"). Families picnic and play in the river, so most of the traffic late in the day is making its way—slowly—out of the gorge below the town of Klickitat. You'll avoid almost all of the traffic

The road makes a series of curves through Klickitat Gorge.

by riding through the gorge early, during the coolest part of the day. Besides, we prefer to ride curves going uphill rather than down, leaning in and powering through.

Follow WA 142 as it sticks to the Klickitat River. As it makes its way to the top of the gorge, it bisects Klickitat and Wahkiacus, so watch your speed. As your trip odometer clicks off to about 22 miles from the turn onto WA 142, the pavement will turn away from the Klickitat River, cross the Little Klickitat River, and make a sharp 180-degree turn, crossing Canyon Creek before ascending rapidly. Before you know it, you pop out of the gorge onto a plateau of open grasslands.

Hang on—you're not done with this ride yet! Continue on WA 142 for about a mile to a 90-degree turn. Stay alert, because about 200 yards after that right-hand curve, you're going to make a left onto the Glenwood Highway. The signage isn't great, but it's the only left you can make. From here you'll go about 5 miles, passing a few farms and ranches, before dropping back into the Klickitat Gorge. The road descends to the bottom of the gorge, then crosses the Klickitat River and follows its course before beginning a rapid but easy climb out of the gorge through a series of big sweeping turns.

Continue west on the Glenwood Highway for about 6 miles to Glenwood. There isn't much going on in Glenwood—it's a sleepy

Steve: Mount Adams, topping out at 12,281 feet above sea level, doesn't get the respect and attention a volcano of its size rightfully deserves. It seems to be the forgotten stepchild in a family of impressive Pacific Northwest volcanoes. Perhaps that's because its peak doesn't loom over a major city, or because it's the second-highest volcano in the state of Washington, with Mount Rainier reigning supreme at 14,410 feet. My guess is that because Mount Adams is surrounded by remote wilderness, with few roads allowing access to its flanks, it simply lacks the "wow" factor people get when they're up close and personal to a peak. At any rate, as with all of the Northwest's volcanoes, it's an impressive sight. ●

Catch a good look at Mount Adams from the road between BZ Corner and Trout Lake.

little town—but it does have the full range of services. As a bonus, you'll get your first real views of Mount Adams.

Head west out of Glenwood on Trout Lake-Glenwood Road, just another name for the road you've been riding. It meanders around Quigley Butte, one of several on the lower flanks of Mount Adams that will obscure your view of the volcano for most of the ride to Trout Lake. That's okay. Concentrate on the curves with the knowledge that a cool, smooth, and sweet treat awaits a mere 16 miles down the road.

If you are in need of a rest and a snack here, you're in luck. This part of Washington is Huckleberry Central, and a huckleberry milkshake makes a tasty addition to this ride. One of the best places to get a huckleberry milkshake, short of picking your own berries and making one at home, is KJ's Bear Creek Cafe in Trout Lake. If you want something more substantial, KJ's also has good burgers and sandwiches so you can have lunch and feed your sweet tooth as well.

If by chance you do feel like picking your own huckleberries, head to the ranger station in Trout Lake for a map of the best locations. You're allowed to harvest up to three gallons of berries free of charge—any more than that and you'll need to get a permit. The most sought-after berries are a deep purple color, plump, and sweet.

From Trout Lake, head south on WA 141 toward BZ Corner, really just a quick stop if you need to gas up or grab a snack. It's also a popular starting point for local outfitters and members of the public who raft the White Salmon River (remember, you passed the mouth of it on your way to Lyle). There's a well-developed public put-in right in town along the east side of the road. You'll see the outfitters' vans parked in the good-sized lot. Take the short walk down to the river from the parking lot and watch rafters and kayakers who've put in farther upriver navigate a set of narrow rapids. A word of caution: mist and spray from the rapids make the rocks right along the river very slippery. If you're not careful, you could go for an unexpected wet and bumpy ride on the White Salmon River sans raft or kayak.

The rapids at BZ Corner are a popular place for rafters and boaters to put in, or for anyone to watch those who've put in farther upriver.

Continue south on WA 141 from BZ Corner toward the confluence of the White Salmon and the Columbia and the intersection with WA 14. Back on WA 14, the ride back to Portland is fun and easy, a reverse repeat of what you rode to get here.

You have other options if you have the time. Cross the Columbia River to Hood River, Oregon, and ride to the backside of Mount Hood (ride 5), or pick up one of the roads to the east side of Mount St. Helens (ride 25). A word of warning: The roads on Mount St. Helens's east side are pretty technical, with bad road conditions and lots of tight turns, so they're not for everyone.

Restaurant

Trout Lake
KJ's Bear Creek Cafe
2376 WA 141
(509) 395-2525

OREGON CASCADES

The Oregon Cascades are wild and rocky, but they're laced with roads ranging from highways in good condition to logging routes that would be questionable for anyone to try. In between are entertaining back roads featuring plenty of ups and downs and winding sections. They run around big peaks, along mountain lakes, and next to rivers and waterfalls, making for a lot of relaxing and entertaining riding.

You can get to this great riding from almost anywhere in the state—the coast, anywhere along Interstate 5, or eastern Oregon—within a couple of hours. At the end of the day, you can pitch a tent or stay in a nice hotel. And before you turn in, you can take a dip in one of the many hot springs that bubble out of the hillsides.

This is nature at its most majestic. The Oregon Cascades are dominated by steep peaks, including plenty of volcanic cones like the Three Sisters and Mount Jefferson. Crater Lake, the deepest lake in the United States, is nestled in the remnants of a massive caldera that erupted nearly 8,000 years ago.

Big rivers, including the Santiam, McKenzie, Rogue, and Umpqua, stream through valleys they cut into the rock. Western slopes are covered in lush vegetation, while things dry out on the eastern side, where evergreen forests eventually give way to open grassland and sagebrush.

Unlike many mountainous regions, the Oregon Cascades also offer plenty of amenities, many of them in funky little towns like Oakridge or Sisters and growing cities like Bend. With everything from skiing to river-rafting, Bend is a recreational paradise and increasingly a playground for the wealthy, the retired, or both. But that also means good food, locally brewed beer, and all kinds of supplies.

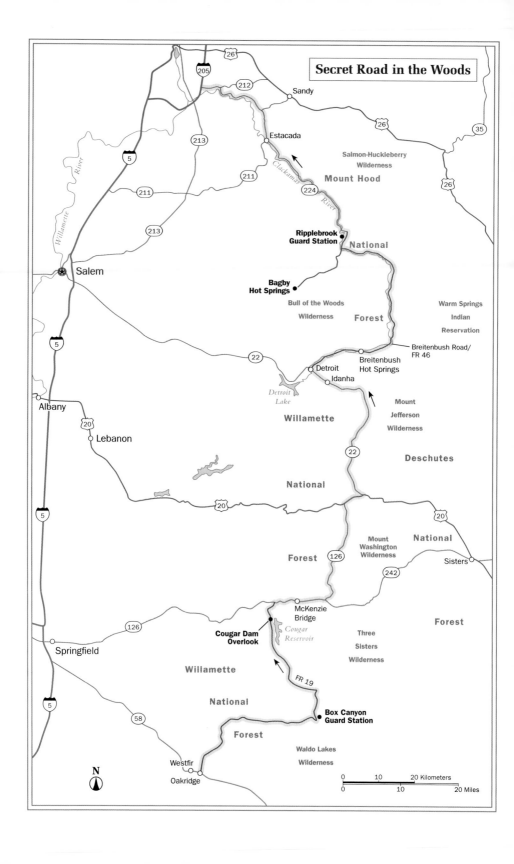

Secret Road in the Woods

RIDE

7

Secret Road in the Woods

Directions:

(from Oakridge):

north on FR 19 to OR 126

east on OR 126 to US 20

east on OR 126 / US 20 to OR 22

north on OR 22 to Detroit

north on Breitenbush Road / FR 46 (becomes OR 224), to
OR 212

north on OR 224 / OR 212 to I-205

Distance:

from Oakridge to Portland: 243 miles

from Oakridge to McKenzie Bridge via FR 19: 85 miles

from McKenzie Bridge to intersection of OR 126 / US 20
and OR 22 (North Santiam Highway): 27 miles

from OR 22 (North Santiam Highway) intersection to
Detroit: 32 miles

from Detroit to Estacada via FR 46 and OR 224: 72 miles

from Estacada to Portland: 27 miles

Time:

a full day

Services:

Oakridge, McKenzie Bridge, Detroit, Estacada, Portland

Best Time of Year:
late spring to fall

Highlights:
quirky little towns; Office Covered Bridge; beautiful scenery
on little-known back roads; rivers and a reservoir

The mountain town of Oakridge in east-central Oregon is the
jumping-off point for this ride. Starting near Oakridge, you'll
meander north through the Willamette National Forest on the
Cascades' west side. The first leg is a back road, Forest Road 19,
that skirts the western edge of the Three Sisters Wilderness and
follows several rivers designated as "scenic waterways." You'll
pick up sections of Oregon Highways 126, 20, and 22, tracking
north through the national forest east of Mount Washington and
Mount Jefferson into the town of Detroit on the shores of Detroit
Lake. From Detroit it's back onto national forest roads that work
their way north, then west, and become Oregon Highway 224.
The name changes but the scenery doesn't as the road follows the
Clackamas River toward Estacada and the outskirts of Portland.

Oakridge is easy to get to; it lies 36 miles southeast of Eugene
on Oregon Highway 58, which passes through the middle of

Steve: Although it's surrounded by the Willamette National
Forest and all the activities a national forest has to offer,
Oakridge, like most small towns in Oregon, seems to
be struggling to stay alive. I get the feeling it's trying to
remake itself, but it still looks a little weary and torn and
tattered around the edges. I can't put my finger on exactly
why it is, but Oakridge has grown on me. Every time I pass
through this town, I like it just a bit more than I did the last
time. ●

The bright red Office Covered Bridge is a sign you've found the "secret" road to begin this ride.

town on its way to south-central Oregon. FR 19, the first leg of this route, is a fun road through rich forest, following scenic rivers with plenty of curves. While Oakridge is easy to find, FR 19 is a different story—hence the "secret" in this ride's name. The first time we tried to find the southern terminus of this road, a couple of guys at a local gas station had trouble providing clear directions. We'll do our best to give you better guidance than the Oakridge boys gave us.

Here's the easiest way to find FR 19: From the west, take OR 58 into the hamlet of Westfir. Watch for the Middle Fork ranger station on your right. Directly across the street from the ranger station is Westfir Road. Make a left on Westfir and cross the green trestle bridge. As soon as you're off the bridge, take the hard left that drops down and begins to parallel the river you just crossed, and you'll be on FR 19. Do not follow Westfir Road as it curves off to your right.

From the east, take OR 58 through Oakridge. About a mile past the west end of town, look for the Middle Fork ranger station on your left; make a right onto Westfir Road, and follow the directions above. If you think you're on FR 19 but don't see a red covered bridge spanning the river, you've made a wrong turn.

The beautiful Office Covered Bridge, so named because it was built by the Westfir Lumber Company to connect the mill and its office, is Oregon's longest at 180 feet. It's well worth parking the bike and taking a peek from a few different angles. If you're there when raspberries are ripe, you'll get the bonus of a sweet treat.

Past the covered bridge, you'll encounter a long stretch of 25- to 35-mph curves. It's best to obey the speed limit: The forest grows right to the shoulder, and the canopy completely covers the road in places. You're bound to encounter twigs, pinecones, and small tree branches—all hazards that can do you harm if you're going too fast. We've even come across a tree blocking one lane or the other.

The pavement is not perfect, either: small cracks, heaves, and slumps add an extra challenge to the tighter curves. Despite that, this is a fun road and very much worth riding. The first time you ride it you may be asking yourself why you didn't find out about it sooner.

The road follow the contours of the North Fork of the Middle Fork of the Willamette River (yes, that cumbersome name is correct), crossing from one side to the other via a series of narrow bridges. Although we're not advising that you stop on any of them, the best views of the river are from the bridges. Traffic is sparse but a fair share of it is empty logging trucks and pickups pulling campers, so stay alert if you do stop.

About 25 miles into the ride, you'll cross to the other side of the North Fork of the Middle Fork of the Willamette River for good. The road straightens and opens up a bit before a short, steep climb away from the river and up Box Canyon. It tops out at the Box Canyon Guard Station, one of many structures built throughout the Northwest to house on-duty first-responder firefighters.

Past the guard station, the road drops through a series of steep and sharp S curves, with a tight 180-degree turn at the bottom. Within about 3 miles, it descends about 1,200 feet in elevation,

One of the most charming things about the Northwest is the fire guard stations and lookout towers scattered throughout its forests. Built mostly through the first half of the twentieth century (many by the Civilian Conservation Corps during the Depression) to fight fires that could kill people and destroy property, they were usually staffed by a small crew. Upon hearing about a new fire from one of the fire-spotters in a lookout tower, guards would dash off to fight them, often on horseback, until they put the fires out or reinforcements arrived.

Although some have fallen apart or been torn down in intervening years, many are preserved and now available for use by the general public. Usually perched in high places with good visibility, some of them are only accessible by four-wheel-drive roads or long hikes. Others are right off paved roads. Reservations through the forest service are required to stay there overnight; if you're interested, check well in advance at www.fs.fed.us/r6/recreation/rentals/. Rental fees pay for maintenance of the sites.

The cabins sleep anywhere from four to twelve people or so, and have basic amenities (the Box Canyon station has a portable toilet, a picnic table, and a fire pit). A sign clearly states that no camping is allowed in the immediate area around this cabin (there are several campgrounds just down the road), but the restroom and picnic table make it a perfect place for a little rest in the forest. ●

into the cool air and thick, lush vegetation of a river valley. You are now following the South Fork of the McKenzie River.

About 17 miles past the Box Canyon station, the road crosses to the river's west side. The pavement becomes only slightly less civilized than it has been so far as it winds through a series of 20- to 25-mph curves along the western edge of Cougar Reservoir. These are tight, mostly flat curves with the usual array of debris

Cougar Reservoir is a nice place to stop, relax, and ponder your next move.

found on any mountain road, so take it easy. It's a short 6 miles to the Cougar Dam overlook and you don't need to push it, so sit back, relax, and enjoy the scenery.

If you enjoy hot springs, watch for signs for Terwilliger Hot Springs, aka Cougar Hot Springs, on your left about 3 miles north of where FR 19 meets Cougar Reservoir and about 4 miles before Cougar Dam. The hot springs are about 0.25 mile from the trailhead. They're clothing-optional, so you may want to take a pass if you're shy.

From the view areas at the dam overlooking the reservoir, it's only about 3.5 miles to the intersection with OR 126. There are many ways to finish this ride from here, and the Cougar Dam overlook isn't a bad place to ponder your next move. For us, the final leg of this ride heads to Portland.

From the Cougar Dam overlook, follow FR 19 as it curves to the left just before the dam. Take a right at OR 126. North of its intersection with Oregon Highway 242 (just a few miles down the road), OR 126 is also part of the McKenzie-Santiam Loop described in ride 8. Follow OR 126 for about 32 miles to the inter-section with U.S. Highway 20. Take a right on US 20 / OR 126 and go northeast for about 3.5 miles to the intersection with OR 22, aka the North Santiam Highway. OR 22 winds, climbs, then descends its way north through the Willamette National Forest. You'll ride west of Mount Jefferson through Marion Forks and Idanha before reaching Detroit. About halfway between the two little towns, the road picks up the North Santiam River and fol-lows it all the way to Detroit.

As you enter Detroit, downtown is off to your left, on the shores of Detroit Lake. Just past downtown, the road makes a Y with OR 22 as the left arm, heading to the northwest. Breitenbush Road (Forest Road 46) is the right arm and heads to the northeast. The Rt. 22 Gas and Mini-Mart sits in the center where the road splits. This is a great place to fuel up, get a snack, and relax before hitting the road for the final leg to Portland. It has a good-sized deck out back overlooking the Detroit Lake Marina and the moun-tains to the northeast.

Steve: This area is filled with hot springs, and many of them are clothing-optional—you can wear a bathing suit if you desire, but be prepared for those who don't. It's one manifestation of the laid-back live-and-let-live philosophy that pervades the Northwest (Oregon also has a couple of nude beaches).

As well as the springs mentioned in this ride, there's also Bagby Hot Springs, run by the National Forest Service, the turn for which is about 30 miles south of Estacada. An unimproved set of springs lies somewhere right along FR 46 about halfway between Detroit and Estacada. Bruce, a biker from Newport I kept running into on rides, said all you have to do to find clothing-optional hot springs in summer is look for parked cars and people in all stages of nakedness. ●

Riders take the curves on OR 224 along the Clackamas River.

OR 22 heads west toward Salem. We won't go that way, since it leaves the national forest about 6 miles west of Detroit and gets progressively uglier the closer it gets to Salem. Instead, follow Breitenbush Road to the northeast. You are still in the mountains, riding through rugged terrain and dense forest, so the usual warning about humps, bumps, cracks, and debris still applies.

About 10 miles from the intersection of OR 22 and Breitenbush Road is Breitenbush Hot Springs, a worker-owned resort community offering spiritual retreats and a conference center. The resort—including the hot springs, spas, and saunas—is clothing-optional.

About 7 miles past Breitenbush, FR 46 will turn north and begin to climb and roll through the forest, eventually descending to the banks of the Clackamas River, the course and contours of which the road follows, whether we know it or not, almost all the way to Portland.

Although the road looks the same, FR 46 changes to OR 224, also called the Clackamas Highway, at the intersection of FR 46 and Forest Road 57, about 45 miles from Detroit. The turn for FR 57 cuts in from the right as you make a tight left-hand curve. A couple hundred feet past the curve, the Ripplebrook Guard Station sits back off the road on your right (although it's closed, the station makes a good reference point).

It's 27 miles of twists and turns from the guard station into Estacada. At times, the surrounding forest is so dense you'll almost forget the river is beyond the trees to your left. Other times, tree-topped cliffs tower to your right over you and the asphalt, and spectacular views of the river are below you to the left. A few miles before Estacada, the road passes the North Fork Reservoir. OR 224 climbs rapidly over a ridge and away from the reservoir before dropping back toward the Clackamas River and into Estacada.

Because Estacada is on the southeastern fringe of Portland's southeastern suburbs, it's not the best part of the ride. It is a great place to fuel up or get a meal or almost anything else. From Estacada, follow OR 224 north through the little town of Eagle Creek, where it twists its way northwest through the tiny enclaves of Barton and Carver, intersecting with Oregon Highway 212 about 3.5 miles east of Clackamas. Take a left onto OR 224 / OR 212 and, after half a dozen or so traffic lights, you'll reach Interstate 205 into Portland.

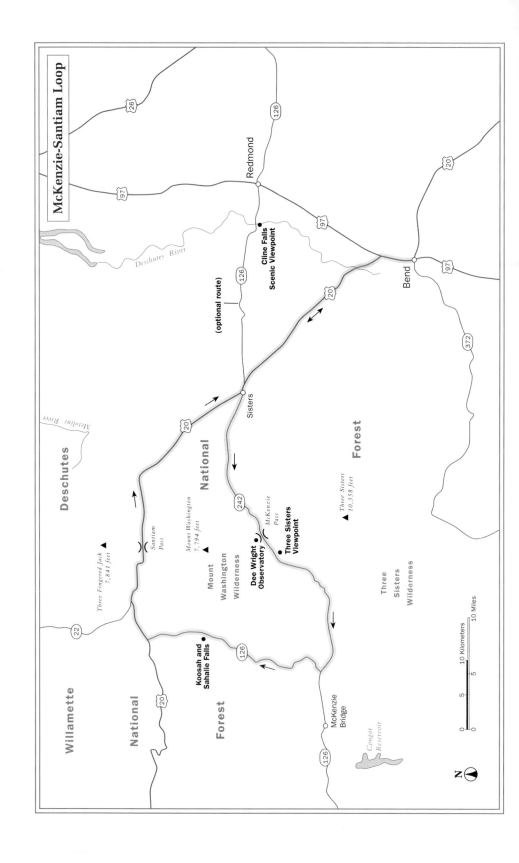

McKenzie-Santiam Loop

Deschutes

Willamette

National

Forest

Metolius River

Deschutes River

National

Forest

Redmond

Bend

Sisters

McKenzie Bridge

Three Fingered Jack
7,841 feet

Santiam Pass

Mount Washington
7,794 feet

**Mount
Washington
Wilderness**

**Dee Wright
Observatory**

*McKenzie
Pass*

**Three Sisters
Viewpoint**

Three Sisters
10,358 feet

**Three
Sisters
Wilderness**

**Koosah and
Sahalie Falls**

**Cline Falls
Scenic Viewpoint**

*Cougar
Reservoir*

(optional route)

26

126

97

20

97

126

20

372

22

20

126

242

126

126

N

10 Kilometers
10 Miles
5
5
0
0

RIDE

8

McKenzie-Santiam Loop

Directions:

northwest on US 20 from Bend to Sisters

west on OR 242 to OR 126

north on OR 126 to US 20

east on US 20 / OR 126 to Bend

(option) OR 126 from Sisters to Redmond

Distance:

total distance: 121 miles (about 79 miles round-trip from Sisters)

Bend to Sisters: 21 miles

Sisters to McKenzie Pass: 15 miles

McKenzie Pass to intersection of OR 242 and OR 126 (Belknap Springs): 22 miles

Belknap Springs to intersection of OR 126 and US 20 (Santiam Junction): 21 miles

Santiam Junction to Sisters: 21 miles

Sisters to Bend: 21 miles

Time:

three to four hours

Services:

Bend, Sisters, Redmond

Best Time of Year:
late spring through fall; some roads are closed in winter

Highlights:
quaint town of Sisters; massive lava flows; views of surrounding mountain peaks; waterfalls

This is a relatively easy loop to do in a morning or afternoon if you find yourself in Bend with time on your hands and the itch to ride. It's not a long loop, but some of the roads are narrow and winding and thus slow. There's also a fair amount to stop and see, so allow yourself a good three hours—a little less if you start in Sisters rather than Bend.

We like to ride this from Bend. Sisters is a nice little town, full of shops and galleries in restored old downtown buildings,

As you can tell on this ride, and from pretty much anywhere around here, this is prime volcano territory, with a number of peaks rising sharply up from the forest floor to domi-nate the landscape. The Three Sisters—three successive peaks each rising more than 10,000 feet—are the third- to fifth-highest mountains in the state (after Mount Hood and Mount Jefferson).

Early settlers called them "Faith," "Hope," and "Char-ity," but now they're more commonly called "North," "Mid-dle," and "South." The north and middle volcanoes are considered extinct, but the South Sister has shown signs of recent activity, including a 2004 earthquake swarm that had people wondering if it was going to become the next Mount St. Helens. Not much has happened since, so your ride should not be disturbed by the prospect of riding through ash clouds or lava flows. ●

Lava-tube windows at Dee Wright Observatory frame and identify the volcanic peaks that dominate this landscape.

but we enjoy returning to Bend at the end of the day and heading for the Deschutes Brewery pub for a tall cold one.

Pick up U.S. Highway 20 just north of downtown Bend and head northwest. The road between Bend and Sisters is not exceptional, but it does offer excellent views of the surrounding peaks, most notably the Three Sisters and Mount Washington.

On a short stretch of the highway about 10 miles southeast of Sisters, you may also catch a brief view of Mount Jefferson, which tops out at 10,497 feet. As you ride along US 20, the mountain appears to loom large over the road and between the ponderosa pines that line the highway. Mount Jefferson is only visible for about 0.5 mile before it disappears behind the trees. Given how big it appears to be from here, you might think it would loom even larger once you reach Sisters, but it won't. Its apparent size must be an optical illusion created by perspective, similar to the way the moon always appears larger when it is near the horizon. Mount Jefferson actually sits about 20 miles north of the Santiam Pass summit, which is about 15 miles northwest of Sisters.

In Sisters, you have a choice of which direction to ride the loop. We prefer riding McKenzie Pass, then Santiam Pass (that is, south to north). To go that way, pick up Oregon Highway 242 on the west side of town. If traffic in Sisters is slow or stopped completely, which it often is, bypass it with a little local trick. Sisters is laid out on a grid pattern, so once you're a block or two into town, take a left, go one block to Hood Street, and take a right. Follow Hood Street all the way to its end, where it curves to the right and intersects with OR 242. Make a left onto OR 242 and you're good to go.

The summit of McKenzie Pass is only 15 miles from Sisters. You'll wind your way through a very healthy ponderosa pine forest, climbing ever so slightly for the first few miles. Before long the road ascends more noticeably and gets progressively narrower. The turns are considerably tighter, with many of them marked as 15- to 30-mph maximum. The curves are so tight and the road so narrow that vehicles over 35 feet long are prohibited. That's a good thing because it means you won't meet any huge semi trailers or monster RVs taking up your lane on a curve.

A paved interpretive trail winds through the lava flows near Dee Wright Observatory on McKenzie Pass.

This is rugged country, but the road is in surprisingly good shape. OR 242 over McKenzie Pass is closed in the winter and does show signs of decay in places. The forest is thick and grows right up to the edge of the pavement, leading to the occasional fallen tree or branch in your lane. As with all mountain roads, watch for the usual array of debris—rocks, roadkill, and gravel in the turns. In other words, it's best to obey the suggested speed limits.

At the summit, a series of massive lava flows comes right to the asphalt in places, and the occasional chunk inevitably makes its way onto the road. One stretch of pavement cuts through the lava flow—if you can't build around it, you've got to build through it. This stuff is hard and can break off with sharp edges. You don't want to try riding back to Bend or Sisters with a slice in your tire, so watch for chunks of lava in your path.

At the summit, take a break, get off the bike, and walk the steps to the top of the Dee Wright Observatory, built by the Civilian Conservation Corps during the Depression (it's named after the project's crew foreman). The entire structure is constructed from lava, with little lava-tube windows that frame and identify the various peaks surrounding the pass. A paved 0.5-mile interpretive trail wanders through the lava flows and gives more information about their origins.

For most of the 22 miles from the observatory to the intersection with Oregon Highway 126, the road heads downhill through turns that are as tight if not tighter than the ones on the east side. The pavement is newer and in better condition, and the forest is thicker and much more lush than that on the east side. The verdant vegetation is clear evidence of the moisture from the Pacific Ocean that gets dumped as rain on the Cascades' western slopes.

At the intersection with OR 126, make a right and trade in the tight switchbacks of OR 242 for big, smooth, sweeping turns. After the 15- or 30-mph turns of McKenzie Pass, it's easy to pull back the throttle and roar through this section of tarmac without stopping. But as you climb and wind your way north, the

Sahalie Falls is the most accessible in a series of waterfalls along OR 126.

McKenzie River is just off to your left, and as it works its way south it creates a series of waterfalls that are worth a peek. The turn for Sahalie Falls is on the left about 14 miles north of the turn onto OR 126. It is by far the most picturesque of the three and the easiest to find.

Continue north on OR 126 to the intersection with US 20, which will lead us back to Sisters and Bend. A few miles after the intersection, Oregon Highway 22 cuts off to the northern leg of the West Cascades Scenic Byway, which heads north and west toward Salem. From OR 22, forest service roads lead to the south side of Mount Hood and Portland.

After the intersection with OR 22, US 20 / OR 126 is pretty much a four-lane divided racetrack, a high-speed madhouse with cars, trucks hauling campers, RVs, semi-trailers, and who knows what else, all vying for the same two or three lanes, all trying their best to gain speed on the downhill sections and keep enough momentum on the uphill to get up and over the pass as quickly as possible. In other words, the best part of this ride is over.

A word to the wise: Watch your speed after you've left the steepest part of the descent behind and entered the ponderosa pine forest on the way back to Sisters. This is where law enforcement officers like to remind you that while they may let you get away with 10 or 15 over on the pass, that kind of behavior isn't tolerated everywhere. (The same holds true in the westbound lanes leaving Sisters.) ●

Sisters offers your pick of watering holes, restaurants, art galleries, and bookstores. When you leave Sisters, you have a couple of road options: OR 126 to the east leads to Redmond, the next town north of Bend on U.S. Highway 97, where you can pick up U.S. Highway 26 east to the John Day area (rides 12–14). Although it's a change from the route into Sisters, it doesn't offer a whole lot beyond that. The Cline Falls Scenic Viewpoint overlooks a Deschutes River waterfall whose water supply has been largely diverted for a power plant. The falls might be worth a look in spring, when flows are highest. From Bend, US 97 heads south toward Crater Lake and south-central Oregon. You could also stay on US 20 toward Burns in southeast Oregon and explore the high desert of the Oregon outback.

Restaurant

Bend
Deschutes Brewery & Public House
1044 Bond St.
(541) 382-9242

RIDE 9

Crater Lake Connection

Directions:

north and east on OR 138 from Roseburg to North Crater
Lake Highway
south on Crater Lake Highway to Rim Drive
Rim Drive around the lake
south on Crater Lake Highway to OR 62
west on OR 62 to Union Creek
north on OR 230 to OR 138
west on OR 138 to Roseburg

Distance:

total distance: 137 to 219 miles, depending on exact route
Roseburg to Diamond Lake: 82 miles
Diamond Lake to Crater Lake: 6 miles
Crater Lake to Union Creek: 21 miles
Union Creek to Diamond Lake (via OR 230): 28 miles

Time:

two days

Services:

Roseburg, Glide, Diamond Lake, Crater Lake National Park,
Union Creek

Best Time of Year:

summer; the park can be snowed in from October to late
June

Highlights:

a curvy climb through the forest; rivers, lakes, and waterfalls; the deep blue splendor of Crater Lake

This ride is an enticing mix of curves, climbs, scenic rivers,
waterfalls, high mountain lakes, and extinct volcanoes. Beginning in Umpqua Valley wine country, it climbs through national
forest while the North Umpqua River tumbles beside it from the

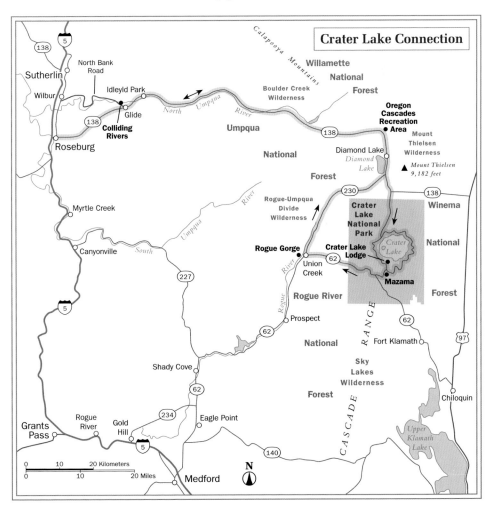

high Cascades. The route ascends to Diamond Lake and Mount Thielsen, makes a loop around Crater Lake, then returns to national forest, following the Rogue River past a series of recreation-happy small towns. Much of the ride follows the Rogue-Umpqua Scenic Byway—which heads from Roseburg to Diamond Lake to Gold Hill on Oregon Highways 138, 230, and 62—and adds Crater Lake National Park, a destination no one wants to miss.

With a lot of ground to cover and much to see, it makes sense to break this ride into two days, allowing for plenty of time to stop and explore the beauty concentrated in this part of Oregon.

One challenge of multiday rides through national forests is limited lodging options. Campsites abound, but sleeping indoors will take a little planning. Three or four places offer lodging between Roseburg and Crater Lake National Park. The national park, near this ride's halfway point, is a logical base, but park accommodations are limited to Crater Lake Lodge at Rim Village and Mazama Village Motor Inn near the Annie Spring Entrance Station. Lodging in the park can fill up early, especially on the weekends, so reservations are a necessity.

Just north of the park, privately owned Diamond Lake Resort, just off OR 138 at the north end of Diamond Lake, offers lodging. Finally, Union Creek, about 18 miles west of the park's south entrance on OR 62, has a lodge and cabins. Towns southwest of Union Creek on OR 62 have plenty of lodging and dining options but are too far from Crater Lake to be convenient.

There are three well-maintained forest service campgrounds around Diamond Lake and several near Union Creek. Camping in Crater Lake National Park fills up fast, so plan ahead to secure a site (call 888-774-2728 to book a room at park lodges or campgrounds). ●

You've probably noticed that some of the best riding is through national forest, and this route is no exception. It enters national forest about 18 miles east of Roseburg, and most of it sticks to national forest or national park lands. This means many miles of great roads, beautiful scenery, and minimal development.

Begin in Roseburg. Arriving from the south on Interstate 5, take exit 124 toward OR 138, the city center and Diamond Lake. Take a right and follow signs for OR 138. Follow OR 138 (also called Oak Avenue) for about 0.5 mile and make a left on Stephens Street, then a right on Diamond Lake Boulevard,

North Bank Road is a worthy shortcut from I-5 north of Roseburg to Glide.

which becomes OR 138—also known as the North Umpqua Highway—shortly before it turns northeast toward the town of Glide.

From the north on I-5, a fun shortcut skirts Roseburg and joins OR 138 just west of Glide. Take exit 135, marked for Sutherlin and Wilbur. Make a left and head east over I-5 to the frontage road. Take a right on the frontage road / Old Highway 99. Go about 4 miles, take a left on North Bank Road, and follow it through hills and valleys for about 17 miles until it intersects with OR 138. Take a left on OR 138 and you'll be in Glide in a couple of miles.

OR 138 closely follows the course of the North Umpqua River, so the 22 miles of asphalt from Glide to Steamboat serves up a taste of curves to come. Because both towns sit in the Umpqua Valley, though, the pavement is relatively flat.

Steve: Glide is home to the Colliding Rivers, where a unique geological formation causes the North Umpqua and Little River to meet head-on—reportedly the only place in the world where this occurs. It's most spectacular during winter and early spring, when rain and melting snow cause the rivers to rise—which is not the best time of year to be on a bike. Before riding here, I pictured two rivers, water traveling in opposite directions, hitting head-on to dramatic effect.

I visited in late summer when the water volume was near its lowest, and despite being a visual person, I had a difficult time picturing the spectacle. I had an impossible time trying to capture it photographically. I rode away thinking I just didn't get it. I did a little more research and discovered that the rivers don't meet "head-on" as I'd imagined, but at more of a 90-degree angle, perpendicular to each other. I may return in spring when both rivers are raging, but I fear I'll be disappointed yet again. ●

It's possible to pass through Steamboat without knowing it since the only landmarks are the Steamboat Inn on the right and Steamboat Creek crossing under the road on the left, joining the North Umpqua beyond.

The real fun begins after Steamboat, as the road shoots into the mountains with serious determination. The stretch of pavement from Steamboat to Diamond Lake is excellent, combining curves and climb. Prepare to lean hard and power through the turns. There are about 41 miles of linked turns between Steamboat and Diamond Lake, most of which are nicely banked and not too tight. There's a particularly nice stretch above Toketee Falls, where buff-colored cliffs loom above the highway. Aside from one or two black-and-yellow 35-mph signs, most of the curves are 45 mph or better, so get ready to pull back on the throttle and enjoy.

Don't be too hasty in the race to the top. OR 138 is known as the "highway of waterfalls." Between mile markers 22 and 72, you've got ten of them. For a list of the falls and simple directions, go to www.oregon.com/trips/northumpqua.cfm. The most accessible are Whitehorse Falls at mile marker 65.9 (visible from the Whitehorse Falls Campground parking lot) and Clearwater Falls at milepost 69.5. Throughout summer, salmon shimmy up many of the waterfalls.

Just past Toketee Falls, the North Umpqua River turns sharply to the northeast. OR 138 follows the Clearwater River for about 7 miles before making its final ascent, tossing in a few big, sweeping turns as it heads south toward Diamond Lake and Mount Thielsen.

Rising to 9,182 feet, the horn-shaped peak of Mount Thielsen is a distinct landmark and the centerpiece of the Mount Thielsen Wilderness area. Glacial erosion has ground the core of an extinct volcano—which last erupted about 250,000 years ago—to its current sharp, curved shape. Sometimes called the Lightning Rod of the Cascades, its rocky spires attract more than their share of lightning strikes.

Mount Thielsen's sharp peak is actually the hardened core of a volcano. Melted rock on the summit testifies to its status as a natural lightning rod.

Take a look at Crater Lake's deep blue waters from Phantom Ship Overlook, named for the lake's ship-shaped island.

The ride from Roseburg to Diamond Lake is only about 80 miles, so expect to arrive at Diamond Lake by mid-afternoon. That allows plenty of time to get acquainted with Crater Lake National Park. Visiting the park in the afternoon will enhance your return to it the following day.

Crater Lake is like most national parks: We ride here not for the quality of the roads but for the sights and the atmosphere. Like all national parks, Crater Lake offers more recreational opportunities than anyone can reasonably be expected to pack into one visit. Some helpful information:

Traffic: Crater Lake generally gets busier as the day progresses, and congestion from an entry kiosk to the rim could add as much as a half-hour to your ride. The north entrance seems less congested than the Annie Spring entrance, where traffic begins backing up by late morning. You're bound to encounter gawkers, slow drivers, and good-sized RVs. In our experience, most drivers are courteous and quick to use turnouts to let others pass.

Boat Tours and Swimming: The Cleetwood Cove Trailhead parking area is the only place where it's safe—and legal—to hike down to the lake's edge. Boat tours of the lake depart from this spot (buy tickets at the trailhead). Swimming is also allowed here. Note that accessing the lakeshore for any activity requires hiking 2.2 miles round-trip on a steep, strenuous trail!

Fishing: Six fish species were introduced to the lake between 1888 and 1941, but only rainbow trout and kokanee salmon remain. Fishing is not only allowed, it's encouraged. No license is required and there is no limit, but you must use artificial bait to avoid accidentally introducing any other species into the lake.

For complete information on all the park's activities, refer to the visitor's guide you get when you enter, or stop at either the Steel Visitor Center (located where Rim Drive meets the Annie Spring entrance road) or Rim Visitor Center in Rim Village. ●

Follow OR 138 for 3 or 4 miles past Diamond Lake to the intersection with Crater Lake Highway. Head south on Crater Lake Highway for about 9 miles to the junction with Rim Drive. The park entrance fee for bikes is $5 and is good for seven days, so hang on to your receipt.

This is a national park, so the quality of the roads is decent but inconsistent. The maximum speed limit is 45 mph, which is fine because the roads are not designed for speed. Besides, we're here for the scenery.

There's no need to rush and attempt the entire Rim Drive tonight. Instead, take your time at some of the scenic overlooks on the rim's west side. Watchman Overlook provides great views of Wizard Island in the middle of the lake. The Sinnott Memorial Overlook offers expansive views of the lake and a view of Wizard Island from a different perspective. Spend a little time wandering Rim Village: Head to the cafe for a snack, meander over to Crater Lake Lodge, or swing by the visitor center and learn more about this stunning deep blue lake and the collapsed volcano in which it sits. Relax and enjoy the immense crater as the late-afternoon light casts long shadows along the rim and paints the clouds with the pink hues of sunset.

The next day, hit the road early to avoid the inevitable traffic flooding the park by late morning. Having spent a little time getting acquainted with the park the night before, you can ride the Rim Drive loop at your own pace, stopping whenever one of the numerous scenic viewpoints appeals to you. Most are right off the road; Cloud Cap Overlook, located a little less than a mile off Rim Drive, is an exception. With its expansive, unobstructed vista of the lake below, it's well worth the short detour. Allow at least two hours to ride the entire 33-mile loop.

The turnoff for the Pinnacles Overlook, which is about 14 miles round-trip down a well-paved road, is near the Phantom Ship Overlook. These unusual formations developed when hot gas escaped through layers of volcanic debris in vertical cracks called fumaroles. Extreme heat of up to 750 degrees worked with minerals in the gases to weld and cement pumice into vertical

The fossilized fumaroles in Godfrey Glen along OR 62, southeast of the national park's Annie Spring entrance, are similar to the Pinnacles inside the park.

tubes or pipes. The pinnacles are harder than the surrounding material and resisted further erosion. If you don't have time to make the trip to Pinnacles Overlook, a smaller version of them is visible at Godfrey Glen along OR 62, southeast of the Annie Spring entrance.

After the park, your next move depends on your destination. One choice is to reverse course; the ride back to Roseburg is as much fun going downhill. We go with a second option and leave the park via the Annie Spring entrance. Pick up OR 62 heading west through the Rogue River National Forest toward Union Creek, about 23 miles from Crater Lake.

Union Creek transformed itself from an old Civilian Conservation Corps camp into a laid-back resort outpost with lodging, a small general store, an ice-cream shop, and Beckie's Cafe (known for homemade soups, chili, sandwiches, and pies). Listed on the National Register of Historic Places, its buildings retain the rustic look of the early 1900s. It's a great place to have lunch, grab an ice-cream cone, and wander over to the Rogue Gorge viewpoint, a short walk up OR 62 across from the resort.

OR 62 (and, later, Oregon Highway 234) follows the Rogue River for 55 miles south of Union Creek to Gold Hill, the southern tip of the Rogue-Umpqua Scenic Byway. Once the highway leaves the national forest (at the tiny town of Prospect, about 12 miles south of Union Creek), peace and serenity disappear, the road widens, and the terrain opens up to residential development, agriculture, and commercialized recreation.

In the summer, Shady Cove—right on the banks of the Rogue River—takes on an almost carnival atmosphere: It's got RV parks, innumerable restaurants, and storefronts touting fishing guides, rafting outfitters, and T-shirts. Gold Hill and Rogue River are considerably more sedate. Unless you need to head south or you like tourist towns, it's not as rewarding as the rest of the byway. Rather than ride all the way to Gold Hill, we prefer to make a loop back to where we started, heading north on OR 62 from Union Creek for about 2 miles to the junction with OR 230. Go north on OR 230 until it intersects with OR 138, about 25 miles to the northeast near Diamond Lake. Make a left on OR 138 and enjoy the ride down to Roseburg as much as you did on the ride up.

EASTERN OREGON

Most people blow past eastern Oregon, sticking to the highway on their way to someplace else. That's a shame. But it's also an opportunity, because it means we don't have to share its backroad byways with hordes of cars.

This area's regional highways cross diverse territory—including deserts, mountains, and the nation's deepest canyon. Even better, the roads are fast and entertaining, with smooth, well-banked curves, and many of them seem engineered with bikes in mind.

Earthquakes and volcanoes shaped this landscape of canyons, mountains, and semi-arid highlands eons ago, and the dry hills preserved millions of fossils. During the nineteenth century, it was shaped by the fur trade, the Oregon Trail, and the Northwest gold rush. More recently, ranching, logging, and tourism have dominated the economic landscape even as the physical landscape retains a relatively unspoiled feel.

Bluffs, valleys, swells, and canyons range from wooded to sagebrush-covered to rocky and inhospitable. Temperatures can vary widely from summer to winter (to above 100 degrees Fahrenheit or well below freezing), with the occasional summer thunderstorm or blizzard.

Although the territory isn't consistently green and there's not an ocean in sight, this is still the Northwest. For one thing, it may feel like a whole different world, but this region is about a day ride from pretty much anywhere in the Northwest. It's easy to get here from the population centers of Portland or Seattle—or Bend or Spokane, for that matter. The area around John Day is especially popular with riders from Bend and Portland, or even from the coast. If you're into camping, there's loads of it in the national forests.

Eastern Oregon's small towns are quintessentially Northwestern, with attractive, well-preserved downtowns. Best of all, the people here take Northwestern friendliness to a whole new level. The folks you'll meet as you ride in eastern Oregon are some of the nicest and most helpful you will run into anywhere.

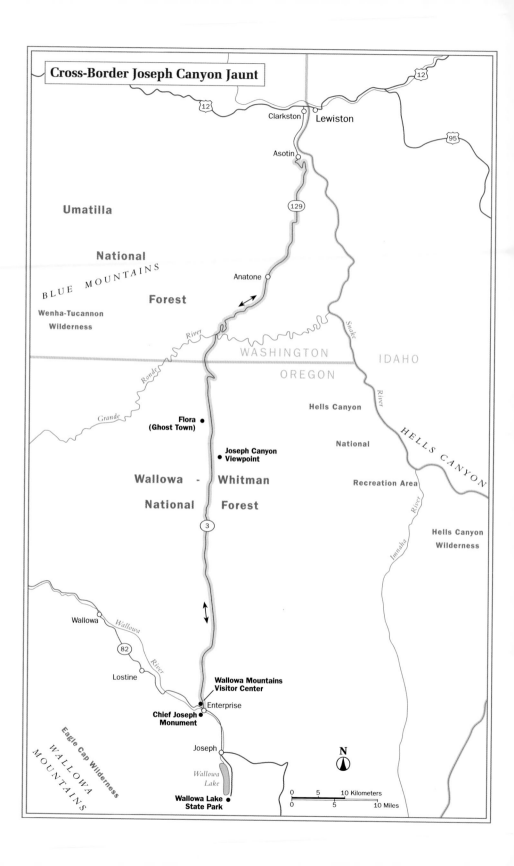

Cross-Border Joseph Canyon Jaunt

RIDE 10

Cross-Border Joseph Canyon Jaunt

Directions:
north on OR 3 from Enterprise, Oregon, to Asotin, Washington, and back

Distance:
total distance: 80–86 miles one way
Enterprise to Asotin, Washington: 80 miles
Asotin, Washington, to Clarkston, Washington: 6 miles

Time:
half a day or more, depending on how far you go into Washington

Services:
Enterprise, Oregon; Asotin, Washington; Lewiston-Clarkston on the Washington/Idaho border; most towns along the Hells Canyon Scenic Byway

Best Time of Year:
late spring/early summer and fall; it can get damn hot as early as June

Highlights:
a pleasant, remote, and sometimes exciting mountain and canyon ride; expansive views of the Wallowa Mountains, Joseph Canyon, the Grande Ronde River, and the sun-baked hills of southeastern Washington; picturesque ghost towns

We don't like out-and-back rides and usually do our best to avoid them. But after several people said we would be crazy not to ride Oregon Highway 3 from Enterprise, Oregon, to the Lewiston-Clarkston area on the Washington/Idaho border, we finally broke down and did it. It makes a good half-day detour; Steve left La Grande, set up camp at Wallowa Lake, rode both directions on OR 3, and was back in Joseph in time for dinner. You could also do this ride as a one-way if you were headed to or from Spokane or the Idaho panhandle.

This part of Oregon is agricultural, a mix of ranching and farming, and the territory around OR 3 north of Enterprise is no exception. You won't find services from Enterprise until you reach Asotin at the other end of OR 3, so make sure you fuel up before you leave. The Wallowa Mountains Visitor Center in Enterprise has maps and up-to-date information about road conditions—especially helpful when it comes to the many unpaved or rarely maintained roads north of town.

OR 3 is NW 1st Street in the center of Enterprise. It's also known as the Lewiston Highway and the Enterprise Lewiston Highway. The ride starts innocently enough in the soft rolling hills that you've come to know and love traveling through this region. If you glance in your mirrors, you'll get an eyeful of the Wallowa Mountains. You'll face them on the return trip.

OR 3 is an average rural road; it has some nice curves and climbs and a couple of interesting and unexpected surprises along the way. The pavement quality is not as good as the roads around Baker City, La Grande, or John Day, but few roads anywhere are. The roadside fields just north of Enterprise are dotted with the occasional ramshackle-yet-charming farmhouse or other remnant of the small towns that used to act as way stations and suppliers for travelers through here.

Within about 10 miles, the road climbs out of the agricultural country and into the national forest. If it's hot in the valley below, this is a nice opportunity to escape. As the locals say, you'll be riding in the trees! After riding in the trees for a while

You'll hardly know you're riding next to a canyon until you pop out of the trees at Joseph Canyon Viewpoint.

you may wonder, as we did, why everyone raves about this road. Since you are riding in the trees, you have no idea what's happening with the terrain beyond what you see in front of you. Keep enjoying the scenery you do have, but look for the Joseph Canyon Viewpoint about 33 miles from where you turned onto OR 3 in Enterprise. The turnoff can pop out of the trees pretty quickly, so be alert.

This is a popular stop for travelers of all sorts and very popular with bikers. You'll get your first views of a small section of Joseph Canyon, and, if you read the displays, a brief but informative history lesson about the Nez Percé Indians who once called this area home. But this is not the best part; you aren't far from the real reason bikers from all over the state consider this a must-do ride.

If you're ready for a longer break and money is burning a hole in your pocket, stop at the RimRock Inn about 2 miles north of the Joseph Canyon Overlook and avail yourself of its of soups, salads, sandwiches, and burgers. The lunch menu prices are pretty

Joseph, Joseph Creek, Joseph Canyon, and other local landmarks are named for two legendary Nez Percé chiefs, father and son, both known as Chief Joseph. When white settlers moved in, the tribe agreed to leave the Wallowa Valley and live on a sizable reservation around where Oregon, Washington, and Idaho meet. But when gold was discovered nearby, the whites broke the agreement and made the reservation one-tenth its original size. The elder chief, who angrily resisted, died in 1871 as tensions escalated.

Realizing he wasn't going to get a better deal, his son agreed to move hundreds of his tribe members to the reservation. In 1877, before that could happen, bloodshed erupted between the Nez Percé and whites when rogue Nez Percé warriors killed some settlers, forcing a heated chase as Chief Joseph led his followers across 1,000 miles of territory, all the while pursued by soldiers. Finally, after several victorious battles, the outnumbered Nez Percé capitulated in Montana with Chief Joseph's solemn speech: "Hear me, my chiefs; my heart is sick and sad. From where the Sun now stands, I will fight no more forever."

The tribe was moved to a barren reservation in Oklahoma, where many died from illness, before being relocated to other reservations in Idaho and Washington. Chief Joseph spent the rest of his life trying to get better conditions for his people, but he was never allowed to return to his homeland in Oregon. The chiefs' story is all the more tragic because both father and son were seen as statesmen and widely admired by whites for their honor, integrity, and fairness. Old Chief Joseph lies buried near Wallowa Lake, about a mile south of Joseph; his son died and was buried in Nespelem, Washington, a few miles north of the Grand Coulee Dam. ●

reasonable; dinner is a bit pricey but not outrageous, especially considering that it's the only game in town. It calls itself a "destination" restaurant, and when you know that its Web site provides directions for cars, motorcycles, planes, and helicopters, you get a better sense of why they can charge what they do. The inn also has RV sites and "fully outfitted tipis" if you choose to spend the night.

About 40 miles into the ride, or about 10 miles north of the overlook, you're in for a surprise. As you come around a curve, one minute you're in the trees and the next, you're looking over the guardrail, staring at one of the most twisted sections of road you'll ever have the pleasure of seeing. Welcome to the descent into the Grande Ronde Valley, a drop officially known as the Buford Grade.

Most maps will say that you have about 9 miles of twists and curves ahead. Our guess is that this number is as the crow flies and doesn't take all the curves into account. If you take that 9 miles of twists and straighten them out, the distance is closer to

Heading north, OR 3 snakes down the hillside into the Grande Ronde Valley.

17 miles between where your front wheel enters the canyon to where it leaves the other side.

As you make your way to the bottom of the canyon, you'll come around curves that give you a full-face view looking across to the walls beyond. The next set gives you an eagle's-eye view of the zigzagging road below. You'll drop to the bottom of the canyon having crossed into the state of Washington about a third of the way down (the road name changes to Washington Highway 129 as you enter Washington).

At the bottom of the canyon, you'll encounter the Grande Ronde River, a tributary of the Snake River that begins its journey about 20 miles south of La Grande. There's just enough time to catch your breath before it all begins again, now climbing rather than descending. The road twists through about 7 more miles of curves before you exit the canyon as abruptly as you entered— only this time, rather than looking down on the road you're about to ride, you're looking up toward the shiny guardrail of the road above.

Shortly after leaving the canyon, the road pops out of the trees and into the vast agricultural lands of southeastern Washington. Anatone, the next town, doesn't appear to have much going on apart from a few houses and abandoned buildings.

From here, the ride is pretty much a straight shot across the sun-baked hills and fields of southeastern Washington. There are a couple of soft turns and several miles of tighter ones as you drop into Asotin. If it was hot back in Enterprise, Asotin will be sweltering. Asotin has all the services you'll need to make the return trip. You've seen the best of what this ride has to offer by the time you reach Anatone, so unless you have a personal reason for making the 6-mile trip to Clarkston and Lewiston (towns on the border with Idaho, named for explorers Lewis and Clark), just fuel up and head back. Before you head south, you can dip your toe into the Snake River at a riverfront park in the heart of Asotin.

From the looks of it, the residents of Anatone pride themselves on their lack of attractions. While most municipalities post a small green-and-white road sign with the town's population listed just below its name, Anatone put up a large green-and-white sign in a field in the center of town listing the population of people, dogs, cats, and horses. There are half as many dogs as people, almost as many cats as dogs, and about one horse for every four people. ●

With more animals than people, Anatone seems proud of its rural feel.

Obviously, the return trip to Enterprise is the reverse of what you just rode, but things always look and ride different from the other direction, and the road through Grande Ronde Valley and past Joseph Canyon is no exception. So enjoy the view, and remember that the next time bikers tell you a particular ride that doesn't look like much on the map is a "must-do," there's probably a very good reason.

Dining and Attractions

Oregon Highway 3
RimRock Inn
just north of Joseph Canyon Viewpoint
Lunch and dinner at a scenic spot overlooking the canyon

Joseph

Breakfast:
Cheyenne Cafe
209 N. Main St.
(541) 432-6300

Mountain Air Cafe
4 S. Main St.
(541) 432-0233
Both Cheyenne and Mountain Air cafes are reasonably
priced, though the Cheyenne Cafe has larger portions

Wildflour Bakery
103 N. Main St.
(541) 432-7225
Fresh-baked bread and other baked goods

Lunch and Dinner:
Embers Brew House
206 N. Main St.
(541) 432-2739
Good pub food and perhaps the largest selection of
microbrews in this part of the state

RIDE

11

Hells Canyon Loop

Directions:
northeast on OR 82 from La Grande to Joseph
east on East Wallowa Avenue / Imnaha Highway from
Joseph to FR 39
south on FR 39 to OR 86
east on OR 86 to Oxbow/Copperfield (option: Hells Canyon
Dam on Hells Canyon Road / FR 454)
west on OR 86 to Baker City

Distance:
total distance from La Grande to Joseph to Baker City: 125
miles
La Grande to Joseph: 70
Joseph to Hells Canyon Overlook: 45 miles
Hells Canyon Overlook to Oxbow/Copperfield: 23 miles
Joseph to Baker City: 125 miles

Time:
about two days

Services:
at La Grande, Baker City, Wallowa, Enterprise, and Joseph

Best Time of Year:
any time but winter

Highlights:

unusual scenery, Native American history, Hells Canyon and the Snake River, interesting little towns, Wallowa Lake and the Wallowa Mountains

Some of the region's best riding roads go through the blandest scenery, bisecting vast agricultural spreads outside Baker City and La Grande. If you expect that same high-quality pavement on the roads around Hells Canyon, they'll disappoint you—but this ride is not about the roads. It's about seeing the sights—including

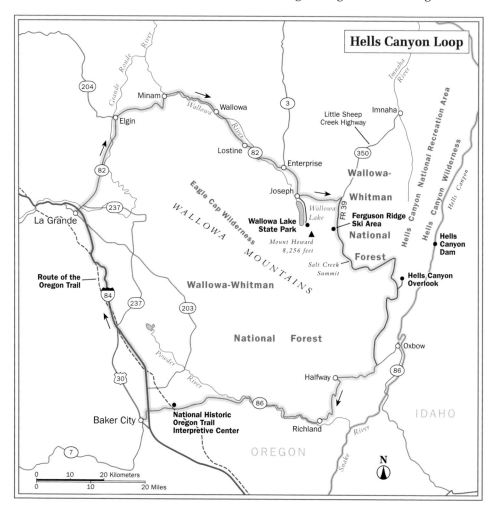

spectacular Hells Canyon—and dipping into the Old West feel that this part of Oregon offers. Since each town has its own flavor and flair and reasons for visiting, you don't pay much attention to the quality of the asphalt.

For good reason, this corner of the state is called "Oregon's Playground" and "Oregon's Little Switzerland." You'll find out why when you get near Enterprise and Joseph. This region also has a rich and somewhat tumultuous history. It played a major role in the Oregon Trail migration, but its history extends much further back than that: Evidence of Native peoples dates back about 7,000 years.

In the more-recent past, the Grande Ronde Valley—essentially Baker City to La Grande—was used seasonally by a variety of Native nations. The valley was a sort of Switzerland-style neutral meeting place for members of the Umatilla, Yakima, Shoshone, Cayuse, and Bannock nations. All parties enjoyed the hot springs, grazed their horses, gathered plants for food, and hunted the abundant big game. The Wallowa Valley was especially beloved by the Nez Percé. Conflicts between European and Native Americans arose here when gold was discovered; treaties were broken, and the United States and its military representatives claimed or reclaimed land that Native Americans had used for thousands of years.

To do this unusual corner of Oregon justice, you'll want at least a couple of days to cover the ground, soak up the vibe, and see all the scenery. Chances are you rode in from a considerable distance, so slow down, relax, and enjoy. Two days will give you time to explore the little towns, perhaps take some side trips, and make important stops at places like the Terminal Gravity Brewery and Public House in Enterprise, which brews some of the best beer in the Northwest.

We suggest riding the first half of the loop, which should only take a few hours, then finding lodging or a campsite in Wallowa, Enterprise, or Joseph. Wallowa Lake State Park, just 6 miles outside Joseph, has a large campground at the far end of the lake. The campsites fill up early on weekends during the summer, so we suggest making a reservation if camping appeals to you. For something a bit more rugged, there's national forest camping

Joseph is a showcase for public art, especially the bronze sculptures throughout town.

outside Wallowa and Enterprise, as well as along the scenic route just before the Hells Canyon Overlook.

If you hit the Enterprise/Joseph area at a reasonable hour, after you find a motel or set up camp you'll have plenty of time to ride Oregon Highway 3 (see ride 10) from Enterprise to the Washington border and be back in time for dinner. If you make it to this region and don't ride OR 3, you'll be doing yourself a disservice. Finish the second half of this loop on the second day.

Now for the ride: We're following the Hells Canyon Scenic Byway, and there are five points of entry to the loop: Baker City, La Grande, Elgin, Enterprise, and Oxbow/Copperfield. Baker and La Grande are good-sized towns with both local businesses and the usual array of fast-food places right off the interstate. We start the loop in La Grande and head northeast on Oregon Highway 82, which intersects U.S. Highway 30 in the heart of La Grande and runs diagonally to the northeast, passing under Interstate 84 about a mile out of town. You'll be on OR 82 all the way to Joseph.

The road and the scenery get decent shortly past Elgin, about 24 miles out of La Grande. After Elgin you'll drop into Minam, which doesn't seem to be much more than a launch spot for boaters and rafters. However, the descent to the river signals that you are leaving the sun-drenched hills of eastern Oregon's farmland and ranching land.

Farther on, you encounter Wallowa, Enterprise, and Joseph, each with its own charm. Wallowa is quaint but seems a little run-down and forgotten, although there are some appealing small motels right in the heart of town. One of the nicest is Bear Creek Lodging, a couple blocks off the main street. Enterprise is functional and feels like a community built around serving the needs of the farmers and ranchers.

Joseph is the jewel of the Hells Canyon Scenic Byway loop: It's done an excellent job of restoring the buildings that line Main Street and is a showcase for public art, especially the bronze sculptures that are well placed throughout the town. South of Joseph, Wallowa Lake State Park features a tramway whose

Steve: Pay attention to speed limits as you pass through the small towns that lie along the scenic byway. In an area where most people are just passing through, it's always good karma to show some respect to the locals—you never know when you might need their help.

I did encounter several downright crazy drivers of the four-wheeled variety. The posted speeds are reasonable, but these folks apparently thought otherwise. One couple looked like older tourists who must have had a tight schedule to keep and wanted to drive the entire scenic loop in one day. They were passing everything in sight, tailgating, speeding up, then braking. Another driver tailgated me for a while, then passed me only to get stuck behind a line of traffic down the road where I eventually met up with him again. Both drivers attempted to pass me just as the passing lane was ending, taking up most of what was rightfully my lane. If I hadn't seen it coming, braked, and swung to the right, I would have been forced off the road. ●

A rider cruises through the outskirts of Joseph near Ferguson Ridge.

gondola ascends 3,700 feet to the summit of Mount Howard. It's a popular picnic spot that offers views of the lake and the surrounding peaks and wilderness (go to www.wallowalaketramway .com for hours and rates).

After you leave Joseph, climb out of the valley toward Ferguson Ridge Ski Area, aka "Fergi's," off to your right. Beyond the ridge, the road drops quickly into Sheep Creek Canyon. If you're not paying attention, your instinct will tell you to follow the river, in which case you'll end up in the little town of Imnaha. If you don't want to go to Imnaha (and you do want to stay on the scenic byway), turn right on Forest Road 39. This is an easy turn to miss. It's not well marked, and since this is a scenic byway, you'll expect more from the road than it appears to offer at first glance.

FR 39, which runs through the heart of Hells Canyon National Recreation Area, is not a typical well-engineered eastern Oregon road. As the main road through the recreation area, it ought to be much better maintained than it is. Long sections, especially in the Salt Creek Canyon area, look and feel like old logging roads someone decided ought to be paved. It's about 24 miles of bumps, humps, and heaves. You'll be dodging rocks, gravel, the occasional tree branch, and potholes big enough to eat your head.

The scenery is a crazy mix of heavily logged national forest interspersed with canyons offering an amazing diversity of vegetation. On the way to your goal, the Hells Canyon Overlook, climb to the top of Salt Creek Summit, then descend through a series of canyons dug out by rivers with names like Salt Creek, Lick Creek, Gumboot Creek, Dry Creek, and Lonesome Creek.

The nation's deepest river gorge (yes, deeper than the Grand Canyon) yawns below the Hells Canyon Overlook as the Snake River cuts a channel a mile below the surface plateau. The 8,000-foot Seven Devils Mountains rise steeply off to the east on the other side. This is rugged country, with few paved roads leading into or out of it from anywhere. A few dirt roads may be accessible with an adventure bike capable of handling serious off-road conditions. Check with the forest service before heading into the backcountry, and only attempt it if your bike-handling skills are up to the challenge. Keep in mind that the weather can be unpredictable any time of year, and off-road conditions could change dramatically.

If you miss the turn onto FR 39 and end up riding the Upper Imnaha Road to Imnaha, you'll find it exceptionally small. Technically only about twelve people live here, though it's well known for fishing and hunting. It also came up with an interesting way of raising money for a favorite charity of one of the residents. Dave Tanzey started the Bear and Rattlesnake Feed—feeding bear and rattlesnake meat to people, not the other way around—in 1988 as a fund-raiser for the Multiple Sclerosis Society. It eventually evolved into a fund-raiser for the Imnaha School scholarship fund. The event was retired in 2004.

Imnaha is the end of the pavement. A gravel road leads to the Hat Point overlook at the edge of Hells Canyon. Check on conditions and plan for a several-hour side trip if you want to try it. ●

Hells Canyon Overlook lets you peer into the deepest river gorge in the United States.

Leaving the overlook, you'll be following the Imnaha River almost all the way to the town of Halfway. Depending on the time of year, be prepared for the temperature to rise, sometimes considerably, on the descent. From the overlook, it's about 15 miles to the intersection with Oregon Highway 86.

Do yourself a favor and ride down to Oxbow/Copperfield, where OR 86 meets the Snake River. You'll be just below the Oxbow Dam and 22 miles, or about 45 minutes, from the Hells Canyon Dam. From here, you can get a reasonable view of the Snake River as it enters Hells Canyon. If you have the time and inclination, cross the bridge over the Snake River and follow Hells Canyon Dam Road / Forest Road 454 for 22 miles to Hells Canyon Dam. The Snake River is wild and scenic below the dam, and this detour will give you a chance to see the canyon and the river in all their glory. We've heard the best way to see the river and the canyon is by jet boat. We're not typically much for powerboats on rivers, but may return one day for a raft trip.

If you only make it as far as Oxbow/Copperfield, you're still in luck, because you'll have a chance to stop in at Hells Canyon Inn. It looks questionable from the outside, but once you get into the air-conditioned dining room or bar, you'll be glad you stopped for a great half-pound burger with homemade fries. If you need supplies, you're only a few steps from the Hells Canyon Store, whose motto is "If we ain't got it, you don't need it."

Reversing course on OR 86 will remind you why you ride in this part of the country and what a good motorcycle road should look and feel like. From Oxbow, it's about 17 miles to Halfway, which earned its name back in the day as the halfway point between the town of Pine and the gold mines of Cornucopia.

By Halfway, you've seen the best the scenic loop has to offer. Halfway may be the gateway to Hells Canyon and the Wallowas, and it offers the full complement of services, but the couple of times we've been there (even on the Friday before the Fourth of July), it was a little too quiet for our taste.

From Halfway, it's a throttle-open run into Baker City, about 54 miles to the west on OR 86. From Richland almost all the way to Baker City, you'll be following the Powder River as it carves a series of canyons through the hills of eastern Oregon. Five miles east of Baker, the National Historic Oregon Trail Interpretive Center offers lots of information about the trail through reenactments and a preserved section of the trail itself.

From here, it's easy to hop onto I-84 for a quick ride back to La Grande or to head south toward the rides around John Day.

Restaurants

Copperfield
Hells Canyon Inn
53945 OR 86
(541) 785-3383

Enterprise
Terminal Gravity Brewery and Public House
803 SE School St.
(541) 426-3000

RIDE

12

Susanville Road

Directions:
east on US 26 from John Day to OR 7
north on OR 7 to Middle Fork Road (known as Susanville Road)
northwest on Susanville Road to US 395
south on US 395 to US 26
east on US 26 to John Day

Distance:
total miles: 111
John Day to Susanville Road: 29 miles
Susanville Road to junction with US 395: 41 miles
junction of US 395 and Susanville Road to Mount Vernon: 33 miles
Mount Vernon to John Day: 8 miles

Time:
two to three hours

Services:
John Day, Prairie City, Mount Vernon

Best Time of Year:
late spring, summer, and early fall

Highlights:

gold-mining history; hot springs, rich river valleys and narrow alpine canyons; fast roads through wide-open spaces.

The Susanville Road ride gives some insight into the history of the Blue Mountain region's "gold belt" from about the Idaho border to John Day. Here, miners dug and panned and sometimes struck it rich, and Chinese immigrants did much of the dirty

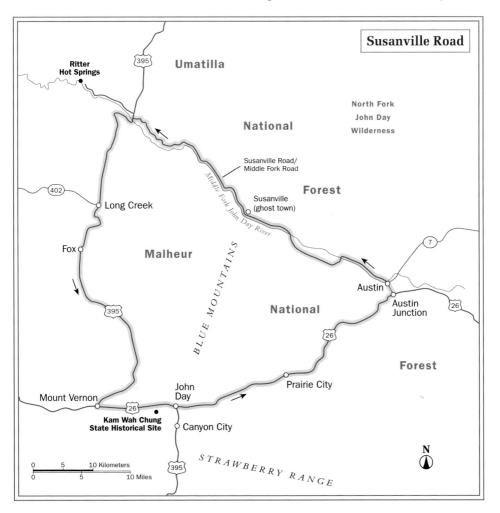

work. An acquaintance suggested this as a "must-do" ride for the area. Although it's a pleasant ride, we wouldn't put it in the "must-do" category. The scenery is good but not spectacular, and Susanville Road is not nearly as well engineered as many others in the area. Most of the turns are not banked, and there are a couple of tight curves with cattle guards right at the turn's apex. It's a very popular ride for the sport-bike crowd, and if we were riding a sport bike, we'd probably enjoy it more. If you decide to break a longer John Day Loop (ride 14) into two days, this could easily be tacked onto the Vale-to-John-Day leg.

The ride takes you east from John Day on U.S. Highway 26, then northwest on Susanville Road to the intersection of U.S. Highway 395, then south back to John Day. If you're looking at a map, it creates a triangle with the town of John Day as the lower left corner.

From John Day, head east on US 26 for about 32 miles. Be sure to fuel up in John Day or Prairie City, because you won't find any gas stations along the ride once you leave US 26. Look for a left turn onto Oregon Highway 7. Stay alert, as this turn can sneak up on you. Take the left on OR 7 and go about a mile.

A covered wagon keeps the region's theme going at this rest stop and view area on US 26 near Dixie Summit, east of John Day.

There is a Susanville—or at least, there was. It was founded in about 1864 as a mining camp during the gold rush that brought hopeful miners streaming into eastern Oregon. And they had reason to look here: The Armstrong Nugget, found near Susanville in 1913, weighed a whopping 80 ounces—the largest nugget of pure gold ever found (now on display at the U.S. Bank in Baker City).

In the early days, many of Susanville's residents were Chinese, and at one point they made up about 85 percent of the population. Despite the town's name, census records show most residents were men. Susanville-area mines eventually produced 50,000 ounces of gold before logging took over as the area's main industry. Some of the old buildings remain, though they are now little more than piles of weathered wood, and gold seekers still occasionally roam these hills looking for their own fortunes. ●

At the small green-and-white sign that reads SUSANVILLE, with a small arrow pointing left, take the left and you're on the Middle Fork Road, commonly known as Susanville Road. (If after the turn onto OR 7 you get to Austin, you've gone a little too far. If you get to Whitney, you've gone way too far.) Strangely, Google Maps lists Susanville Road as "Up Middle Up Fork Road" and MapQuest lists it as County Road 20. The road follows the middle fork of the John Day River for the rest of the ride.

In stark contrast to practically every other road in the area, the pavement here is almost dead flat. There is no cant or camber, and this includes the curves, few if any of which are banked.

Shortly after the turnoff for OR 7, the road feels well off the beaten path, and the valley into which it leads seems remote but not forgotten. Perhaps because the road runs so close to the river, or maybe because we had dropped speed a bit, the narrow valley felt quiet and a little isolated despite the muffled roar of the bike's engine. We were struck with the impression that we had

The Susanville Road makes a good side trip on the way from Vale to John Day.

discovered a tranquil, lesser-traveled trail through a part of the state that we know is very well explored by bikers.

A word to the wise: Sections of this road are open range. We've never seen any livestock in the road here, but in a couple of tight curves, cattle guards are unfortunately placed right in the turn's apex. We're not big fans of steel cattle guards, and for the most part do our best to cross them with the bike fully upright. We hit at least one somewhat unexpectedly, causing the bike to lose a little traction and wobble a bit. After that we cooled things down and crossed the rest of the guards with the bike as upright as possible and at a more reasonable speed.

At the intersection of Susanville Road and US 395, if you like hot springs and want to explore a bit more, make a very soft right across US 395 and check out Ritter Hot Springs. They're quaint, with an old-fashioned hospitality you don't find much anymore. The owners provide a tranquil and relaxed setting that will allow both body and mind to unwind from the stress they build up on the road. Prices are reasonable and well worth paying.

If you aren't the hot-springs type, make a left, heading south on US 395 back toward Mount Vernon and John Day. The road ascends rapidly to the top of Ritter Butte Summit, where you'll have a clear view of the road laid out in front of you and the distant peaks beyond.

US 395 crosses a broad, semi-arid, high alpine plateau specked with juniper and small patches of forest. It passes through the small town of Long Creek, which has its own school and post

Steve: A few miles into our ride through the valley, my sense of calm was destroyed when a sport bike came screaming full-on from around a partially blind corner, hugging the yellow line and leaning full tilt well into our lane.

Don't get me wrong; I have nothing against sport bikes. I've owned them and ridden them with great joy and sometimes reckless abandon. One of the things I like most about the Buell Ulysses I ride is that it handles something like a sport bike. It loves the curves, falling into a tight right-hander only to pop up like a Weeble toy to take the upcoming tight left-hander.

The issue I have with this particular sport bike on this particular road was that he was hugging the centerline— and so was I. I was not leaned over as far and perhaps not going as fast as he, and I brought the bike upright and avoided a potential disaster. He, on the other hand, continued along the line he had chosen, apparently oblivious to the potential for disaster. I have no idea how fast he was going; my guess is considerably faster than the legal limit, and surely too fast to allow for any correction of operator error. No matter what you ride, the time and place to ride as if you are at the track is at the track!

Once I recovered, the rest of the ride was pleasant. With my sense of soothing serenity gone, I came to grips with the fact that this road is no undiscovered gem as we crossed paths with numerous individual riders and multiple packs enjoying the road as much as we were. ●

office but not much else, then up and over Lost Creek Mountain Summit, where you might not even notice the slight change in elevation. Fox and Beech Creek are places too small to be called towns. After Beech Creek Summit at the southern edge of the plateau, you'll drop into a richly forested, narrow alpine canyon that yields a long series of linked curves and sweepers as it drops gradually into Mount Vernon, about 8 miles east of John Day.

When you get back to John Day and want to get off the bike for a little change of pace, swing by the Kam Wah Chung Museum. For anyone interested in Oregon history, this is a must-see attraction. It's just north of the main drag on NW Canton Street; look for the signs. The museum presents artifacts and displays that preserve and share the struggles and legacy of the Chinese workforce in Oregon. It also highlights the lives of Chinese businessman Lung On and herbal doctor Ing Hay, both of whom worked out of this building. Using traditional Chinese remedies, Dr. Hay cared for the Chinese gold-mine workers and others from the surrounding area.

RIDE
13

A Picture-Perfect Day

Directions:
west on US 26 from John Day to OR 19
north on OR 19 to OR 207
south on OR 207 to US 26
west on US 26 about 3 miles to John Day Fossil Beds
National Monument, Painted Hills Unit
east on US 26 back to John Day

Distance:
total distance: 174 miles
John Day to John Day Fossil Beds National Monument
visitor center: 35 miles
Visitor center to Spray: 31 miles
Spray to Service Creek / OR 207: 13 miles
Service Creek to Mitchell: 25 miles
Mitchell to John Day: 70 miles

Time:
half a day to a full day, depending on stops

Services:
John Day, Spray, Service Creek; Mitchell has all services,
but gas is sometimes unavailable

Best Time of Year:
late spring through early fall

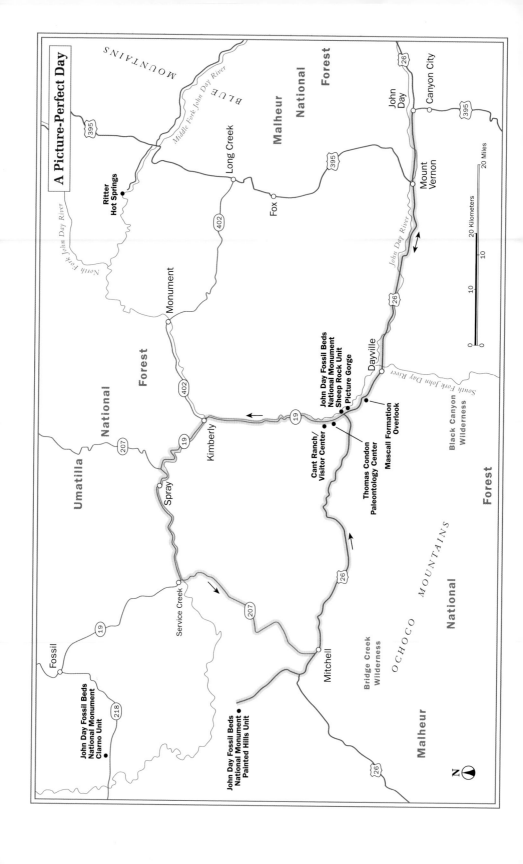

A Picture-Perfect Day

BLUE MOUNTAINS

BLUE John Day River

Middle Fork John Day River

North Fork John Day River

Ritter Hot Springs

395

Long Creek

402

Fox

Monument

Malheur National Forest

395

John Day River

26

Mount Vernon

John Day

Canyon City

26

395

20 Kilometers
20 Miles

10   10
10   10

0

Umatilla National Forest

207

19

Kimberly

19

402

John Day Fossil Beds National Monument Sheep Rock Unit
Picture Gorge

Dayville

South Fork John Day River

Black Canyon Wilderness

Cant Ranch/ Visitor Center

Thomas Condon Paleontology Center

Mascall Formation Overlook

Spray

Service Creek

19

Fossil

218

John Day Fossil Beds National Monument Clarno Unit

John Day Fossil Beds National Monument Painted Hills Unit

207

26

Mitchell

Bridge Creek Wilderness

OCHOCO MOUNTAINS

National Forest

Malheur

26

N

> **Highlights:**
> less-traveled back roads; the rugged beauty of Picture
> Gorge; incredible natural history, geology, and geography;
> no need to hurry

If you have time and are on the road reasonably early, this could be combined with ride 12, the Susanville Road ride, for a great day of riding—you could call it a John Day day, since both routes loop back into John Day. If you only have time for one ride or are headed to points farther west, this one, with its dramatic scenery and paleontological history, is the must-do of the two. Do it as either a loop from John Day or a one-way westward route out of the area.

The John Day Fossil Beds National Monument is spread out over three sites: the Clarno Unit, the Painted Hills Unit, and the Sheep Rock Unit. All three are dedicated to preserving and studying the ancient history that is so close to the surface here. Sheep Rock, the closest to John Day and the site of the monument's visitor center, is the first this ride explores.

Heading west on U.S. Highway 26, follow the course of the John Day River, which you'll continue to track on Oregon Highway 19 and through Picture Gorge. One fork or another of the river seems to be everywhere in this part of the state. The terrain is familiar—a broad agricultural and ranching river valley flanked by ever-present soft rolling hills with higher peaks in the background.

Around Dayville, the John Day River appears to be gaining in volume and velocity. By the time you reach Picture Gorge, the result is obvious: Over the span of unimaginable eons, the force of the water has cut through a basalt uplift of about 1,000 feet. You'll see the gorge's cliffs before you're sure what you're seeing.

Be sure to stop at the John Day Fossil Beds Overlook (also known as the Mascall Formation Overlook). It's off US 26 about 1 mile south of the mouth of the gorge, and the turn is well marked.

> **Steve:** Picture Gorge is named for the pictographs found through here. Since I love to photograph pictographs and petroglyphs, I asked the rangers at the visitor center to give me some specific locations. They politely told me that due to concerns about falling and unstable rock, they are reluctant to tell visitors exactly where the pictographs are. One of the rangers also pulled out photos of a series of pictographs that vandals covered with spray paint three times recently. The chemicals that remove the spray paint also destroy the pictographs. I understood why they were hesitant to disclose exact locations.
>
> After I promised I would be cautious and wouldn't tell anyone where the pictographs were, the rangers eventually gave up the goods. I am a man of my word, so that's as much as you'll get out of me. ●

You'll get a brief but informative overview of the geography and underlying geology of the area, where volcanic activity lay down basalt rock flows and layers of ash in a series of valleys and ridges.

Between those periods of violence, plants and animals populated these valleys, which at the time were well watered. Strange creatures, including horse- and elephant-like animals and giant cats, lived here and left their bones when they died. Now, paleontologists comb the area looking for their preserved remains. Pondering the immense span of time and the catastrophic events that created this beautiful vista can twist your mind into a knot, but it's fun to think about!

The Thomas Condon Paleontology Center, essentially the visitor center for all three sections of the national monument, is on your left about 2 miles north of the intersection of US 26 and OR 19, after the road leaves the gorge. It has more information than you could ever begin to absorb in a month of Sundays, but even a brief visit will afford you a basic understanding of the significance of the terrain through which you're traveling (for more

At John Day Fossil Beds National Monument, even the view from a rest stop 6 miles north of the visitor center is unexpectedly good.

information, go to the monument's Web site, www.nps.gov/joda/index.htm).

The center has a viewing window into a lab where scientists work on extracting fossils from the stone in which they have lain for millions of years. This is a must-see for any youngster who wants to be a paleontologist—or for any of us older kids who still dream about being one. The view of the uplifted rocks from the parking lot is pretty cool, too.

If by this time you're in need of a break or a snack, stop by the historic Cant Ranch, about 0.5 mile down the road from the visitor center. The ranch chronicles the saga of human settlement in this region. Keep going past the ranch and there's a picnic area and rest stop about 6 miles to the north. It's worth a stop: The short road into the parking area has some nice curves, there's a picnic table under a tree if you need to get out of the sun, and the view of the surrounding area is above average.

As you cruise along through the twists and turns of OR 19's path through the John Day River valley, it's sometimes difficult to keep your eyes on the road. The valley is a study in contrasts: the relatively serene waters of the John Day River; the colorful hillsides, slowly revealing secrets of the ancient past through countless eons of erosion; high basalt-fringed ridges, topped by views of distant mountain peaks. The beauty of this short section of road is rivaled by few other places we've been. You'll want to ride slowly to savor your journey through time.

The monument's Clarno section, about 20 miles west of Fossil, preserves cliffs and ancient volcanic rock flows in an arid sagebrush-and-juniper landscape. It's an optional trip up OR 19. To paleontologists, these formations are exciting because they contain fossilized remnants of prehistoric animals, including four-toed horses and crocodile-style lizards, trapped in the mud. For the rest of us, it's a chance to take some short hikes up to the cliffs (which means it's not as easy to appreciate from the road as the other two units of the monument). The appropriately named town of Fossil is home to the nation's only public fossil-hunting bed and a couple of small museums, but not many people.

Fuel up in Spray, especially if you're headed down Oregon Highway 207 to the Painted Hills Unit of the national monument (fuel in Mitchell is available only sporadically, so if you have any doubt, fill up here). It's a little more than 10 miles from Spray to

The John Day National Monument's Painted Hills Unit is a beautiful and colorful landscape of striped rock dunes.

the intersection of OR 19 and OR 207. Take a left on OR 207 going south. OR 207 is a fun ride up and over a series of ridges as it makes its way to the tiny hamlet of Mitchell and the intersection with US 26.

A word of caution: OR 207 is a secondary road that isn't maintained as nicely as the region's major highways. On the other hand, some of its curves are banked so well they look as if they were designed for a luge or a bobsled, and it features some big sweepers and very tight turns. Some of the tight curves are well banked and marked with suggested speed limits; others are not. Steve found himself coming

The 0.25-mile Painted Cove Trail, part of which is boardwalk, allows for a closer look at the monument's vibrant claystone hills.

in a little hot on a few of the unmarked curves. Don't exceed your or your bike's ability to navigate turns.

The turn for the national monument's Painted Hills Unit is about 3 miles west of the intersection of US 26 and OR 207, and it can sneak up on you. The Painted Hills are another 8 miles or so off US 26. The first 6 miles are paved and the last mile or two is well-graded gravel that any bike can handle without a problem.

Overlooks give you expansive views of soft-looking hills striped with subtle hues of red, gold, black, and purple. The colors seem to change with angle and intensity of the light. Short trails, the best of which is the Painted Cove trail, let you visit them in person. The Painted Cove Trail, about half of which is a boardwalk, allows you to walk into the claystone hills; they don't look quite so soft when viewed close up.

Back on US 26, head west toward the Cascades or east to return to John Day.

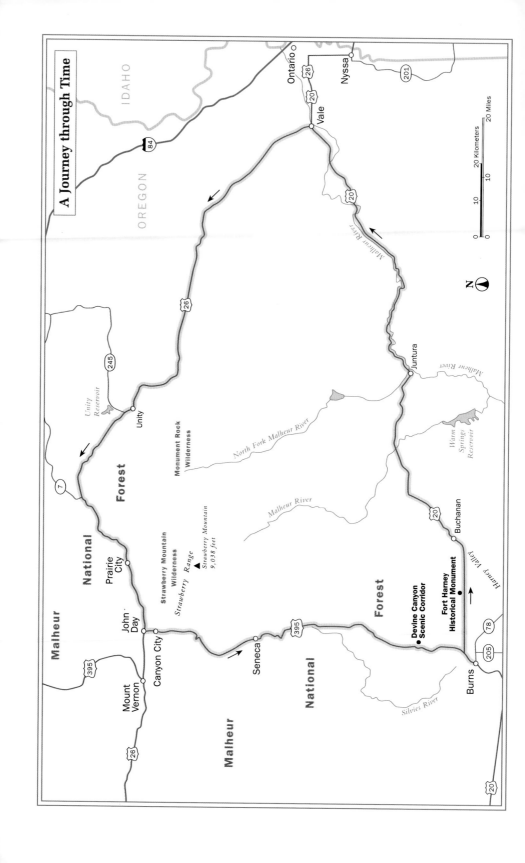

A Journey through Time

Directions:
south from John Day on US 395 to Burns
northeast on US 20 to Vale
northwest on US 26 (the John Day Highway) from Vale to
John Day

Distance:
total distance: 299 miles
John Day to Burns: 71 miles
Burns to Vale: 114 miles
Vale to John Day: 114 miles

Time:
one very long day or two nice days, depending on how
much time you spend exploring

Services:
Burns, Vale, Prairie City, and John Day / Canyon City;
limited between towns

Best Time of Year:
late spring, summer (which can be hot), and fall; the ride
passes through lots of snow zones

Highlights:
tidy small towns populated by friendly and helpful people in classic cowboy country; eons of geological, paleontological, and Oregon Trail history; some of the best motorcycle roads in the region; good food and the added bonus of decent coffee outside the java meccas of Portland and Seattle

This ride gives you a taste of what makes this part of the state so interesting and fun to ride. It encompasses mountainous terrain and high alpine twists and turns on its way to Burns. Heading northeast out of Burns, it skirts the northern edge of the weird and wonderful high desert of southeast Oregon. On its way to Vale, it climbs over two passes that provide expansive views of distant canyons and mesas, then leads directly to Malheur Gorge—a 40-mile playground of curves that serves as a gateway to the open and serene agricultural lands ringing the historic town of Vale.

You can start this loop from any of the bigger towns in it, but John Day is an excellent home base for exploring this part of Oregon, so we start there. The loop could easily be broken into two days, with the first taking you from John Day to Burns to Vale. On day two, ride from Vale to John Day, possibly making the Susanville Road side trip (ride 12) on your way.

From John Day, head south on U.S. Highway 395 and through Canyon City toward Burns. To get here, you've come in on U.S. Highway 26 from the east or west, or US 395 from the north or south, so you should already have a good idea of what you're in for. Anyone who wouldn't remember those roads probably shouldn't be at the controls of any vehicle, much less a motorcycle. In short, starting about 8 miles down the road, you've got 70 miles of great alpine riding ahead, beginning with a steep and winding climb up to 5,152 feet.

Roll from the summit through Bear Gulch, hitting a series of gullies and canyons and nice curves before dropping into the Bear Valley. This is simply good, solid alpine riding the way it was meant to be. The Bear Valley is a high alpine desert with wide-open views of the mountain peaks that surround it and sparse vegetation consisting mostly of sage and the occasional pocket of juniper.

There are a few named dots on the map between here and Burns, but these are generally just wide spots in the road, ghosts of towns that used to supply a few ranches and the busy mining district this once was. None of them have services now. At the valley's southern rim, you'll hit the little town of Seneca. Don't count on it for fuel, but if you were in a pinch and needed help, friendly Seneca would be the place to find it.

Just south of Seneca, the landscape changes rapidly. The wide vistas of the Bear Valley disappear as the road drops into the Devine Canyon Scenic Corridor. Devine Canyon is a relatively narrow, ponderosa-pine-lined canyon sliced by the Silvies River. US 395 follows the Silvies River for about 15 miles until it tumbles toward Burns.

About 15 miles outside Burns, you'll hit your final summit at 5,340 feet. US 395 intersects with U.S. Highway 20 a few miles northeast of Burns. Make a right on US 20 if you're looking for gas or food; it will bring you into the heart of Burns and right down the middle of Broadway.

If it's breakfast or lunch you're after, look for Bella Java & Bistro near the end of Broadway on your right. The food is good, the staff is friendly and helpful, and for those who need to stay connected to the outside world, they have wireless Internet. For dinner, go to the south end of Broadway and take a right onto West Monroe Street. Your destination is the Meat Hook Steak House, on your left just before West Monroe makes a soft bend to the left and turns into Hines Boulevard. For more choices, don't hesitate to ask someone in this very friendly small town.

From Burns, find your way back to US 20 eastbound. The first 25 miles or so are flat as a griddle and straight as an arrow. Anyone can handle straight and flat for a while, right?

You'll pass the site of Fort Harney, set up in 1874 to battle Native American tribes. More than 500 Paiute Indians were rounded up in 1879 and held here until they were shackled and marched off to other forts in the Northwest. It closed in 1880, and the remnants of the old cemetery are all that's left.

Just past Buchanan, the road begins to climb, taking you up and over Stinkwater Pass at 4,648 feet before dropping a little. Then it's up and over Drinkwater Pass at 4,212 feet before you dive into the little agricultural town of Juntura. The Oasis is a friendly little cafe in the center of town at the RV park, and its diner-style food is popular with both travelers and locals. Get a refreshing cold drink or a milkshake (a specialty) and cool off in the shade of one of the massive cottonwood trees.

Back on the road, it's all fun and games from Juntura to Vale. From the moment it enters Malheur Gorge, and for about the next 40 miles until it drops down from Vines Hill Summit, the road will follow the path carved by the Malheur River (which has plenty of forks but does not, strangely enough, connect with nearby Malheur Lake). The curves on this road are fun and fast (obey the posted speed limit if you can).

Malheur is derived from the French term meaning "bad hour" or "misfortune." French trappers gave the river its name after they stashed a cache of beaver pelts in the area only to have them discovered and stolen by the local Native Americans. The river has lived up to its name once or twice since, including a time when a group of northbound travelers left the river looking for an Oregon Trail short-cut, couldn't find any water on the high desert, and died. This area, a misfortune for trappers and travelers from the past, is good fortune for those of us on two wheels. ●

Vale's impressive murals, painted on buildings all over town, celebrate its history. *Patriots on Parade* depicts an old-fashioned Fourth of July.

The entire length of the gorge is a seemingly endless series of long, open right- and left-hand sweepers that go on for so long you'd swear you were about to make a full circle and end up where you started—at which point the road changes direction and you find yourself leaning hard into another beautifully banked curve on the opposite side, taking a little rubber off the other side of the tire. There are a few nice S curves thrown in for good measure. We have no idea who engineered this road, or most of the roads in this part of the state, but we can only assume he rode a motorcycle. The scenery is not spectacular, but this is one of the most fun and easy-to-ride roads you'll encounter anywhere.

After dropping from Vines Hill Summit, the road is back in agricultural country and on the outskirts of Vale. Vale has a rich history, most notably as the first Oregon Trail stop in Oregon. You'll immediately notice the city's motto emblazoned on flags around town: BORN AND RAISED ON THE OREGON TRAIL. The town proudly displays the history of the Oregon Trail through a series of approximately thirty murals painted on the sides of buildings. Four more murals greet visitors as they enter town.

Surrounding hot springs were popular with travelers, and the Rinehart Stone House Museum, built in 1872, has served as an inn, a Pony Express stop, and a stage stop between Boise and the Willamette Valley. Now restored, the museum offers a display of historic relics and photos.

Leaving Vale, pick up US 26 heading toward John Day, climbing steadily through rich ranch and agricultural lands surrounded by the soft, round, bare hills ubiquitous in this part of the state. The road follows Willow Creek for a short time before cutting more sharply west on its way toward Unity, Prairie City, and John Day. There are no services to speak of between Vale and Unity, except for gas in the little town of Brogan about 25 miles outside of Vale. Unity has gas, a store, and a small RV park. Shortly after Unity, the soft rolling hills and grasslands ascend to higher elevation and more rugged alpine terrain similar to that around US 395.

When the weather is clear, you can gaze off to your left into the Monument Rock and Strawberry Mountain wilderness areas. The highest of the peaks you'll see in order from east to west are Table Rock at 7,815 feet, Lookout Mountain at 8,033 feet, and Strawberry Mountain at 9,038 feet.

You'll be climbing and descending and twisting and curving from just past Unity to John Day and beyond. The asphalt in this part of the state tends to be manicured and nicely banked, and this section of US 26 is no exception. The quality of these roads allows even a timid rider to pull back the throttle and enjoy the ride. If it's summer and the thermometer is rising, you'll find some relief from the heat as the road climbs up and over Dixie Pass at 5,279 feet. You'll be leaving the sights and smells of the alpine environs as you begin your descent toward Prairie City and John Day, but the excellent roads and riding don't cease when you drop to a little lower elevation.

A sign of good grub: bikes outside the Silver Spur Cafe in Mount Vernon, about 8 miles west of John Day.

If you're running low on gas or need snacks, you will find what you need in Prairie City. John Day, with all amenities, is only 11 more miles down the road.

If you're new to this part of the country, or to Oregon, you're probably wondering, "Who was John Day, and why are so many things named after him?" Even though four forks of a river, a dam, two towns (John Day and Dayville), a wilderness area, and a national monument carry his name, surprisingly little is known about the man. It's widely known that he was a hunter from Virginia and that he arrived in the West in the early 1800s. He's perhaps most famous for the fact that he and Ramsay Crooks were robbed and stripped naked by Native Americans on the Columbia River, not far from the river that now bears his name. ●

Dining and Other Amenities

John Day

The Grubsteak and Mining Company
149 East Main St.
(541) 575-1970
Full menu, bar in the back, friendly staff, and decent food at good prices

The Outpost
201 West Main St.
(541) 575-0250
Pub food, steaks, and pizza

The Squeeze-In Restaurant & Deck
423 West Main St.
(541) 575-1045
Big menu, reasonable prices; can get busy

Mount Vernon

The Silver Spur
150 South Ingle St.
(541) 932-4545
Breakfast, lunch, and dinner; big sandwiches, salads, and pizza; fast and friendly service

Vale

The Starlight Cafe
152 Clark St. North
(541) 473-2500
A diner on the west end of town, on your left if you're coming in on US 20 from Burns; very popular with travelers and locals, and the place for homemade pies

RIDE 15

High Desert Discovery

Directions:
southeast on OR 78 from Burns to New Princeton
southwest on Lava Beds Road (becomes Diamond Lane)
from New Princeton to OR 205
south on OR 205 to Fields
(option) northeast on East Steens Road; north on OR 78
back to Burns

Distance:
Burns to Fields: 112 miles (224 miles round-trip)

Time:
one long day or two nice days, depending on where you
spend the night

Services:
Burns, Crane, The Narrows RV park, Frenchglen (limited and
sporadic), Fields

Best Time of Year:
late spring / early summer and fall; summer can get damn
hot

Highlights:
classic tales, historic buildings, and other remnants of the
Old West; varied landscapes of mountains, deserts, hot
springs, and volcanoes; the Malheur National Wildlife Refuge, complete with wetlands and water birds; some of the
friendliest and most helpful people you'll find anywhere

The riding in this region is not for the faint of heart, nor is it
ideal for those who crave in-your-face dramatic landscapes.
The beauty of southeastern Oregon can be subtle and may take
time to notice and appreciate; it's a mix of terrain and vegetation combined with changing light as the day progresses and variable weather. In the same day you'll find pancake-flat, wide-open
high desert and rolling, sagebrush-covered hills flowing into rich
ranch land and farmland. You'll encounter basalt cliffs hanging
above one side of the road and wetlands on another. There are
steep, glacier-carved mountains towering over bone-dry deserts
and just about every possible combination in between. You must
be prepared for long distances between services and harsh, unfor-
giving weather any time of the year. But the area is appreciated by
some who pass through and by all who remain.

This ride begins in Burns, a little town at the north end of the
High Desert Discovery Scenic Byway. Its location gives you a few
options for the ride. The first is as an out-and-back from Burns to
the outback town of Fields, with the option of spending the night
in Fields or Frenchglen. The second is a loop involving about 65
miles of reasonably decent gravel-packed dirt road that is usually
well graded. The third is down and out of the area via Oregon
Highway 140.

Let's start with the out-and-back: Leave Burns heading southeast on Oregon Highway 78 toward Crane and New Princeton.
Shortly after leaving Burns, you'll pass Crystal Crane Hot Springs
on your left. It doesn't look like much, but it's been around a long
time and is a great place to soak after a long day on the road and

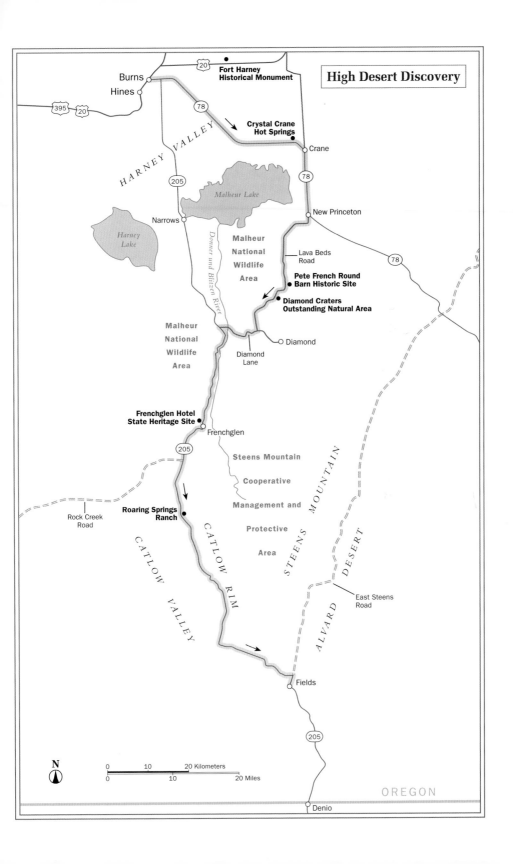

High Desert Discovery

Fort Harney
Historical Monument

Burns

Hines

395 20

20

78

HARNEY VALLEY

Crystal Crane
Hot Springs

Crane

205

78

Malheur Lake

New Princeton

Narrows

Malheur
National
Wildlife
Area

Lava Beds
Road

78

Harney
Lake

Donner and Blitzen River

Pete French Round
Barn Historic Site

Diamond Craters
Outstanding Natural Area

Malheur
National
Wildlife
Area

Diamond

Diamond
Lane

Frenchglen Hotel
State Heritage Site

Frenchglen

205

Steens Mountain

Cooperative

Management and

Protective

Area

STEENS MOUNTAIN

Rock Creek
Road

Roaring Springs
Ranch

CATLOW RIM

ALVARD DESERT

East Steens
Road

CATLOW VALLEY

ALVARD DESERT

Fields

205

N

0   10   20 Kilometers
0   10   20 Miles

OREGON

Denio

The interior of the Pete French Round Barn south of Burns shows the craftsmanship that's kept it standing for many decades.

for reasonably priced lodging near Burns. It has RV hookups, tent sites, and rustic cabins, plus a huge soaking pool that's about 7 feet deep in the middle. Cost is $3.50 for a day pass, or free for overnight guests. It has private soaking tubs if you prefer your hot springs a little less public.

Just past New Princeton—really not much more than a couple of buildings near the road—OR 78 makes about a 40-degree turn to the left. Go straight on Lava Beds Road and follow signs for the High Desert Discovery Scenic Byway; you may also see signs for the Malheur National Wildlife Refuge and the Pete French Round Barn. The barn is about 14 miles down Lava Beds Road, which winds its way through surprisingly rich agricultural lands. Follow signs directing you to the round barn or Diamond and make a left onto a short gravel road to the Round Barn and its visitor center.

Cattle baron Peter French built the round barn, one of two or three built in the area and the only one still standing, in the late

1870s or early 1880s. It's innovative in its design and construction: The center area of the barn was used as a stable for horses, with an outer ring to break and exercise them in the winter.

The visitor center is on the right as you approach the barn. You can stop here on your way in or out, but you must stop. Richard "Dick" Jenkins, the owner of the visitor center, is perhaps the most friendly, knowledgeable, helpful person you'll ever meet. His family has lived in the area since the 1880s, so even longtime locals defer to him for accurate information. This is also one of the most impressive visitor centers/gift shops you'll ever set your riding boots in. It's well stocked with all kinds of interesting and high-quality merchandise related to the West, including books, the work of local artists, and Jenkins family heirlooms. When you find something you like that's too big or fragile to strap to the back of your bike, he'll be happy to ship it for you.

Leaving the round barn, you'll take a left on Lava Beds Road and continue until Diamond Lane. Follow Diamond Lane until it intersects with Oregon Highway 205. The tiny town of Diamond, long a supply center for travelers and the families running surrounding ranches, is now home to the Hotel Diamond (which serves meals by reservation only). You'll pass signs for Diamond Craters, a complex containing a diverse array of easy-to-reach volcanic features, from 6,000 to 60,000 years old. If you have in interest in geology and volcanic activity, this is a great place to stop and look around—or you may simply make note of the interesting lava flows blanketed by fields of sage and keep on riding (see www.blm.gov/or/districts/burns/recreation/diamond_craters.php).

Make a left when you get to the intersection of Diamond Lane and OR 205 and head south toward Frenchglen.

If you need fuel and don't want to risk not getting any in Frenchglen, head north from the intersection of OR 205 and Diamond Lane to The Narrows RV Park, where services are consistently available. It's only about 16 miles up a nice stretch of pavement that winds its way along the base of cliffs formed by ancient basalt flows.

Steve: Frenchglen is a quaint little place local brochures and Web sites encourage tourists to visit. Depending on whom you talk to locally, this is either a great idea or a complete waste of time, but anyone headed south on OR 205 toward Fields will go right through the middle of it.

The main attraction of Frenchglen is the Frenchglen Hotel, now owned by the state of Oregon as a historic site. Built in the mid-1920s to house stagecoach travelers and visitors to the "P" Ranch (the headquarters for Pete French's livestock holdings), the hotel is a typical example of American Foursquare architecture, complete with a big screened porch across the front. It's a simple design, and the porch is a popular place for visitors and hotel guests to hang out. I thought about taking a little break and having something to eat and drink, but the porch was full of folks not quite twice my age. I imagined a sweaty, bug-covered biker in their midst would disturb them, so I kept on riding.

If it's early, you may be able to get a hearty breakfast served family-style at the hotel, but little else is likely to be open. Fuel may be available, but only sporadically, and very much at the whim of the proprietor. If you do need gas, you should probably have cash—and if it's after hours, be prepared for a minimum charge that is too steep to justify filling the tank of any bike. I suggested a hostile takeover of the gas station to a couple of locals, simply for the sake of more-predictable services. My comments were met with the dry laughter and wry smiles of those who have considered the same. ●

At the Narrows, OR 205 greets the Malheur National Wildlife Refuge. Harney Lake and Mud Lake lie off to the southwest, and Malheur Lake sprawls to the northeast—or at least, they should. Southeastern Oregon had suffered through an extended dry spell when we visited, so there was no water in sight. But the RV park

The Catlow Rim rises behind an old building near Roaring Springs Ranch.

remained. With water elsewhere nearby, the wildlife refuge is an oasis in an otherwise arid landscape. It's host to some 320 bird species, among them white-faced ibis, trumpeter swans, grebes, and a plethora of other waterfowl, shorebirds, and songbirds.

If you have plenty of fuel at the intersection with OR 205 and Diamond Lane, head south on OR 205 toward Fields, the next town with services. You're at the southern tip of the wildlife refuge, following the course of the Donner und Blitzen River (yes, that is its name). Steens Mountain is visible in the distance on your left as you ride, with the Catlow Rim on your right. Even

One end of the Steens Loop Tour Route begins in Frenchglen. It's not paved and not open all the way through to the other end. Our bike can handle well-graded dirt and gravel, but Dick Jenkins at the Round Barn Visitor Center advised against going more than a few miles on a fully loaded motorcycle. Perhaps we'll give it a go when we're not as heavily laden. ●

when the lakes to the north are mostly dry, there is lots of water here. Lots of water tends to bring lots of bugs and lots of birds. Be alert: Some of the birds enjoy sitting in the middle of the road, playing their version of chicken, not getting out of the way until the very last minute. We've come very close to hitting several and have had to duck more than a few times to avoid being hit in the head as birds veered off to avoid the bike.

The road makes a sharp turn at Frenchglen, twisting and climbing for about 3 miles up a 14 percent grade. This is some of the steepest road we've been on, but it's in good condition with the curves well banked. You're passing through a gap in the Catlow Rim, coming out on the west side of the rim just north of the Roaring Springs Ranch. You'll now be riding with the Catlow Rim on your left and the Catlow Valley stretching off into the distance on your right. OR 205 (also known as Catlow Valley Road here) follows the base of the rim for the next 38 miles or so, and if you've ever done any sailing, it may feel like tacking down-valley.

The road runs straight northwest-to-southeast for a few miles before turning to run northeast-to-southwest. It repeats this zigzag

Although East Steens Road is usually in good condition, heavy rains on Steens Mountain can send muddy water washing over it.

many times on its way to the south end of the valley. There, it makes a relatively sharp turn to the southeast through a tight gap in the rock, once again climbing up and over the Catlow Rim before descending gently into the little outback of Fields.

Owned by Tom and Sandra Downs, Fields Station is a combination store, cafe, gas station, campground, and hotel. It's also the only reliable place for services through here and a one-stop shop for adventures in this part of the state. Throw in a few houses and a post office, and that's the entire town of Fields. Everyone we've met in Fields, including other visitors, has been warm and friendly, usually on adventures of their own but equally interested in hearing about ours.

You have several options here: You could spend the night in Fields or turn around and ride back to Frenchglen or Burns.

You could also choose to pick up East Steens Road just north of Fields. It's about 62 miles of gravel-packed dirt road that's sometimes well graded and other times not. There are no services until Crane, about 40 miles to the west from where East Steens Road intersects with OR 78. Steve rode it once on a rainy spring day, and stretches of the road were in reasonably decent shape, while others were washboard or corduroy, with puddles filling depressions in the road.

We wouldn't recommend it unless you're riding an adventure-style bike or are comfortable taking your cruiser or touring bike off-road and are willing to risk uncertain conditions. The road is very lightly traveled with a few ranches nestled up against the base of the mountain, so if you did blow a tire or dump your bike, help could be a long way off and a long time coming. The upside is that East Steens Road runs west of the Alvord Desert and just east of Steens Mountain, offering close-up views of the mountain's rugged eastern edge.

The other option is to head south on OR 205, now called Fields-Denio Road, to Denio Junction in Nevada. There, you can pick up OR 140 westbound to Lakeview or southbound to Winnemucca, Nevada.

Restaurants and Accommodations

Burns

Bella Java & Bistro
314 North Broadway
(541) 573-1460
Good bakery, salads, sandwiches, and coffee (Samantha is the owner, and her family has lived in the area for a long time. Ask her about Burns and the surrounding area, and if she doesn't know the answer off the top of her head, she knows someone who does, and will quickly pick up the phone on your behalf.)

Meat Hook Steak House
673 West Monroe St.
(541) 573-7698

Crane

Crystal Crane Hot Springs
About 16 miles east of Burns on OR 78
(541) 493-2312
www.cranehotsprings.com
RV spaces, tent camping, cabins, soaking pool, and private tubs

Fields

Fields Station
22276 Fields Dr.
(541) 495-2275

Frenchglen

Frenchglen Hotel
OR 205, 60 miles south of Burns
(541) 493-2825

WESTERN WASHINGTON

When people think about this part of the world, they think about rain—and water is a big part of the landscape here. But Western Washington also has mountains, islands, cities, farmland—and even some relatively dry spots.

Actually, Western Washington is drier than people think it is. With a mere 37 inches of rain a year, Seattle gets less precipitation than Houston, New York, or Atlanta. And summers here are glorious, luring more bikers out onto the roads than you would think could possibly live in a place with such a dreary reputation. (Since it's so close to the border, you'll meet a lot of Canadian riders, too.) As soon as the weather clears in early summer, the hills and valleys are alive with the sound of roaring engines and the sight of bikes hitting the road. Some hardy folks ride year-round here, no matter what the conditions; it helps that the weather is cool but generally mild, and snow is rare.

With so many bikers living or visiting here, Western Washington is home to many clubs, most of them welcoming to riders visiting or new to the area. Businesses, especially roadside eateries and watering holes, tend to be overwhelmingly motorcycle-friendly.

This is also home to Seattle, the biggest metropolitan area in the Northwest. More than 3 million people live around the Puget Sound. That means lots of bikers and motorcycle shops, all kinds of amenities—and lots of suburban sprawl, with the traffic headaches that begets. Still, there are lots of places to get away from it all, and they're within a couple hours of the big city.

The landscape is dominated by the rugged and remote Olympic Peninsula to the west, the strategic and economic hot spot of Puget Sound, and the Cascades on its eastern edge. In between are cities, towns, farms, wineries, and a network of semi-rural highways that make attractive alternatives to the slow, often-clogged mess that is Interstate 5.

Those roads include Washington Highways 9 (the Valley Highway), 92 to Granite Falls, 203 through Carnation, 18 and 169 near Issaquah . . . we could go on. And those roads have even more remote ones branching off from them. They give us lots of chances to get out of the city and feel as if our everyday lives are far away. Short rides along their foothills are so close we can do them during our lunch hours—if our bosses are nice.

Bikes line up on the ferry from Mukilteo to Whidbey Island.

San Juan Jaunt

Directions:
north on I-5 from Seattle to US 20
west on US 20 to Anacortes
Washington State Ferry to islands

Distance:
depends on which islands you visit and how much riding
you do on each
Seattle to Anacortes—about 80 miles

Time:
one full day to two or three days

Services:
Anacortes, Friday Harbor (San Juan Island), Eastsound
(Orcas Island)

Best Time of Year:
early spring to late fall; San Juan Islands are fairly dry and
have good weather much of the year

Highlights:
gorgeous locales and a laid-back vibe; possible whale and
other wildlife sightings; first dibs on the ferry

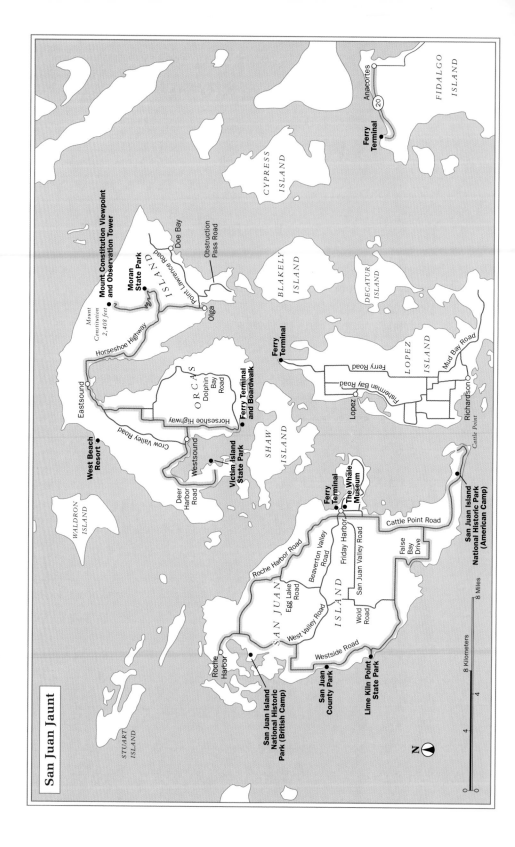

San Juan Jaunt

FIDALGO ISLAND

Anacortes

20

Ferry Terminal

CYPRESS ISLAND

Mount Constitution Viewpoint and Observation Tower

Doe Bay

Mount Constitution 2,408 feet

Point Lawrence Road

Moran State Park

Obstruction Pass Road

BLAKELY ISLAND

Horseshoe Highway

Olga

DECATUR ISLAND

ORCAS ISLAND

Eastsound

Dolphin Bay Road

Ferry Terminal

Ferry Terminal and Boardwalk

West Beach Resort

Horseshoe Highway

Crow Valley Road

Westsound

LOPEZ ISLAND

Mud Bay Road

Fisherman Bay Road

Ferry Road

Lopez

Deer Harbor Road

Victim Island State Park

SHAW ISLAND

Richardson

Cattle Point

WALDRON ISLAND

Ferry Terminal

The Whale Museum

Friday Harbor

Cattle Point Road

San Juan Island National Historic Park (American Camp)

Roche Harbor Road

Beaverton Valley Road

San Juan Valley Road

False Bay Drive

Egg Lake Road

SAN JUAN ISLAND

Wold Road

West Valley Road

Westside Road

Roche Harbor

STUART ISLAND

San Juan Island National Historic Park (British Camp)

San Juan County Park

Lime Kiln Point State Park

N

0   4   8 Kilometers

0   4   8 Miles

The San Juan Islands sit like gems in the waters between the U.S. mainland and Vancouver Island. There are many islands in the group, though only a few—notably San Juan, Orcas, Shaw, and Lopez—are large enough for human habitation. They sit in the Olympic Mountains' "rain shadow," which means they get less precipitation than most of the region, and the best way to tour this beautiful, friendly, popular getaway is by bike. Not because it features sweeping, fun-filled roads; for the most part, those don't exist in the San Juans. And not because the islands' small scale is ideal for motorcycle travel, although it is. It's because touring by bike takes a lot of the stress out of a trip that can be a pain by car.

Here's how people in cars get to the San Juans in summertime: They try to leave as early as possible to miss northbound traffic on Interstate 5. Join what seems like a million other cars, all headed the same place at the same time and drive for at least a couple of hours, maybe more. Wait in line for a ferry for a couple hours, maybe more, and hope they get a spot on the next one out. After arriving on the islands, they fight for parking at the islands' popular locales.

Here's how motorcyclists do it: Take the HOV (high occupancy vehicle) lanes out of Seattle. Arrive at the Anacortes ferry twenty minutes before it departs. Use priority boarding for bikes, which allows you to hop on without having to wait

Motorcycles get first-on, first-off privileges on most Washington State ferries, including this one on its way to Orcas Island.

Anacortes is also home to Washington's biggest motorcycle event—the Oyster Run. It started out as a spur-of-the-moment ride by "Limp" Lee and a few buddies (you'll have to ask him where the nickname comes from) who rode to grab some oysters at a favorite Marysville hangout. Within a few years, the event grew so much by word of mouth that it eventually overwhelmed the original route on WA 9. The slightly larger, tourist-oriented Anacortes graciously (if at first suspiciously) agreed to host what had become a major rally.

Now, bikers choose their own paths to the main event. Held the fourth Sunday of each September, it caps off the summer riding season with loosely organized events usually centered around food and drink at motorcycle-friendly local establishments throughout the region. Go to www.oysterrun.org for information on an event you should plan on joining if you're in the area come September. ●

in line with cars. Then enjoy your compact, agile, and efficient mode of exploring while fully experiencing the islands' beauty in 360-degree, open-air style.

Between the highway and the ferries, it would be difficult to see much of the San Juans in a single day, so most people make a two- or three-day trip of it. Lodging can be expensive or fill up on busy weekends, so most visitors book trips well in advance. Another option is to stay in Anacortes and then jump on the ferry first thing in the morning. Anacortes offers a plethora of discount hotels, plus lots of good restaurants and a historic downtown district of its own. Even if you're staying on the islands, it's a nice place to grab a bite before the ferry.

We head first to San Juan Island, home of the islands' biggest town, Friday Harbor. Since you only pay for westbound ferry rides, it makes sense to go to San Juan, the westernmost island, first, thus only having to pay once. The ferry lands on Friday

Harbor's doorstep—go straight a block and you're in the middle of downtown. It's a quaint, genteel place with lots of shops and real estate offices selling vacation homes to those in the thrall of the islands' beauty. Pick up a free map of the islands at one of the businesses in Friday Harbor; a road map will make navigating the islands much easier. You can also use the islands' official Web site, www.visitsanjuans.com, to plan ahead.

This is a place to wander. Roads are slow, and everything is small and tidy. Farms and ranches fill most of the landscape. You can stop (or not) to check out anything from roadside art to the lavender and alpaca for which the islands are famous.

Several main roads cross San Juan Island, and they're all pretty straight two-lane, double-yellow affairs. Those around the

Christy: San Juan Island National Historical Park actually encompasses two sites on the island, American and British camps. The camps were established by the American and British militaries when the islands were disputed territory claimed by both. While the British up north were busy setting up their version of a civilized town in a sheltered bay, the American soldiers were going crazy from constant winds and government neglect. Badly paid and provisioned, with no job to do and nowhere to go without facing court-martial, some of them were literally bored to death (one panel notes the high number of suicides).

An interpretive trail around American Camp tells the tale of how the "Pig War" got started—an American shot a Brit's pig in 1859—and how it progressed into a standoff during which a lot of military men postured but no actual fighting erupted. The matter was finally settled in 1872 when both countries agreed to let Kaiser Wilhelm of Germany determine the islands' fate. He decided in favor of the Americans, and the British left to pursue interests elsewhere. ●

island's edge are more interesting. We'll do a counterclockwise tour of San Juan, starting at Friday Harbor. Things are so close that you can always break away or backtrack if you miss something.

From Friday Harbor, turn left on Argyle Road past the Friday Harbor Airport (the biggest of several in the San Juans—people here love their small planes). Follow Argyle to Cattle Point Road and signs for San Juan Island National Historical Park and American Camp. At the end of Cape San Juan, the Cattle Point Lighthouse makes for nice photos from a distance. It's not open for tours, nor is it very easy to access from the road (via a hike that's not well marked). If you're here during the day and want more information, visit the interpretive center between the lighthouse and the east end of American Camp.

Also between the lighthouse and American Camp, South Beach is a broad, windswept, driftwood-strewn pebble beach—the longest public beach in the islands. It's a popular spot for picnicking, barbecues, and walks.

From here, backtrack to the intersection with Bailer Hill Road (for views over False Bay, take False Bay Drive, a maintained gravel road). Bailer Hill Road turns into Westside Road.

Picturesque Roche Harbor is a convenient lunch spot for tourists circumnavigating San Juan Island.

Whale watchers can spend many happy hours looking for wildlife in the waters off Lime Kiln Point State Park.

The two-lane road curves around the edge of the hilly coastline—a pleasant change from the straight, flat valley pavement. It's narrow, with some bucks, pebbles, and patches, and traffic can be slow along the water as drivers gawk at the scenery.

Lime Kiln Point State Park is one of the islands' must-do stops. This is the islands' most popular (and reliable) whale-watching point. It also features a pretty lighthouse and the remnants of an old industrial kiln. On summer days, a naturalist can answer questions about the plant and animal life here, and a sign tells when whales were last spotted. If you wait long enough, your chances of seeing whales on any given day in summer are pretty good. That plus nice restrooms and short trails make it a perfect spot for a lunchtime picnic. Just up the road, San Juan County Park is pretty much the only option for camping on the island.

Continuing north, take a right on West Valley Road and follow signs for the British Camp section of the national historical park. Informational panels tell more about the history of this place, where more of the buildings have been preserved than at

American Camp. Signs will also direct you to a midden (a big pile of empty shells left by ancient people over the course of many oyster dinners).

For a look at a picturesque little settlement and some good lunch or dinner possibilities, make a left onto Roche Harbor Road. Once the site of a massive lime factory owned by John McMillin, Roche Harbor is home to some pricey vacation houses, a beautiful small harbor, and a handful of restaurants. The lime kilns are silent now, but it's still sort of a company town—all the businesses are owned by a group of investors who now cater to tourists arriving by boat and airplane.

Back on the road, veer left on Roche Harbor Road and follow it around as it meanders back to Friday Harbor.

On to Orcas Island. Sleepy San Juan is bustling compared to the bucolic landscape of Orcas. Here, the slopes are steeper and things have a wilder, less-civilized feel. The only town of any size, Eastsound, is in the narrow middle of an island many describe as being saddlebag-shaped (horses', not motorcycles').

Bring your binoculars if you love wildlife: Three pods of killer whales (orcas) frequent the area May through September, drawing thousands of tourists who hope to see these magnificent creatures up close. Countless outfits on San Juan and Orcas islands offer trips out by motorboat, many offering money-back guarantees that you'll spot a whale. You have almost as good a chance of seeing whales from onshore lookouts like Lime Kiln Point. (Boats are required by law to stay 100 yards away, since the noise and disruption they create can be harmful.) At any time of year, you may also see eagles, seals, sea lions, and porpoises along the islands' coasts. If the weather turns rainy or you miss the whales in person, or you just want to know more, consider visiting the informative Whale Museum in Friday Harbor. ●

It's a reliable bet if you need fuel.

Like San Juan, Orcas is crisscrossed with narrow, meandering roads that either end at the water or connect with each other. The island's main road, the aptly named Horseshoe Highway, goes around from one side of the island to the other and through Eastsound. On the west side of the island, Deer Harbor Road leads to beach parks with intriguing names like Skull Island, Massacre Bay, and Victim Island, which give you the idea life here was not always easy. Now, though, these are pretty spots to wander the shore and for kay-akers to put their boats in the water. Farther north, on the west coast, West Beach Resort usually has ice cream for sale.

The road up Mount Constitution, the San Juans' highest point, is full of tight switchbacks.

The most impressive thing about Orcas, and the must-do adventure of the island, is Moran State Park on the island's east side. It surrounds Mount Constitution, the highest point on the islands, at 2,408 feet. You don't have to be a mountain climber to enjoy the view from the top: There's a road all the way up. As one of the islands' most popular attractions, it gets a lot of traffic, but the twisty-turny ride is pretty and the views from the summit are stunning. On a clear day, you can see all the way to Mount Rainier to the south and Mount Baker to the northeast.

Continue to the end of Olga Road and you'll find another couple of beach-access parks and the tiny artsy enclave of Olga, where a small and often busy cafe run by the artists serves good food (don't expect super-fast service—they are artists, after all).

Christy: On top of Mount Constitution, an observation tower gives even more eye-popping views. Information panels inside tell about the park's origins: Robert Moran, the Seattle businessman who owned this land, donated it for a public park in 1921. Moran felt this beautiful landscape should belong to everyone. Reading his story, I was touched by his selfless gift, one that ensured this place would be accessible for us decades later.

At the time, Washington had no state parks, and the state wasn't even sure what to do with the gift. But it quickly became a beloved spot for hiking, swimming in several lakes, and camping. The Civilian Conservation Corps built many of the classic log structures still in use here. Moran's grand mansion, at the end of a road that branches off just outside the state park's west entrance, is open to the public. ●

On a sunny day, islands, the mainland, and faraway volcanic islands are visible from the top of Mount Constitution.

Head east on Point Lawrence Road to get to Doe Bay Resort, a retreat with cabins and a cafe (and massage and yoga, if you're feeling stressed).

The third most popular island for motorized vehicles is Lopez Island. It's another beautiful place, with more parks on the water. But the island has few amenities (a handful of cafes and guesthouses), is mostly residential, and has no especially appealing roads for motorcyclists—just a grid of mostly straight lanes through rolling farmland. If you really want to get away from the urban grind, though, this is a good place to escape. It's known for its friendly residents (who wave at pretty much everyone they see), and it's popular with bicyclists tired of fighting traffic elsewhere. Its most interesting spot is the historic town of Richardson, at the island's south end, and pretty views from nearby Agate Beach County Park.

Shaw Island, the smallest of the ferry-accessible islands, is worth a little time if you have some to spare but also doesn't have much in the way of amenities. There are about 800 islands in the San Juans, total, and riding the ferry will give you a chance to see the houses built by those rich and lucky enough to have their own. Other islands have been set aside as wildlife reserves, while many are just specks of land left to the birds.

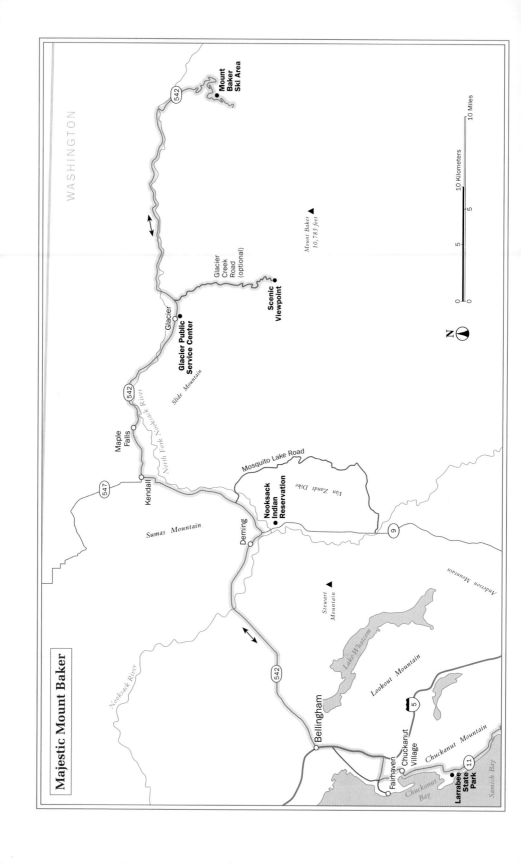

Majestic Mount Baker

WASHINGTON

Mount Baker Ski Area

542

Glacier Creek Road (optional)

Scenic Viewpoint

Mount Baker 10,785 feet

Glacier

Glacier Public Service Center

Slide Mountain

542

Maple Falls

North Fork Nooksack River

547

Kendall

Mosquito Lake Road

Nooksack Indian Reservation

Van Zandt Dike

Sumas Mountain

Deming

9

Stewart Mountain

Anderson Mountain

Nooksack River

Lake Whatcom

Lookout Mountain

542

Bellingham

5

Chuckanut Village

Chuckanut Mountain

Fairhaven

Larrabee State Park

11

Chuckanut Bay

Samish Bay

N

10 Miles

10 Kilometers

5

5

5

0

RIDE
17

Majestic Mount Baker

Directions:
out and back on WA 542 from Bellingham to Mount Baker
Chuckanut Drive: South from Fairhaven on WA 11

Distance:
total distance for a Mount Baker round-trip: 124 miles
Bellingham to Maple Falls: 28 miles
Maple Falls to Mount Baker summit: 34 miles
Chuckanut Drive: 21 miles one-way

Time:
half a day or more (a full day from Seattle)

Services:
Bellingham and suburbs, Deming, Maple Falls, Glacier
(limited)

Best Time of Year:
late June through September

Highlights:
Mount Baker's snowcapped peak; a rare chance to take a
paved road up much of a big mountain; charming historic
and motorcycle-friendly towns; cliff-hugging, oceanfront
Chuckanut Drive

We do this as an out-and-back to Mount Baker (there is no other option to get to Mount Baker), and then head back to Chuckanut Drive for a little sunset ride. You could combine this with a jaunt up or down Whidbey Island (ride 19), especially if you have a couple days and are coming from the Seattle area.

Bellingham is a beautiful little city, the last of any size before the Canadian border. It's surrounded by farmland, and beyond that, by mountains on the east side and water on the west. Much of the town is well preserved from its boom days at the turn of the twentieth century, and it's full of shops and good restaurants. Consider staying overnight here at one of many inexpensive motels to get a good start on the road to Mount Baker the next day. That plan would also allow you a chance to ride Chuckanut Drive—one of Washington's most lovely and beloved stretches of road, and for good reason. While it's pretty any time, Chuckanut Drive at sunset is one of life's great pleasures.

Mount Baker is considered a relatively young, active volcano. Although it hasn't historically erupted violently a la Mount St. Helens, a couple vents blow off steam at the top and occasional

This couple brought a picnic to watch the sunset from Chuckanut Drive—a popular activity along this scenic route.

underground magma flows cause earthquakes and avalanches. Don't worry too much; seismologists keep a close eye on the volcano, and if something was imminent, officials wouldn't let anyone near it.

There aren't many amenities at the top of Mount Baker (its ski resort doesn't offer summer activities), so in summer, most people go to drink in the views, take photos, and appreciate the majesty of nature. Plan to eat before or after you climb the mountain road—or take your own picnic. If you dislike traffic, try to start out fairly early in the day. This is one place where you won't have to worry about piling on too much gear, as Mount Baker's weather is always cool.

Take exit 255 from Bellingham, following signs for Washington Highway 542 (called Sunset Drive in the city suburbs). There are plenty of places to fuel up or buy picnic supplies. If you're headed directly from the Seattle area and want to miss some of

Christy: Mount Baker might seem like just another pop-up volcano in the Cascade chain, but it holds a special fascination for weather nerds like me. All the moisture coming in from the Pacific, plus quick elevation changes, make this a great place for snow. I wanted to visit Mount Baker ever since I learned it holds the record for the most snowfall ever measured in the United States in a single season—a whopping 1,140 inches, or 95 feet! (It's also a world record for a scientifically verifiable amount.) That year, the 1998–99 season, piles of snow crushed trees and damaged structures at the resort.

It's not surprising that other mountains around here do well in the precipitation category: The record Mount Baker broke, 1,122 inches, was held by Mount Rainier. This explains why you might not get a chance to ride these mountains if you wait until late fall or try in early summer. Even if valleys are dry, snow is likely up top. ●

The fertile valleys around Bellingham are full of family farms, some with traditional red barns.

Interstate 5, Washington Highway 9 along the foothills of the Cascades is a popular and pretty alternative that also connects with WA 542.

A few miles out of town, a sign welcomes you to the Mount Baker Scenic Highway—and this is where things do get scenic. Leaving the suburbs behind, the road enters hilly, forested country interspersed with the occasional small farm producing berries, horses, or Christmas trees. The Cascades' steep peaks are visible in the distance, as is Mount Baker itself on occasion. Following the Nooksack River, the road curves around hills and straightens through valleys. The two-lane highway is generally in surprisingly good condition almost all the way to the top, with just the occasional rough patch—an accomplishment considering this area's winter weather. In summer, you may experience the downside that makes good roads possible: construction crews stopping traffic as they work to undo the damage snow does in winter. Fortunately, they seem to try to keep delays short.

Several small towns pop up along the route. Deming's claim to fame is that it hosts the annual Deming Logging Show each June—a big deal in a place where the timber industry is a financial lifeblood. Maple Falls and Glacier both offer decent food options (if you started early and haven't had breakfast yet, stop in at the Harvest Moon bakery in Maple Falls). Maple Falls is also your last chance for reliable fuel.

After Maple Falls, the road is a series of big curves in and out of the forest, sometimes dropping the speed limit to 40 mph. Road conditions deteriorate a bit, with the occasional fairly major dip. There are few chances to pass, which can be aggravating since no one seems to want to go anywhere near the speed limit. But that's okay; curves are not very well banked on this stretch, and the surface can be rough in spots. In fact, it's either pretty rough or really good, depending on whether a given section was recently visited by one of those maintenance crews. The scenery is mostly just dense evergreen forest, with an occasional cabin or small resort popping out of the trees. The air is clean, cool, and deliciously fragrant with the scent of pines.

As well as the last flush toilets before the summit, Glacier is home to the Glacier Public Service Center, a very helpful visitor center with all kinds of information. It's open Thursday through Monday, 9 a.m. to 3 p.m., which makes it one of the all-too-rare forest service offices that recognize people might want help on weekends. It's an especially good idea to stop in if you'd like to try one of the secondary roads nearby or the mostly paved Glacier Creek Road (described later), or if you're coming relatively early or late in the season, when snow might be a problem.

As the road continues its steady climb, some sections can be fun, especially when they're not crowded with traffic. Curves along here are mostly well-banked and only occasionally bumpy.

Until you're higher on the mountain, there won't be many scenic overlooks (or should that be underlooks?). Nooksack Falls is one possible turnoff, but getting to the falls requires navigating about 0.5 mile of steep, packed (but pitted) gravel. And while the falls are pretty, the rocks around them are so steep and slick that they've been fenced off, giving only partial views (a sign lists the names of people who have slipped and fallen to their deaths here, and surrounding trees are plastered with DO NOT ENTER! warnings).

The road climbs more quickly now, wiggling its way up the mountainside in a series of switchbacks, with some occasional gravel across the surface. The vistas open up, and you get the feeling you're heading for the top of the world. A few pullouts allow you to take a more-substantial look.

Just after the blink-and-you'll-miss-it Mount Baker Ski Resort lodge, the road reaches a relatively flat meadow and circles Picture Lake, with the surrounding peaks (most notably Mount Shuksan) reflected in its surface. You know what to do here.

The road climbs a few more miles to Heather Meadows and Artist Point, where most summer visitors park and take one of many short hikes to views of mountains in every direction. These high alpine meadows were settings for movies including *Call of the Wild,* starring Clark Gable, and Robert De Niro's *Deer Hunter.* Stop in at the visitor center for informative displays. (Note that even if the weather is good into October, the visitor center—and its potties—close at the end of September.)

After spending some time at the top, all you have to do is turn around and enjoy the relative free-fall back down.

Since the Mount Baker out-and-back doesn't take an entire day, it's a perfect ride to combine with the short but beautiful

Mount Shuksan rises impressively over Picture Lake.

The surface is rough, but the views from the top of Glacier Creek Road are spectacular. We took this photo for those who don't want to try it.

Christy: One possible detour off the Mount Baker Highway is Glacier Creek Road (FR 39), which heads off southward from WA 542, just east of Glacier. While most maps will show it as a paved road, that's not entirely true. The river next to the road is prone to flooding and has washed out pavement in a couple of places. Those are now gravel that may or may not be in great condition. Both the gravel and the paved road are narrow and have developed a few enormous potholes, so it's imperative that anyone using any kind of transportation go slowly (I had to slam on the brakes a couple times to avoid falling into one). The good news is that those on athletic bikes shouldn't have too much trouble steering away from the really rough spots, which are usually on flat stretches.

This slog up the mountain would not be worth doing if it weren't for the amazing views at the top (you'll know you're there when the pavement ends for good at the Heliotrope Ridge trailhead parking lot). From this vantage point, Mount Baker and its surrounding crags look so close they seem on the verge of falling into your lap.

If you consider attempting this detour, first ask rangers at the Glacier Public Service Center about conditions, and don't even try if you're not confident in your bike-handling skills. ●

Chuckanut Drive, a must-do excursion if you're going anywhere near Bellingham. Locals like to pull off at one of the vistas along the 21-mile stretch of Washington Highway 11 to watch the glorious sunsets over the San Juan Islands directly to the west.

The scenic drive starts in Fairhaven, a small, historic town that's essentially a suburb of Bellingham (its proud residents don't like hearing this). It's a nice place to grab a bite to eat or wander the streets. Like Bellingham, in around 1890 Fairhaven thought it would become the Northwest's next big city, the port at the end of railroad lines bringing goods to and from the sea. It embarked on a major building boom, erecting thirty-five hotels and many other brick buildings within a couple of years. Unfortunately, Seattle won out as the transportation hub. Fairhaven has hung on as a small town with very consistent architecture ever since, keeping many of those same Victorian buildings in use.

From I-5, take the Fairhaven Parkway exit into the middle of the historic downtown and make a left (south) on 12th Street, which becomes Chuckanut Drive. The road starts to cling to the coast soon after that, and continues to do so for most of the scenic drive. At first, it's hard to catch more than a glimpse of the water below, since it's blocked by trees and the residences of a few lucky homeowners. You get your first good chance with Larrabee State Park, the biggest chunk of public land along the drive. Taking the turnoff to the right (west), you drop into a maze of campgrounds that leads to short beach hikes and a boat launch.

The ride—and the views—are best on the south half of Chuckanut Drive, as the undulating road wraps around the edge of seaside cliffs. Sunset or not, be sure to stop at Dogfish Point and Pigeon Point for the best views on the drive. A handful of restaurants whose cuisine features locally harvested oysters sit right beside the road.

After rounding one last curve, the road suddenly leaves the mountain and becomes straight and flat. It continues this way through fertile farm country until it connects with I-5 at Burlington. If you have a little more time or are connecting with a ride to Anacortes or Whidbey Island, make a right on Samish Island Road and ride the quick jaunt out to more water views from Samish Island. Reconnect with WA 11, or make your leisurely way south along the coast on Bayview/Edison Road, which connects with U.S. Highway 20. This whole area is motorcycle-friendly, and almost any establishment will have bikes parked out front.

Restaurants

Deming
The North Fork Brewery
6186 Mount Baker Hwy.
(360) 599-BEER

Edison/Bow (south end of Chuckanut Drive)
Longhorn Saloon & Oyster Bar
5754 Cains Ct. (Bow)
(360) 766-6330

Glacier
Graham's Restaurant
9989 Mount Baker Hwy.
(360) 599-1964

Milano's Restaurant
9990 Mount Baker Hwy.
(360) 599-2863

Maple Falls
Harvest Moon Bakery
7466 Mount Baker Hwy.
(360) 599-1347

Olympic Odyssey

Directions:

north on US 101 from Aberdeen to Sappho
north on WA 113 from Sappho to WA 112
north and west on WA 112 to Clallam Bay and Neah Bay
east on WA 112 from Clallam Bay to junction with US 101
east on US 101 to Port Angeles
out-and-back on Hurricane Ridge Road from Port Angeles to Hurricane Ridge
east and south on US 101 from Port Angeles to Potlatch

Distance:

total distance from Aberdeen to Potlatch: about 390 miles (includes round-trip mileage to Hoh Rain Forest, Cape Flattery, and Hurricane Ridge)
Aberdeen to Lake Quinault: 43 miles
Lake Quinault to Forks: 65 miles
Forks to Clallam Bay: 29 miles
Clallam Bay to Neah Bay: 21 miles
Clallam Bay to Port Angeles: 50 miles
Port Angeles to Potlatch: 86 miles

Time:

two to three days, depending on stops

Services:
Aberdeen, Lake Quinault Resort Village, Forks, Clallam Bay, Neah Bay, Joyce, Port Angeles, Sequim, Quilcene, Eldon, Lilliwaup, Hoodsport, Potlatch

Best Time of Year:
summer and early fall

Highlights:
the watery woods of the Hoh Rain Forest and Lake Quinault; sandy beach gems; impressive views of the Olympic range and coastline; fun, fast riding along the Hood Canal

The Olympic Peninsula is so enormous and has so much to see and do that it's impossible to describe more than a fraction of it, and trying to ride it in anything less than two days is sheer folly. This route takes us on a clockwise journey from its southwestern side and samples some of what the peninsula offers—which leaves much more to explore on your own.

We'll visit Olympic National Park's old-growth rain forests and remote beaches and wander to the most northwesterly point in the Lower 48. We'll glide east along the Strait of Juan de Fuca into Port Angeles, then scale more than 5,000 feet in 17 miles to get breathtaking views of the glacier-capped Olympic Range, the national park's centerpiece. Rounding the peninsula's northeastern shoulder, we'll coast along the Hood Canal through a string of humble communities where shellfish is king. This is one of those trips we take not necessarily for the great riding but for the intriguing and awe-inspiring features along the way.

Aberdeen is the last city of any significance on northbound U.S. Highway 101 until Port Angeles. Heading west from Aberdeen, Washington Highway 109 is the access road for a bunch of small coastal towns. While this may sound like an enticing scenic

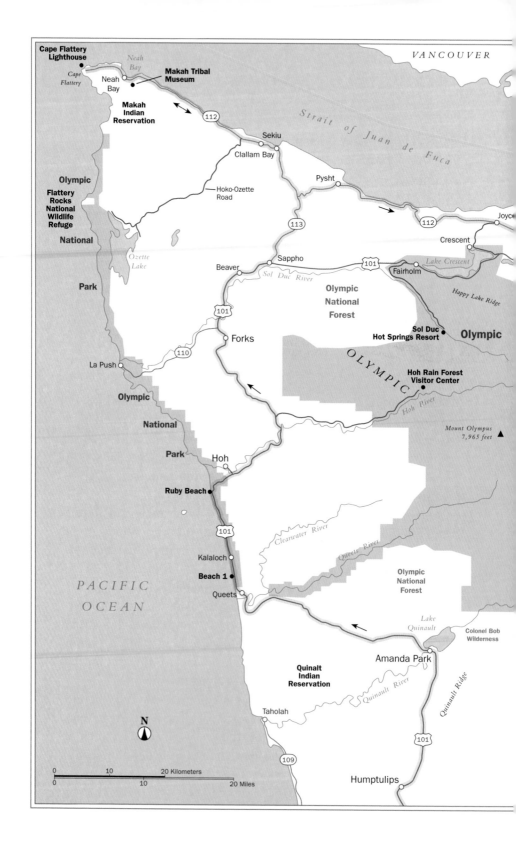

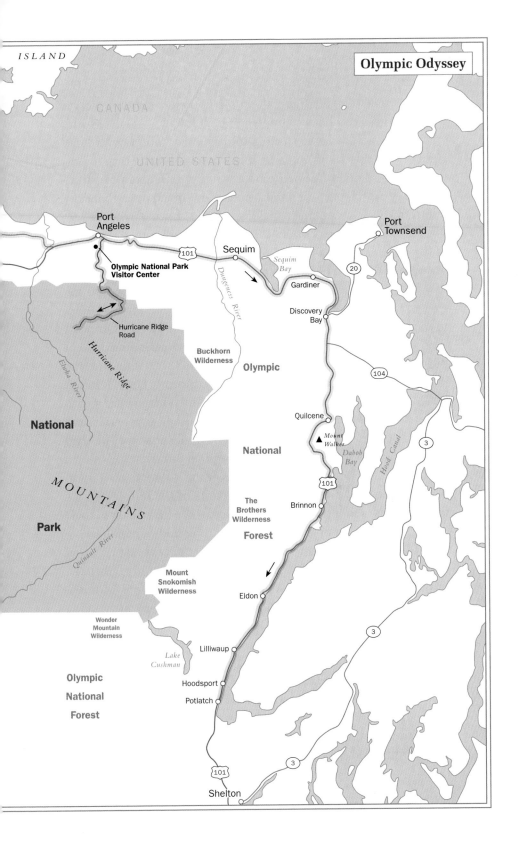

detour, it dead-ends in Taholah on the Quinault Indian Reservation, so unless you have a couple of hours to kill, stay on US 101.

US 101 north of Aberdeen is in decent condition, with long, straight stretches interrupted by the occasional gentle turn to prevent you from nodding off. Summer traffic and frequent construction can slow the pace, and the scenery isn't much more than acre upon acre of clear-cut forest, making this the kind of territory to get through as quickly as possible. The clear-cut extends to the edge of the national forest; across that line, tall trees growing right to the edge of the road remind us that we're in the Pacific Northwest.

About 43 miles north of Aberdeen, US 101 bumps into the edge of Lake Quinault. Carved and fed by glaciers, it marks Olympic National Park's southwestern tip. Surrounded by the Quinault Rain Forest, the lake and the Quinault Valley make an excellent introduction to the peninsula's rain-drenched west side, and the lake's south shore makes a great base for exploring. Lake Quinault Lodge and Lake Quinault's Rain Forest Resort Village offer a variety of lodging. The resort also has a restaurant, a general store with a gift shop, a laundry, and coin-operated showers. The road to the lodge and village passes three national forest campgrounds. Easy hikes lead from the campgrounds or the village to the largest Sitka spruce in the world and other giants of the rain forest. It's wise to check about camping in advance, since the season is short (two of the three campgrounds are closed by mid-September).

From Amanda Park (on Lake Quinault) to Forks, the highway cuts across the Quinault Indian Reservation, running through low hills and curves. Some are nicely banked, allowing for travel at the posted maximum of 55 mph, while others are challenging at speeds well below the limit.

About 27 miles from Amanda Park—after hitting Queets and crossing the Queets River—the road punctures the national park's western fringe and sails past a row of beaches, some named, others numbered. The best is Ruby Beach, at the north end of the string; it's worth the short access hike that's easily done in riding gear. Strewn with piles of driftwood logs washed up against tree-fringed cliffs and sea stacks rising out of the surf, it's an especially captivating scene late in the day as the sun sinks low in the western sky.

After Ruby Beach, US 101 leaves the park and turns sharply northeast, advancing inland along the Hoh River. The rich forest disappears at the national park boundary, and the pavement rambles across clear-cut low coastal hills for about 10 miles.

Don't miss the Hoh Rain Forest, one of America's most spectacular temperate rain forests and one of the park's most popular destinations. It's at the end of Upper Hoh Road, which splits off US 101 to the right about 3 miles after 101 crosses the Hoh River. The Hoh Rain Forest Visitor Center is 18 miles east of US

Ruby Beach is the northernmost in a string of beaches off US 101 before the road leaves the national park and heads inland.

101. The $5 park entrance fee is good for seven days, so hang on to the receipt, especially if you're planning to ride to Hurricane Ridge.

Short hikes easily done in riding boots start near the visitor center. The Hall of Mosses Trail, 0.75 mile each way, winds over a low ridge to a grove of moss-draped maples. This side of the peninsula averages 140 inches of rain a year, so everything may be draped with veils of moss, but the maples are especially so. All that rain makes everything grow like crazy. Even if you don't make it to the grove, there's plenty to see along the way.

The Spruce Nature Trail is a peaceful 1.25-mile loop through a younger part of the forest populated with red alder and cottonwoods to the glacier-fed Hoh River that sculpted this terrain.

A whole spectrum of green is on display in the Hoh Rain Forest's Hall of Mosses.

Longer and more-challenging hikes lead to high alpine meadows and glacier fields. When you've got your fill of scenery (or possibly rain), return to US 101 toward Forks, an old logging town and possible overnight stop 13 miles past the turnoff for Upper Hoh Road.

North of Forks, US 101 continues inland, skirting the national forest but well outside national park boundaries. Just before Sappho, US 101 makes a sweeping turn to the right.

To get to Cape Flattery, the most northwesterly point in the Continental U.S., make a left onto Washington Highway 113, Burnt Mountain Road. The road rises and falls through low hills, twisting through some surprisingly entertaining curves. Local traffic and the occasional logging truck are the most likely obstacles, but they don't affect the quality of the pavement, and some of the trucks take these roads at remarkable speeds that won't slow you down.

Washington Highway 112 intersects from the right about 22 miles north of Sappho, and WA 113 becomes WA 112 before it rolls into Clallam (pronounced clow-lum) Bay about ten minutes

Steve: Forks has lots of overpriced motels, probably because of *Twilight,* the wildly popular vampire-romance book and movie series. Although their creator, Arizona resident Stephenie Meyer, hadn't visited Forks, she chose to set her story here because it's the rainiest town in the Lower 48—a weather pattern apparently conducive to vampire lifestyles.

I'm not a teenage girl, nor do I have daughters, so I know very little about *Twilight.* I do know that I'm a little put out at having to pay far more than I ought to for a dive motel room because a bunch of teen girls invade the area in search of a fictional vampire boyfriend. Having once been a teenage boy, I know they're bad enough without adding dangerously romantic vampire attraction to the mix. At any rate, watch out for starry-eyed daughters (and moms) wandering around Forks on *Twilight* tours. ●

later. The bay and the coastal hamlet of Sekiu (pronounced like C-Q) come into view as the road hangs a left halfway through town. Overlooking the west end of Clallam Bay, Sekiu is a summer tourist destination for fishing, kayaking, bird-watching, and diving.

The road hugs the bay for about 2 miles, passing the turnoff for Sekiu, climbing over a ridge, and dropping back to the water's edge. It snakes through narrow turns, skims the water, and dips close to rocky beaches as birds bob gently in the waves offshore. Other times, it overlooks the sea from a perch carved out of rocky cliffs that couldn't possibly be very stable.

At times, it's difficult to both focus on the road and absorb the enchanting scene. If you find one of the rare pullouts between Sekiu and Neah Bay, you may be rewarded with a glimpse of a gray whale feeding in shallow reefs just offshore or a bald eagle on the hunt. On a clear day, Vancouver Island is visible across the Strait of Juan de Fuca.

Sekiu overlooks Clallam Bay on the Olympic Peninsula's northern edge.

When the road enters the Makah (pronounced ma-caw, like the bird) Indian Reservation, roadside signs list a short set of rules you should follow as a guest of the Makah Nation. The fishing village of Neah Bay is the center of a 27,000-acre reservation that includes Cape Flattery and Tatoosh Island. A $10 pass, available at many businesses in town, is required to visit Cape Flattery or other recreation areas.

The parking area for the Cape Flattery Trail is a 6-mile jaunt from Neah Bay on a good paved road. It's 0.75 mile each way and relatively easy, though sections may be muddy or slippery and moss may coat elevated cedar boardwalks. Boots are probably okay, but switch to more-suitable footwear if you have it.

The hike leads to viewing platforms overlooking the cape's ragged cliffs and coves and rock haystacks dotted with seabirds. Poised on an outcropping, the final platform presents views of Tatoosh Island, spectacular, unspoiled scenery in all directions, and wildlife. Sea otters frolic in the foamy surges and gray whales occasionally make slow, sinuous laps within view of the deck.

Consider rounding out your visit to the Makah Nation with a stop at the Makah Cultural and Research Center. The museum's exhibits include artifacts from the Ozette collection, including dugout canoes; whaling, sealing, and fishing gear; basketry; and other tools excavated from a Makah village that was buried by a mudslide nearly 500 years ago. Carvings, basketry, and jewelry made by Makah artists are available for sale in the museum, which is open seven days a week. If you think local names are hard to pronounce, Makah is much easier than its members' name for the tribe: Qwiqwidicciat. ●

Tatoosh is actually the largest of a small group of islands about 0.5 mile off Cape Flattery. Historically used by Makah fishermen—and, more recently, by the U.S. Coast Guard, Weather Bureau, and the U.S. Navy—it's now home to diverse communities of nesting seabirds, marine mammals, and plants. Access requires written permission from the Makah tribe.

Backtrack on WA 112 past Sekiu and Clallam Bay to the junction with WA 113, where you have two options. WA 113 returns to Sappho, and US 101—which runs through the Sol Duc Valley—enters Olympic National Park near Fairholm, and skirts Lake Crescent's southern shore.

If you're not intent on visiting Sol Duc Hot Springs or the lake, make a left on WA 112 and follow it along the coast for a satisfying and scenic alternative to the peninsula's interior. After the highways diverge, WA 112 winds through the Pysht River valley to the crumbling and vine-shrouded remnants of Pysht, where the road meets the strait. It climbs into the coastal hills through a mix of smooth curves, long switchbacks, and quick, twisting descents, crossing narrow valleys cut by rivers slicing their way to the strait. Traffic is generally light, the pavement is good, and the riding is fast. Again, your most likely impediment is the occasional logging truck chugging up one of the inclines. In the steepest sections, slow-moving vehicles are allowed to drive on the shoulder, and they'll move over when possible.

WA 112 meets US 101 about 4 miles west of Port Angeles, makes a left on Lincoln Street, and tracks straight to downtown and the port.

We're aiming for Hurricane Ridge. If you want to avoid the city center, go straight when US 101 turns left on Lincoln Street and make a right on Race Street. The Olympic National Park Visitor Center will be on your right, and deer may be grazing near the trees on the edge of the lawn.

Before heading to the top of Hurricane Ridge, it's wise to stop at the visitor center to pick up a map and check road and weather conditions. Port Angeles sits in the Olympic Range's rain shadow and averages a mere 25 inches of rain annually. That means the

Spend a little time exploring Hurricane Ridge, where views of the Olympic Mountains are stunning. The distant peaks, surrounded by heavily forested deep valleys, are not especially tall; Mount Olympus is the highest, at 7,965 feet. But because they rise directly from the wettest place in the Lower 48, right next to the Pacific Ocean, abundant precipitation feeds their many snowfields and glaciers. About 266 glaciers crown the Olympics' peaks—about 10 square miles' worth on Mount Olympus alone.

Hurricane Ridge Meadow is an easy paved hike from the parking lot across from the ridge's visitor center. A short, paved walk leads to the ridge's backside, which overlooks the Strait of Juan de Fuca, and from there a gravel trail runs along the ridge to the chairlift and the Hurricane Ridge Ski and Snowboard Area ski-patrol shack. If you're up for it, take a crack at Sunrise Point, visible from the parking lot; although the initial steep grade looks intimidating, it's a relatively short hike. ●

weather in town can be warm and sunny even as 5,240-foot Hurricane Ridge is getting wind, rain, fog, hail, or even snow. Video monitors behind the visitor center information booth display images, updated every fifteen minutes, from a webcam on the ridge (they're online at www.nps.gov/olym/photosmultimedia/hurricane-ridge-webcam.htm).

Head south from the visitor center on Hurricane Ridge Road. Pay the $5 entry fee—or produce your receipt from a previous visit to the national park within the last seven days—at the entry kiosk about 5 miles from the visitor center. Despite the terrain and significant elevation gain, riders of every skill level can handle the 17-mile ascent to Hurricane Ridge. Wide and in excellent condition, the road climbs steadily, rolling through smooth, gentle turns. Because it's in a national park, the maximum speed is 35 mph, so watch the speedometer.

Descend from the heights of Hurricane Ridge and follow signs for US 101 eastbound. Depending on the day and hour, traffic from Port Angeles to Sequim (pronounced squim) can be thick and sluggish. The road bends south around the tip of Sequim Bay and across Miller Peninsula. After the junction with U.S. Highway 20 (the turn for Port Townsend), traffic diminishes with every mile. Beyond the intersection with Washington Highway 104 to the Hood Canal Bridge (the fastest option for a ferry to Seattle), it drops to a trickle on a relatively straight, fast road.

After entering Olympic National Forest about 4 miles south of Quilcene, the highway rounds Mount Walker's west side and zips to the shore of Dabob Bay, one of several internal Hood Canal bays. For the next 39 miles, US 101 hugs the canal's wooded western shore. (If you're thinking this doesn't look much like a canal, that's because it's actually a fjord.) A solid bed of good pavement surges over low hills and flows through big, smooth curves, making this some of the peninsula's best riding.

Whether it's shrimp, crab, oysters, or clams, the Hood Canal is famous for shellfish, and US 101 passes through a succession of small towns selling whatever is in season. Harvest your own

Hoodsport is one of many small towns along the Hood Canal that offer super-fresh shellfish.

or drop in on one of the many local restaurants serving it off-the-beach fresh.

South of Potlatch, the last town on the canal's western shore, US 101 bends east toward Olympia and Interstate 5. With roads heading in every direction, options for continuing your journey are almost endless.

RIDE
19

Whidbey Getaway

Directions:
west on WA 525 or WA 526 from I-5 to Mukilteo ferry
terminal
ferry from Mukilteo to Clinton
west on WA 525 from Clinton to Langley Road
north on Langley Road to Langley
southwest from Langley to WA 525 via Brooks Hill Road /
Bayview Road
west on WA 525 to WA 20 turnoff to Fort Casey State Park
north on Engle Road to Coupeville
west on Madrona Way from Coupeville to WA 20
north, then east, on WA 20 to I-5

Distance:
Seattle to Mukilteo: 26 miles
Clinton to Langley: 7 miles
Langley to Coupeville (via Fort Casey State Park): 30 miles
Coupeville to Oak Harbor / intersection with WA 20 (via
Madrona Way): 13 miles
Oak Harbor to Anacortes: 16 miles
Anacortes to intersection with I-5: 13 miles

Time:
a few hours to a full day, depending on stops and detours

Services:
along all main roads and in all towns

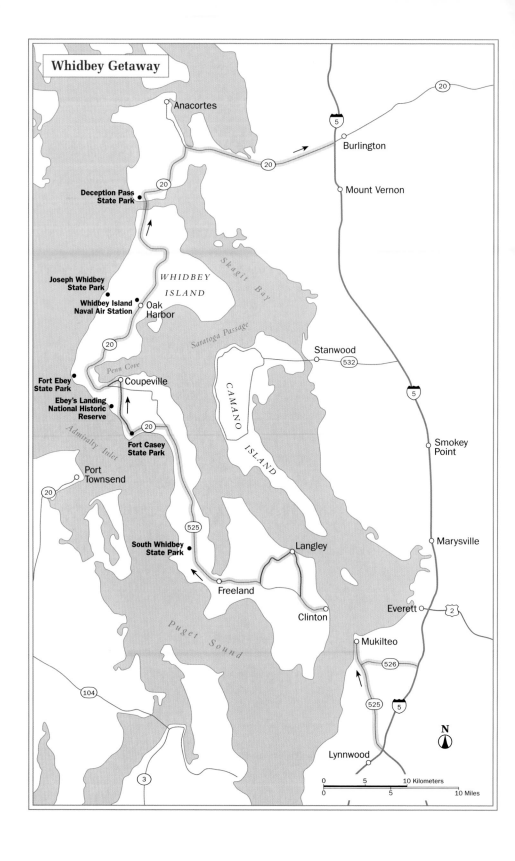

Whidbey Getaway

Anacortes

20

5 Burlington

20

Mount Vernon

20

Deception Pass
State Park

Skagit Bay

20

WHIDBEY

ISLAND

Joseph Whidbey
State Park

Whidbey Island
Naval Air Station

Oak
Harbor

Saratoga Passage

Stanwood

532

5

20

Penn Cove

Coupeville

CAMANO

Fort Ebey
State Park

Ebey's Landing
National Historic
Reserve

ISLAND

Smokey
Point

20

Fort Casey
State Park

Admiralty Inlet

Port
Townsend

20

Marysville

525

South Whidbey
State Park

Langley

Freeland

Everett

2

Clinton

Puget Sound

Mukilteo

526

104

525

5

N

3

Lynnwood

0   5   10 Kilometers

0   5   10 Miles

Best Time of Year:
early spring to late fall

Highlights:
easy riding through pleasing territory; historic military and
cultural sights; tasty treats in sociable settings

Bikers love Whidbey Island, and it's easy to see why. Weather
here is unusually dry and predictable compared to the rest of
Western Washington. Roads are in great condition, with speeds
actually hitting 55 mph (rare anywhere in the Puget Sound region,
even on the interstate). Throw in luscious vistas, historic small
towns and parks, and biker-friendly businesses, and you have a
near-perfect day trip.

Obviously, you could do this ride from south to north or vice
versa, but we like to begin with the ferry on the south end. It gives
us a real sense of leaving everyday life behind and a chance to see
Deception Pass at sunset.

The fun starts with the ferry from Mukilteo, which will take
you to Clinton on Whidbey's south end. Whether you come
into Mukilteo from the north, east, or south, you'll eventually
hit Washington Highway 525, which continues on Whidbey.
Although you'll be riding through a fair amount of development
to the terminal, you shouldn't get lost if you follow ferry signage
and stay on the main road westbound toward the water.

Despite being on the other side of the water, Clinton feels like
a suburb of the mainland. Any dallying here will give all the cars
behind you a chance to catch up, so keep them in your rearview
mirror and ride straight up the hill.

WA 525 is usually a two-lane 55 mph highway with a double
yellow stripe. Unless it's rush hour, traffic generally flows along
well, and the pavement is pristine.

Christy: I'm a ferry fan in general (especially given priority boarding for bikes), and the Mukilteo-Whidbey Island route is one of my favorites. It runs regularly, departing every half-hour from 5 a.m. to 9 p.m., so I know when to get there without looking at a schedule. It's inexpensive (about $3 for bikes) and quick (about 20 minutes). The ferries are small enough that boarding and unloading are fast and easy, but big enough to not get rocked around much.

From the ferry, I get beautiful views of the mainland, Whidbey Island, and the Kitsap Peninsula in the distance. Other ferries, plus any number of pleasure and working boats and possibly wildlife, ply the waters. Although some use this as a commuter ferry, the general vibe feels more as if everyone's headed off on vacation, especially on weekends.

If you take the ferry to Port Townsend (discussed later in this ride), you'll get much the same feel, only more so. That ferry sails less frequently, and motorcycles don't get priority boarding without reservations, so it's wise to schedule in advance if that's your intention. ●

You could just take WA 525 (which merges into Washington Highway 20 on the island's north side) all the way from one end of Whidbey to the other, but the best scenery is on the coast and in the hilly terrain between it and this central plain. A number of roads, almost all in good condition, branch off from the main highway. Many are worth exploring, especially if you want to meander and have lots of time. We'll take you to some of our favorite spots and let you figure out your own detours beyond that. (One hint: Pretty much any road with a state park at the end, or with "bay" or "cove" or "beach" in the name, will eventually take you right to the water and nice views.)

While most secondary roads are in good shape, be aware that the usual assortment of forest debris can be scattered across them, especially after bad weather. Also, some surfaces can be a little corrugated, and some curves are not well banked, so heed your speed.

Our first turnoff from WA 525 is Langley Road, just a couple miles past Clinton. Make a right, following signs for Langley. Langley is full of little shops, bakeries, and galleries. If you need any sort of leather items (and who doesn't?), stop by at Ace Leather Goods, a motorcycle-friendly family-owned business whose wares are crafted right on the island.

After window-shopping, consider grabbing a pastry and coffee and wandering to the waterfront park for nice views. The strip of land to the north is Camano Island, which lies between Whidbey and the mainland. If you get lucky during springtime, you may see gray whales in the Saratoga Passage between the two islands.

You can either backtrack to WA 525 or go to the west end of town and take a pretty, more circuitous route via Brooks Hill Road, which becomes Bayview Road. Back on WA 525, relax and enjoy the pastoral farm-country scenery on the way to Greenbank.

From Greenbank, ride another relatively quick 5 or 6 miles on WA 525 to the intersection with WA 20. Lots of artists and writers live on the island, and you can see why: The rolling hills and toasted fields, broken up by swaths of evergreen and deciduous forest, are inspiring.

Anyone can climb around on the military fortifications that line the Whidbey Island coast at Fort Casey.

The turnoff for Admiralty Bay, the Port Townsend ferry, and Fort Casey is well signed. Make this left and enjoy increasingly expansive views as the road heads downhill onto the edge of a wide, flat tidal plain. WA 20 travels along a narrow strip of land, Keystone Spit, between Admiralty Bay and Crockett Lake (which looks more like a bay) toward the ferry terminal.

Unless it's high tourist season, you may make the ferry without reservations. It leaves every hour and a half or so—unless the tide is out. In that case, you'll have to wait for Puget Sound to fill back up again. It's a half-hour journey to Port Townsend.

If you get here with plenty of time to spare, go the couple miles past the ferry terminal to Fort Casey before you depart (there's a convenient U-turn road right after the park, for just that purpose).

Along with the fortifications and gorgeous views, Fort Casey offers camping and picnic areas and nice restrooms (which are housed, appropriately, in their own hillside bunker). Just up the hill north of the park, beautifully maintained Admiralty Head Lighthouse is a good place to spot the fort's resident deer herd (watch for them on the road, too).

After climbing the battlements for a while, you're probably ready for lunch. For us, that means Coupeville. Rather than making a right from the fort entrance and heading back via WA 20, we go left for a change of scenery and take Engle Road through charming, wide-open farmlands. Keep going straight on this smooth, easy road, cross WA 20, and hit Front Street, Coupeville's historic waterfront, a couple blocks later.

Coupeville claims to be the second-oldest town in Washington. Obviously, early settlers knew a good spot when they saw it. On sheltered Penn Cove, it has easy access to all kinds of natural resources. If you like mussels, you'd be crazy not to grab some famous Penn Cove mussels mere yards from where they're harvested.

The whole Victorian-style downtown is preserved as part of the Ebey's Landing National Historical Reserve. Although tourists flock here during frequent festival weekends, bikes can usually

All of Puget Sound is scattered with military remains, but the ones at Fort Casey are the most impressive—partly because of what was once here, but more because of what still is.

In the 1890s, the American military built fortifications here, at Fort Worden in Port Townsend, and on Marrowstone Island to the south. Throughout this so-called "Triangle of Fire," massive guns were installed in seaside emplacements and aimed toward the middle of the Admiralty Inlet, which could be a route for enemies sneaking toward the mainland.

Fort Casey's guns were on mobile platforms so they could be raised to fire and then lowered behind the bunker. If anyone had tried to invade, it would have been a spectacular show. But within decades, airplanes replaced ships as the likely mode of attack, and all that firepower was essentially useless. While many of the guns were removed and sent overseas to help out in World War II, the fort itself was revived and reinforced during the war. In the 1960s, two of the 10-inch artillery guns were returned from the Philippines, bearing the scars of the action they saw there.

Now, the fortifications make for a grand shoreline vista from the crest of the hill behind them. They would be impressive enough from a distance, but visitors are invited to climb around on them and into the bunkers. More concrete platforms are at Fort Ebey State Park, north of here on the coast. If you take the Port Townsend ferry, you can see the other two points on the "Triangle of Fire" in a matter of hours. While Fort Flagler on Marrowstone Island is a little out of the way, it's a fairly short ride from Port Townsend. ●

squeeze into a parking spot close to the shops and restaurants. There are several good eateries in town; we recommend Toby's Tavern, which often has a line of bikes out front.

The mussels at Toby's Tavern on the Coupeville waterfront come fresh from the cove out back.

Beach access points from Front Street give you better views of the cove. Stop in at the small museum just off Front Street for more about the town, its history, and local attractions.

From downtown Coupeville, you could get back onto WA 20, but for more views of Penn Cove, take the first right onto Madrona Way as Front Street curves uphill from the water. Madrona Way curls around the bay, sometimes just feet from the water, before it ends at a T intersection with WA 20 on the bay's north side.

Where you go from here depends on how much time you have and whether you want to see more of the island's west coast. If you do, go left on WA 20, then right on Libbey Road toward more fortifications at Fort Ebey. From Fort Ebey, backtrack a couple blocks on Libbey and turn left onto West Beach Road, which runs along the coast to Joseph Whidbey State Park. The park possesses beautiful views of San Juan and Vancouver Islands, as well as "Puget Sound's only true surf"—it's the only spot where waves can come in from the Pacific Ocean without interruption.

If you're ready for Deception Pass, make a right at the T onto WA 20 and clip along through some nice 50-mph curves. You're on the outskirts of Oak Harbor, a military bedroom community serving Whidbey Island Naval Air Station. Sprawling from a hillside harbor, the town seems startlingly modern compared to Coupeville. Stay on WA 20, which avoids the tangled city center, and soon you'll be passing the Naval Air Station at a fast clip toward Deception Pass, less than 10 miles away.

At Deception Pass, water rushes between Whidbey's north tip and Fidalgo Island, while WA 20 crosses the Deception Pass Bridge high above the water. With steep, rocky, tree-dotted cliffs on either side, the bridge (originally built as a Civilian Conservation Corps project during the Depression) is one of Washington's most-photographed icons. To really appreciate it, explore Deception Island State Park. For great views of the channel and bridge from below, follow signs in the park for North Beach and take the very short, flat walk to the photogenic log-strewn beach. The roads in the park are paved but sometimes steep and slick with debris.

The beaches at Deception Pass State Park are easy to reach via short paths.

At the very least, park at one of the viewpoints on either side of the bridge and walk out onto it. The deep, churning waters flowing below inspire awe.

End your day by visiting one of the Anacortes area's many motorcycle-friendly establishments for some dinner before taking WA 20 back to the intersection with Interstate 5.

Restaurant

Coupeville
Toby's Tavern
8 Front St.
(360) 678-4222

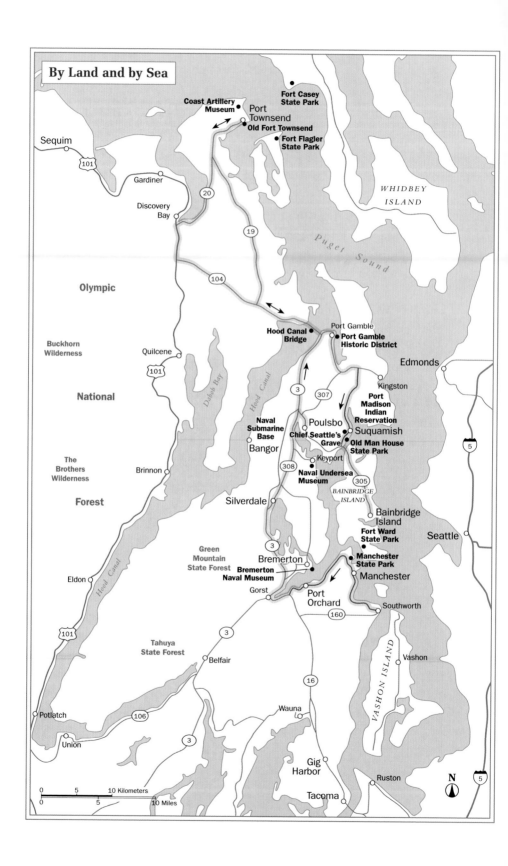

By Land and by Sea

RIDE

20

By Land and by Sea

Directions:

from West Seattle:

ferry from Fauntleroy terminal to Southworth (option: Vashon Island)

north on Colchester Drive to Manchester

west on Beach Road to Port Orchard

west on WA 166/16 to WA 3

north on Silverdale Way/Viking Way to Poulsbo

north on WA 3 to WA 104

west on WA 104, north on WA 19 or US 101 / WA 20 to Port Townsend and back

east on WA 104 to Miller Bay Road to Suquamish

south on Miller Bay Road to Suquamish

south on Suquamish Way to WA 305

south on WA 305 to Bainbridge Island ferry terminal

ferry to Seattle

Distance:

total distance: 147 miles

Southworth to Port Orchard: 13 miles

Port Orchard to Poulsbo: 31 miles

Poulsbo to Port Gamble: 10 miles

Junction Hood Canal Bridge to Port Townsend: 74 miles round-trip

Port Gamble to Bainbridge Island Ferry (via Suquamish): 19 miles

Time:
half a day to a full day, depending on stops

Services:
everywhere

Best Time of Year:
spring through late fall

Highlights:
ever-changing landscapes and seascapes; lots of things to
do and see; funky, artsy, or down-home towns

This ride takes ferries, crosses big bridges, and features more
seaside, forest, and out-of-the-way roads than a person could
possibly desire in a day. It starts and ends with ferry trips—
remember, you're on a bike, so you can skip lines without worries
about getting there early.

With its scattered blue-collar towns and a mostly rural feel,
the Kitsap Peninsula seems father away from Seattle than it is,
for better or worse. It's full of winding country roads—almost all
with excellent surfaces and some right along the water.

This ride is one of those day trips you do for the sights and
things to do, not for the fabulous riding. It isn't very long, but
while most of the roads are in good condition, speed limits are
sometimes lower than we'd like. Add significant time for any
leisurely meals, sightseeing, beach walks, or museum visits. (To
customize your trip, visit the area's surprisingly comprehensive
tourism Web site, www.visitkitsap.com.)

For much of this ride, you have two options: Take the main
roads, which are relatively fast but dull; or explore your choice
of the many alternatives. Anyone taking the back roads should
either plan to bring GPS or plan to get lost. Signs pointing the
way to any given destination are few, and many of the winding,

A typical Kitsap Peninsula road: The pavement is smooth and curves are plentiful, but speed limits are low.

two-lane country paths look similar. The good news: If you do get lost you'll likely end up at water, on a main road, or where you started.

From Seattle, take a ferry from the Fauntleroy terminal in West Seattle to Southworth on the Kitsap Peninsula. Fifteen minutes from Seattle, Vashon Island is an easy detour along the way. It's a quaint place with a homespun atmosphere that doesn't seem possible this close to the big city. The roads are relaxing rather than exciting.

From the Southworth ferry terminal, go up the hill and stay right on Southworth Drive for a little over 3 miles, following signs for Manchester. Make a right on Colchester Drive, which continues around the coast. In downtown Manchester, Colchester Drive ends in a T at Main Street. Go left and then take the first right turn. This is Beach Drive, which runs along the coast all the way into Port Orchard.

Just past Manchester, Manchester State Park, with remnants of military fortifications set up in the late nineteenth century, is a quick out-and-back off Beach Drive and a nice stop for a picnic.

Beach Drive skims right along the water for a while, giving you views of Bainbridge Island to the north and Bremerton to the east. The Puget Sound Naval Shipyard, bristling with giant Navy vessels, is easy to spot.

Beach Road ends at Bethel Street in Port Orchard. Head right on Bethel to Bay Street, an old-fashioned waterfront business district with a nice collection of shops and restaurants. If you're in the mood for a hole-in-the-wall, go left on Bethel to the Bethel Tavern, a friendly old-fashioned biker bar (it's not the cleanest place in the world, so neat freaks beware).

South and west of here, pretty roads meander through forests, hills, lakes, and old-fashioned farmsteads. It's a good place to get lost (on purpose). One nice alternative to our route is to head south from Port Orchard on one of those rural roads, or Washington Highway 16 to the junction with Washington Highway 302 through Wauna. From there, you can either take Washington Highway 3 north or Washington Highway 106 along the south end of the Hood Canal to the junction with U.S. Highway 101 on the east side of the Olympic Peninsula (see ride 18). Those roads are more remote than the route we're about to take—which suits

Christy: For 150 years, Puget Sound has been fortified mightily against an invasion by water that has never happened. White settlers worried about Native tribes. The British pushed out the Spanish. Americans took over in the 1800s and feared the British, the Japanese, and the Russians—a cycle of threats repeated in the twentieth century—and built an elaborate series of defenses along the coastline. This ride is studded with their remnants.

The U.S. military still has a huge presence in Western Washington. The Navy dominates, but the Army (Fort Lewis) and the Air Force (McChord Air Force Base) are also here.

This ride offers a multitude of chances to investigate military history. In Bremerton, a tour of Vietnam-era destroyer USS *Turner Joy* involves climbing ladders and walking on deck (not exactly activities for which motorcycle boots are made), and the Puget Sound Navy Museum houses a collection of naval artifacts. Both are within walking distance of the Bremerton ferry terminal, so they're especially easy to reach if you skip the first part of this ride and instead take a forty-five-minute ferry directly from downtown Seattle to Bremerton.

The intriguing Naval Undersea Museum is in Keyport, just off WA 308, which intersects with both WA 3 and Silverdale Road north of Bremerton and is well signed. One of my favorite museums, it houses the largest collection of naval undersea artifacts in the United States, including the *Trieste II*—a 96-ton deep submersible that descended 20,000 feet—and an 1864 Confederate mine. Bonus: Admission is free. ●

One of the artifacts on display at the Naval Undersea Museum in Keyport is *Deep Quest*, which holds a record for depth reached by U.S.-built submersibles—8,310 feet.

some folks just fine. Of course, the farther you get away from the highway, the more bumpy surfaces will to be.

We're focusing on possibilities to the north. From downtown Port Orchard, follow signs for northbound WA 3 and Bremerton. Washington Highway 166 just west of town joins WA 16, which merges onto WA 3 just before it rounds Sinclair Inlet. You'll get up-close views of the hulking vessels of the Puget Sound Naval Shipyard, which has built and maintained ships and submarines since before World War I. Some of the ships here are mothballed but stored for future service; others are being dismantled. This active military installation is not open to the public.

With its barricade of giant gray ships and equally colorless shipyard buildings, Bremerton feels faded; feel free to bypass it. To escape the soulless four-lane WA 3, exit onto Washington Highway 303 north of Bremerton, then take the first exit onto northbound Silverdale Way toward Poulsbo. Silverdale Way is slower than the highway but rolls pleasantly past old-fashioned farmhouses and fields.

You know you're getting close to the little town of Poulsbo, which proudly calls itself "Little Norway," when Silverdale turns into Viking Way. Suddenly, everything has a Scandinavian theme. In the 1800s, Norwegian immigrants settled this spot that reminded them of the fjords back home, and it's been lutefisk and lefse ever since. Tourists flock to the colorful, historic waterfront for food, trinkets, and entertainments, especially during many festival weekends. To get there, follow Bond Street to Front Street (it's well signed). Parking is plentiful; there's a big lot between the main drag and the waterfront. Scandinavian bakeries can supply you with a pastry as big as your helmet.

Return to Viking Way and follow signs for WA 3 northbound. WA 3 narrows to two lanes and is a straight, quick ribbon of road all the way to the north end of the peninsula.

You're so close to the Hood Canal Bridge by now that Port Townsend, about an hour away on its own peninsula, is an easy detour. It's also a possible full-day excursion, depending on how long you want to spend in town. To get there, go left at the intersection with Washington Highway 104 and cross the Hood Canal Bridge, the world's third-longest floating bridge and the longest in seawater. Built in 1961, it held up pretty well until a 1979 storm generated 120-mph winds and sunk it (no one was on it). It was rebuilt by 1982 and got a major overhaul in 2009.

The most direct route to Port Townsend is Washington Highway 19, a typical farm-and-forest backway with a few curves and rough spots. If you don't want to make this a total out-and-back, you could also go or return via US 101, a few miles west of the WA 19 junction, and Washington Highway 20, which splits off from US 101 to Port Townsend. Both are in fine shape.

Port Townsend is a well-preserved and charming seaside town. Its Fort Worden, with Fort Casey and Fort Flagler, was part of the "Triangle of Fire" that would have rained a hail of bullets onto any attacking ships. From Port Townsend's waterfront buildings, bluffs, and beaches, you can see Whidbey Island across the water (you can also catch a ferry from here to Whidbey; see ride 19 for information). Fort Worden's sprawling collection of military buildings (including the Coast Artillery Museum), now a state park, are just northwest of downtown. Stroll through and check out the buildings, the beach, and Point

In Port Gamble, even the dead have nice views of the Hood Canal.

Wilson Lighthouse before returning to the Kitsap Peninsula via the Hood Canal Bridge.

East of the bridge, WA 104 traces a beautiful broad bluff right beside the water. Historic Port Gamble perches on the cliff's edge, looking much the way it did during a nineteenth-century heyday fueled by lumber exports. The lumber company that still owns the town began restoring it long before mill operations ceased in 1995. Now a National Historic Landmark, it's been converted into shops, restaurants, and lodging to match a lovely waterfront setting that manages to feel serene even when it's crowded with summer tourists.

After you've taken in Port Gamble's Hood Canal vistas, stay on WA 104 south along the water's edge for about 4 miles to its junction with the Bond Road. Make a left on WA 104 and ride east for about 1.5 miles to the intersection with Miller Bay Road. Take Miller Bay Road south as it runs through farms and forest, then along the edge of Port Madison to Suquamish. (If you're ready to

Chief Seattle, also called Sealth or Si'ahl, was a famous warrior, organizer, and orator who befriended whites in the Puget Sound region and acted as an ambassador for Native people. He is also famous for eloquent, oft-quoted speeches, though existing translations may not accurately represent his exact words.

A member of the Duwamish and Suquamish tribes, Chief Seattle befriended white settlers and pursued good relations between Natives and newcomers. When the government attempted to move his people to a reservation, his personal relationships helped him persuade authorities to let them remain on this spot, part of their homeland. His good friend David "Doc" Maynard persuaded fellow settlers to name the city of Seattle after the chief as an act of goodwill. The chief died in 1866; painted canoes above his headstone honor the chief's work. ●

head back to Seattle, stay on WA 104 to Kingston and take the ferry to Edmonds.)

Suquamish, in the beautifully situated Port Madison Indian Reservation, offers a lot of information about Puget Sound tribes. The Old Man House, in the middle of a public park near the water on Division Street, is the site of the largest Native American longhouse ever built. The gravesite of Chief Seattle is at nearby St. Peter's Catholic Church and Suquamish Memorial Cemetery.

If history's not your thing, enjoy the present at the Suquamish Clearwater Casino amid the suburbs that line Washington Highway 305 as you leave town.

Head south on WA 305, across the steel-truss Agate Pass Bridge to Bainbridge Island, where everything is attractive, neat, and pricey. You're only twenty minutes from the ferry if you head straight to it. But some of Puget Sound's most beautiful little beaches—with great views of Seattle on one side and the Kitsap Peninsula on the other—are along the island's edges. Your best

The ferry from Bainbridge Island gives travelers fantastic views of downtown Seattle.

bet to explore them is to grab a tourist map at one of the island's businesses. Be forewarned that those seaside roads can be slow, patched, and pitted, with very poor signage. No matter where you go on Bainbridge, be prepared for bicyclists. They're everywhere.

Catch a ferry back to Seattle from the terminal at the south end of Bainbridge. It's a forty-five-minute trip with gorgeous views of the city, especially at sunset.

Restaurants

Port Orchard
Bethel Tavern
3840 Bethel Rd. SE
(360) 876-6621

Poulsbo
Sluys' Bakery
18924 Front St. NE
(360) 697-2253

WASHINGTON CASCADES

Some of the most remarkable natural beauty in the Northwest exists in the steep, rocky, snowcapped peaks of Washington's Cascades. Part of the Pacific Rim's "Ring of Fire," the Washington Cascades feature a string of volcanoes from Mount Baker in the north to Mount Adams near the Oregon border, all surrounded by craggy ridges uplifted by earthquakes or magma.

The Cascades give bikers a lot of what they live for—nice roads, welcoming small towns, and spectacular vistas. A handful of highways take you out of the cities and suburbs, up through dramatic alpine wilderness, and down into warmer environs. Clouds passing over the Cascades drop their moisture as they rise, so the east side lies in a dry rain shadow that makes for a great way to escape the cool and damp.

Eastern towns can be a long day out and back or a quick overnight or weekend getaway. Since few roads cut through the Cascades, those that do are very popular. A bonus: They're often lined with motorcycle-friendly businesses for whom bikers are bread and butter, meaning these rides offer great opportunities to meet fellow motorcyclists.

While we aren't big fans of interstates, Interstate 90 through the Cascades isn't horrible (in fact, it's beautiful as it crosses the summit) and provides a quick escape hatch or return route. Be forewarned that everyone else sees it that way, too, so it can be a nightmare of clogged weekend traffic. We've seen stop-and-go Memorial Day traffic backed up all the way from downtown Seattle to Ellensburg—a distance of more than 100 miles.

The Cascades are great for recreating, especially fishing, hiking, or camping. Campsites abound, although if you do plan on camping, be prepared for rain and chilly nighttime temperatures, even in summer. To truly experience the Cascades, bring some comfortable shoes and be prepared to take a hike, which here can be anything from 0.25 mile to 2,500 miles (if you hike the entire Pacific Crest Trail, which runs from California into Canada—but that's an entirely different book).

RIDE

21

Cascade Loop

Directions:

east on US 2 from Monroe to Wenatchee

north on US 97 Alt to WA 153

north on WA 153 to WA 20

west on WA 20 to I-5

(option: south and west on WA 530)

Distance:

total distance: about 430 to 450 miles, depending on route

Seattle to Leavenworth via US 2: 118 miles

Leavenworth to Wenatchee: 22 miles

Wenatchee to Chelan: 40 miles

Chelan to Winthrop: 61 miles

Winthrop to Rockport (intersection with WA 530): 95 miles

Rockport to Seattle via WA 20: 105 miles

Rockport to Seattle via WA 530: 94 miles

Time:

one very long day to two or three days

Services:

many points along WA 522 and I-5, Monroe, Sultan, Gold
Bar, Skykomish, Leavenworth, Wenatchee, Entiat, Chelan,
Winthrop, Mazama, Marblemount, Concrete, Darrington

Best Time of Year:
late spring through fall; snow can come early to mountain
passes and stay late, especially on WA 20

Highlights:
impressive and diverse landscapes from mountains to
rivers to canyons; cheerful tourist havens such as Leavenworth and Winthrop; enjoying the company of your fellow riders on some of the most popular bike routes in the
Northwest

This is a famous ride for bikers (as well as drivers), and rightfully so. Though it's possible to make this entire loop in a long,
iron-butt-style day, you'll probably want to stay at some kind
of halfway point if you want to linger anywhere. Many on two
wheels (or four) spend a night or more in one of the warmer, drier
towns on the Cascades' east side. If you like fruit, try to leave
room in your saddlebags for some of the fresh produce for sale
near Wenatchee.

Choosing where to stay can get tricky. Wenatchee has plenty
of budget motels. Chelan is more charming and has lots of lodging (including condos) but can get booked up. Winthrop has a few
lodging options, but you'd probably want to reserve in advance
for this remote town. We once thought about staying in Winthrop,
but we discovered the whole town had been booked for a reen-
actment of Woodstock. That same weekend, much of the power
went out, as did the server that handles most of the town's Internet service, resulting in something closer to the original Woodstock than organizers probably intended. The moral of the story
is that if you want to stay a night along the northern route back
across the Cascades, it might be wise to plan ahead.

Options to make your way north from Seattle all involve getting through the sprawl around the city. One of the most direct,
if not the fastest (with stoplights and strip malls along the way),

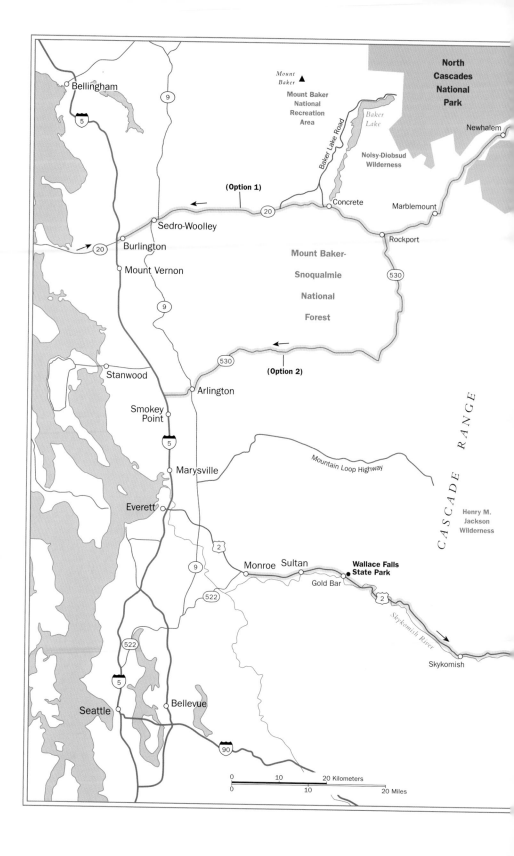

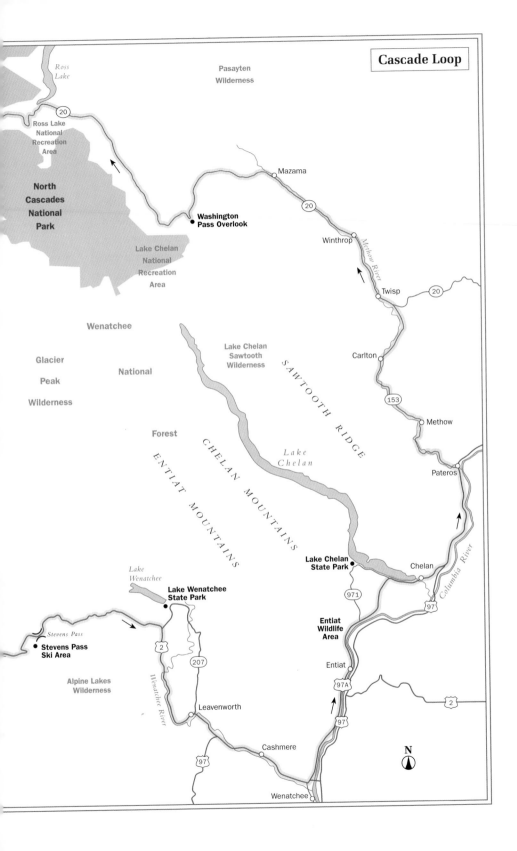

Like the totem pole, Sasquatch is an iconic figure in the Pacific Northwest.

Christy: At a couple points along this ride, statues and signs pay homage to one of the Northwest's most famous and beloved characters: Sasquatch. The thick woods are supposedly home to this hairy, ape-like beast also known as Bigfoot. Although people all over the country have reported seeing such a creature, Washington and Oregon have had more than their fair share, leading local residents to adopt it as a sort of mascot. Lest you think this is just a joke, some people steadfastly believe he (she? it?) really exists. It's not surprising that Seattle is home to the Sasquatch Information Society (www.bigfootinfo.org), which keeps track of reported sightings. I've never seen him in person, though I have to admit I haven't looked very hard (or it's possible I haven't spent enough time drinking beer in the forest). ●

is Lake City Way north out of town. Lake City Way turns into Washington Highway 522, which leads to Monroe and the turnoff to U.S. Highway 2.

On US 2, small towns like Gold Bar replace the suburbs as the Cascades' sharp crags rise majestically ahead. Just outside Gold Bar, 265-foot Wallace Falls is visible from US 2 as it drops dramatically down the face of a cliff to the east; follow signs 2 miles north of Gold Bar to Wallace Falls State Park if you'd like to see them up close (the hike to the highest waterfall itself is about 5 miles round-trip).

The road rises, narrow but in decent shape, surrounded by a variety of trees and following the lovely rock-strewn Skykomish River. The town of Skykomish, whose entire historic downtown seems to be in the midst of a renovation, is the last place to fuel up and grab a bite to eat before hitting the passes—and a lot of riders do, often at one of the delis in town.

A pullout soon after Skykomish at Deception Falls tells of the Great Northern Railway built through the Cascades and finished in 1893, linking the Northwest to Minnesota. Workers kept improving the tunnels and grades until 1929 (the tunnel under Stevens Pass, the longest railroad tunnel in the United States, is 2,000 feet below the surface). The highway that follows the railroad's path continues to be an important east-west route, kept open year-round—except when it's temporarily closed by avalanches, which happens a couple of times each winter.

At Deception Falls, two short trails lead to two waterfalls. The name may come from the fact that the one you get to second—and hence, maybe the one fewer people see—is actually the taller one.

The forest becomes denser as the road climbs at an ear-popping rate toward Stevens Pass. The road is wide and fast, with plenty of passing lanes, and eventually becomes a roaring four-lane highway just outside Stevens Pass Ski Area.

Things quickly get drier, and the mountains less dramatic, on the eastern side of the pass. The road, which narrows back to a two-lane highway and is in great condition through here, makes the descent in a series of long S curves that hug first Nason Creek, then the Wenatchee River. This stretch is very popular with kayakers, rafters, anglers, and folks just taking a dip. A few vacation cabins are scattered along the road as it flattens. It's not as exciting as it was a little way back, and recreation-related traffic increases on the way into Leavenworth.

US 2, here winding alongside the Wenatchee River, is understandably popular with all kinds of bikers.

Leavenworth calls itself "Your Bavarian Getaway," and that's exactly what it strives to be. That doesn't mean just one block in the center of town: Pretty much everything, including fast-food restaurants and grocery stores, is decked out with shutters and pastoral frescoes. It wasn't always this way; Leavenworth was a thriving timber town until the railroad rerouted its tracks away from here. Inspired by the alpine surroundings, town leaders cooked up a plan in the 1960s to reinvigorate their economy by going gangbusters with the Bavarian Alps theme, plastering and painting their old buildings, firing up German-themed restaurants and knickknack shops, and instituting celebrations like the town's annual Christmas-lighting ceremony.

The experiment has been a huge success, which means it's overrun with tourists for much of the year, especially on weekends. It can be tough to find parking on the main streets, even for bikes, though you should be able to find something within a block or two of the center of town. The good news is, Leavenworth has something for everyone, especially when it comes to food—not just traditional German stuff (Munchen Haus), but also Italian (Visconti's is a favorite) and even Mexican, all on or near the main drag.

For some, Leavenworth is more recreational paradise than tourist trap. It's surrounded by lakes, rivers, trails, and trees aplenty. (Lake Wenatchee, with its vacation cabins, campgrounds, and boat put-ins, is north of Leavenworth on Washington Highway

207, also called Lake Wenatchee Road.) Others come to eat, shop, and bask in sunshine that's warmer than anything west of here. If you're considering staying the night, look into accommodations in advance, especially on weekends (and especially on festival weekends, which are many; go to www.leavenworth.org for information on the town).

After Leavenworth, the canyon widens up and becomes a valley that's home to Cashmere, a town famous for its delicious pears. Now completely out of the mountains, roll into Wenatchee, where the undulating, yellow, desert-like surroundings are startlingly different from the environment you were just in an hour ago.

Roadside signs proclaim the Wenatchee area's fruit-related virtues, and the hillsides and valleys surrounding this good-sized town are covered with all kinds of fruit trees. (We prefer fresh fruit to the "applets" and "cotlets," candies made of fruit jelly and nuts that are a much-touted local specialty.) Wenatchee has all the usual amenities, plus the Washington State Apple Commission and Visitors Centers for anyone who just can't get enough of apples.

Some people take U.S. Highway 97 south from here and make a loop with Interstate 90 as the southern leg back into Seattle. While this is rewarding, with beautiful mountain views and attractive old towns along the way, we're not big fans of the interstate—especially at times when people are heading back into the city after a weekend getaway. So we'll stick to the classic Cascade Loop route and head north from here on US 97 toward the junction with Washington Highway 20, this loop's northern half.

We took U.S. Highway 97 Alt along the west edge of the Columbia River (US 97 is on the east side). The two reconnect at Chelan, so which road you choose depends on which view of the river you prefer and whether you want to stop in at the Entiat Valley Pastry and Coffee House, which is on US 97A just north of Wenatchee. The doughnuts, cookies, and everything else are freshly baked and possibly addictive, and the coffee is delicious.

Steve: Scan the hillsides for signs of Rocky Mountain big-horn sheep. They and other wildlife are plentiful along US 97A, which is on the eastern edge of the Entiat Wildlife Area. On a return trip from Canada, I saw a herd trying to cross the highway from west to east. One of the big ewes almost got hit by a semi-trailer while the rest of the herd stayed on the west side. ●

East of here, a series of dams backs the Columbia into man-made lakes that seem out of place in this arid landscape.

Just north of Entiat and nestled at the end of a deep mountain valley, glacial Lake Chelan is a very long (50 miles), very deep (1,500 feet), and well-loved body of water—Washington's version of Loch Ness. With air temperatures topping 100 degrees in summer, this is where Western Washington folks go for reliable hot weather from late April to October.

The lake's shores are encrusted with vacation homes, and Chelan is often full of swimsuit-clad tourists swimming, water-skiing, or even parasailing. At the lake's far end, the little town of Stehekin can't be reached by paved road. Most get to it via the *Lady of the Lake* ferry or floatplane. The Forest Service office in the town of Chelan would seem like a logical place for some information on the area's roads, except that it's open Monday through Friday from 7:45 a.m. to 4:30 p.m.—exactly when tourists and many bikers are not here.

After Chelan, US 97 runs straight and fast through dry farming territory and more orchards. Turning onto Washington Highway 153 orients you once again toward the mountains, which can be an appealing thought on a 90-plus-degree day. This is deer country: Roadside deer kill signs list how many deer usually die on the road here, how many have been hit recently, and how many dollars the resulting damage has cost. It feels as if there's an odd sense of pride about this: "We killed 45 deer last year!" But we assume it's meant as a warning.

Methow has a store and a cafe. The road goes through another few hamlets, some with general stores and the odd motel. Be prepared for off-and-on canyon winds as you head through the Methow River valley.

For being in the middle of nowhere (or maybe because it is in the middle of nowhere), Twisp has a strangely artsy vibe. It also has a couple restaurants. After Twisp, things get noticeably greener, and you finally feel that you're back in the mountains—a feeling reinforced by the occasional view of the peaks ahead.

In sort of the same way that Leavenworth attracts tourists with its Bavarian themes, Winthrop has gone all out in refurbishing itself as an Old West town. (Not surprisingly, the architect who renovated the old downtown was from Leavenworth.) At least Winthrop was at one time an Old West town, as informational signs and museums will attest. But unlike Western towns that tried to keep up with changing times over the years, Winthrop decided to cash in on its history and not change much of anything.

Founded by gold prospectors, it never was very big, which might account for the survival of so many old buildings (others look old but aren't). The result is a few solid blocks of boardwalk-style town where you might feel compelled to tie your bike up to a hitching post. Just park it and head for one of the many saloons or other eateries. Note that if you're coming in from the east, you'll pass a couple of restaurants and other establishments (including a full-size grocery store, in case you need anything) before hitting Winthrop proper.

Pretty much everything in Winthrop celebrates the Old West.

Mazama, just west of Winthrop, is the last place with any kind of services for 70 miles. If that sign doesn't convince you you're in for some serious wilderness, the sharp mountains looming ahead will. The road leaves meadows behind and weaves upward through a canyon flanked by forested rock hillsides, then onto a ridge.

North Cascades National Park is one of those parks where much of what it has to offer is off the beaten path—which means a fair distance from the highway. It's a mecca for hikers and mountain climbers and others wanting to get far away from their hectic everyday lives. Fortunately, you don't have to take a hike to get an eyeful of the pointy peaks the park is all about. Many viewpoints along the highway allow you to look out over the crags that make up some of the most remote and challenging territory in the Lower 48.

This is a low-key place. There's no lodge or cafeteria. If you're coming in from the east, there's not an entrance station

Before the highway enters North Cascades National Park and right after a big hairpin turn, be sure to stop by at the Washington Pass Overlook, on the north side of the road. It has some of the nicest bathrooms we've ever seen in a rest stop, but that's not why we suggest you take a moment here. At the end of a very short trail, the view overlooking the canyon, the massive Liberty Bell Peak, the Early Winter Spires, and the ribbon of road far below you is breathtaking.

If that wasn't enough, you'll very often hear the sweet sound of motorcycles roaring their way through the turn. Their thunder echoes off the canyon walls to spectacular effect. It's a sound worth waiting to hear, though you shouldn't have to wait very long, as lots of bikes come through. We're not sure why this isn't part of the national park, but we're glad someone put it here. ●

Yes, Diablo Lake really is that color. The deep turquoise comes from fine glacial silt suspended in the water.

or much else indicating you've entered a national park. To get brochures or talk to a ranger, you'll have to go to the visitor center in Newhalem. But if you're not interested in the backcountry, mostly they'll tell you to check out the sights along the road. So, to avoid backtracking, just stop at the viewpoints along the road on your way in.

Newhalem is home to a visitor center, rangers, and some employees of the Diablo power station up the road. This part of the national park has long been a major power-producing area. For security reasons, tours of Diablo Dam (once a popular park activity) are no longer possible, but you can see it from several short hikes and overlooks.

After a long stretch without many amenities, Marblemount is a nice change, albeit not a very big one population-wise. At least you can buy fuel here. We also recommend the Buffalo Run Inn and Restaurant. The inn is a combination hotel/hostel, and the restaurant serves good burgers (including a buffalo burger and other exotic-meat specialties).

At Rockport, you can get to Interstate 5 via either WA 20 (west) or Washington Highway 530 (south, then west). If you're headed back to Seattle, it's about sixes, distance-wise. WA 20 takes you through Concrete, named for the cement plant in town, built in 1908, which must have come in handy for building all the dams nearby. Concrete is at the foot of Lake Shannon, which is at the foot of Baker Lake; a paved road (Baker Lake Road, or Forest Road 11) runs up the lakes' west sides and leads to trails, campsites, and a couple overlooks. The lakes are on the western edge of the imaginatively named Noisy-Diobsud Wilderness (named for the Noisy and Diobsud Creeks that run through it).

WA 530 takes you through a broad river valley with a couple of nice but fairly unremarkable small towns, including Darrington, before dropping you into the Skagit Valley at Arlington. The Mountain Loop Highway, which heads south from Darrington and is a popular jumping-off point for hikers, is not paved all the way, so check in with rangers if you plan to try it.

Restaurants

Entiat
Entiat Valley Pastry
2042 Entiat Way
(509) 784-4118

Marblemount
Buffalo Run
60117 WA 20
(360) 873-2103

RIDE 22

Mount Rainier Loop

Directions:

from Puget Sound area: South on WA 7 or WA 161 to junction of 161 and 7

east on WA 7 (becomes WA 706) from Elbe to WA 123

north on WA 123 to WA 410

north, then west, on WA 410 (with out-and-back to Sunrise Point) to Enumclaw

north on WA 169 to I-5

from the south: east on US 12 from I-5 to Morton

north on WA 7 to Elbe, then follow directions above

Distance:

total distance from Seattle: 272 miles

Seattle to Elbe (via WA 161): about 73 miles

Elbe to Longmire (visitor center): 31 miles

Longmire to WA 123 junction (Stevens Canyon entrance): 29 miles

Stevens Canyon entrance to Packwood: 13 miles

Stevens Canyon entrance to Enumclaw: 52 miles

Sunrise Point out-and-back: 32 miles round-trip

Enumclaw to Seattle: about 42 miles

Time:

most of a day to two days

Services:
plentiful along WA 161 and WA 7/706 west of Ashford; Packwood; Greenwater (limited); Enumclaw

Best Time of Year:
late spring through early fall; high elevations are snowy until at least the end of May, and most of the park closes after the first snowfall in late September or early October

Highlights:
innumerable views from all sides of iconic Mount Rainier; short hikes to spectacular vistas and secluded forests; a high-elevation mountain getaway

Mount Rainier, one of the Northwest's most majestic icons, is an ever-present backdrop for the Puget Sound region—that is, when it's sunny, which isn't too often. On the hottest days of summer, people from all over flock to Mount Rainier National Park for a chance to commune with its snowy, 14,411-foot cap. This ride gets you as close to the peak as any paved roads can, allowing you to see its less-viewed eastern faces—again, when it's sunny. Since Rainier's most popular assets are those great views and bountiful hiking opportunities, it's much less appealing on a cloudy day. That's even more true for motorcyclists, since most of the roads in and around the park are not great riding in their own right.

Wildflowers in July and August, plus cooler temperatures at elevation, make this an ideal late-summer ride. Many car travelers, who have to compete for limited parking spaces, take a free shuttle bus from Ashford to the park's beloved Paradise area on summer weekends (it's not offered on weekdays, even though things can get crowded then, too). Bikers shouldn't have any trouble squeezing into designated motorcycle spots or the hidey-holes between cars, so you don't have to take the shuttle, though "free shuttle to Paradise" has a nice ring to it.

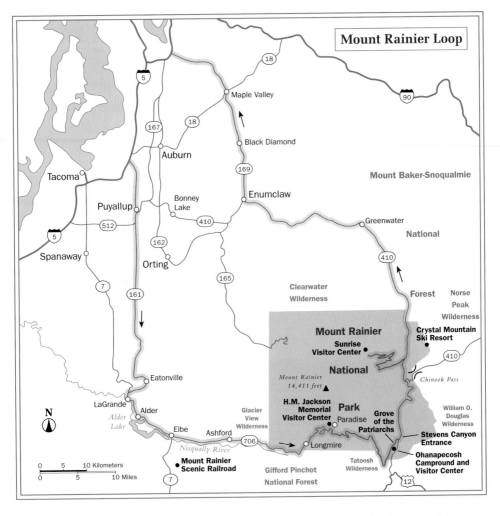

We do this ride as a big loop around Mount Rainier. You could also make a sort of figure-eight and include U.S. Highway 12 and Washington Highway 410 east of the park (ride 23), which are much more fun to ride, though they're a little more out of the way and offer less to do on the side. Spending some time in the park and exploring nearby roads would make for a nice two- or three-day trip. Given the limited lodging around the park, you might want to try to score a room at the National Park Inn in Longmire or Paradise Inn at Paradise.

We head to Rainier's southwestern entrance, the Nisqually entrance, first, then around to Sunrise Point and back to the Seattle area. If you want to see views from Sunrise in the morning (you can probably guess from the name that morning is a good time to see those), reverse this loop. We find Sunrise just as enchanting in the afternoon, so we go to Paradise first hoping to beat the afternoon crowds that build up there.

Since the national park's foremost activity is hiking, consider bringing comfortable shoes. And since food on the mountain is not the greatest, we suggest you eat outside the park or bring a picnic.

Unless you're coming from the south (possibly after visiting Mount St. Helens) or the east, getting to Rainier means dealing with suburban sprawl and attendant traffic before you climb into the Cascades. The best route from Seattle to Paradise is Washington Highway 161 through Puyallup. But on a good day, turning off Interstate 5 onto Washington Highway 7 in Tacoma is also a quick option. Both feel like an endless suburban strip mall.

Craggy peaks around Mount Rainier are visible through the windows of the Jackson Memorial Visitor Center.

Short hikes from the Paradise area, many of them paved, lead to meadows below Mount Rainier that blaze with color in late summer.

WA 7 and WA 161 meet just south of Eatonville. Continue east on WA 7, which becomes Washington Highway 706. The scenery gets more forested, and civilization recedes enough to allow a 55-mph speed limit and chances to pass for a few miles on a typical two-lane highway. Other roads branch off from this route, but signage for the park is pretty good.

The road gets more narrow and twisty, so prepare for braking and downshifting. Heed speed-limit signs: Hills and trees hide whatever's around the corner, and oncoming traffic will likely include large vehicles (especially logging trucks) you don't want to share a lane with. There's not a lot of scenery to speak of, and you seem to spend most of the time facing every direction except toward the mountain that is your goal. In short, riding through here is a bit of a pain.

You'll pass by the shores of glacier-green Alder Lake, which is dotted with trunks of chopped-down trees and campers taking a dip (their similar shapes from a distance might require a double-take). The closer you get to the national park, the more drivers seem to slow down. Good thing you're on vacation.

Although many travelers make Ashford their last stop before entering the national park, we prefer the old-fashioned old town of Elbe (Ashford has more of a hippie-climber commune vibe).

Christy: On one trip to Rainier, I wanted to check out WA 165 into the northwestern corner of the national park (the Carbon River entrance), which maps say is paved. But when I stopped into the ranger station in Enumclaw to inquire, I discovered it had been damaged and was closed indefinitely until money became available to fix it. That question saved me a lot of time and frustration!

The main highways in this area are vital corridors for both tourism and business, so they will generally be well maintained, and damage will be repaired quickly. If you have any intention of checking out lesser roads, including secondary out-and-back roads into the national park or other parts of the mountains, check in with a ranger. The diverse landscape here guarantees heavy snow, avalanches, landslides, floods, and other natural disasters, which severely damage roads. It may take years for nonessential roads to get repaired. ●

The Mount Rainier Scenic Railroad is based in the train-oriented hamlet of Elbe. A historic Lutheran church is in the background.

Elbe, home to the narrow-gauge Mount Rainier Scenic Railroad that chugs southward from here for a few miles, seems to have a general railroad theme about it (you can't miss, for example, Hobo Inn's caboose lodging). A cute little church sits beside the railroad tracks, and the biker-friendly Elbe Bar and Grill is just across the street. Get fuel here or in Ashford, since there's none in the park and possibly none for many miles, depending on your intended route (Packwood, the only place between Mount Rainier and the Yakima Valley with reliable services, requires an out-and-back detour of 13 miles each way).

Around Ashford, you know you're getting into serious mountains when you see narrow-shoulder warnings and signs reading WATCH FOR PEDESTRIANS AND ELK. We didn't see or hit any elk, but we did see lots of pedestrians, many too busy looking through their camera lenses to pay attention to us.

WA 706 enters the park and finally hits a serious incline as it skirts the Rainier foothills. Huge trees line the road, and the air is fragrant with that piney national-park smell. Not far from the entrance, historic Longmire is a typical national-park-style lodge and visitor center nestled in the pines.

From the park entrance to Paradise, WA 706 is narrow, much-patched, and sometimes rutted, with few guardrails. It would be hard to exceed the 35-mph speed limit, even if you wanted to, so sit back and take time to enjoy some of the many pullouts that feature increasingly dramatic views as the road follows the Nisqually River and climbs along cliffs and canyons. The major pullouts are obvious, and include Ricksecker Point (just before Paradise) and Narada Falls (just after it).

Paradise is the park's most popular spot, and crowds crawl all over it in summertime. It's a great place to gaze up at Rainier's piled-on glaciers and even hike on the mountain. Some short but steep paved hikes originate at the Henry M. Jackson Memorial Visitor Center (just completed in 2008 to replace an old concrete structure that looked like an alien spacecraft) and let you stretch your legs without even changing out of your boots. Paradise Inn's dining room features the best food in the park. The Jackson visitor center has a cafeteria and some exhibits about the mountain.

Christy: There's definitely something special about the national parks. As soon as I ride through the entrance gates, the trees get bigger, the air seems to smell cleaner and stronger (I call that clean, sharp scent of pines "that national-park smell"), and the scenery automatically gets better. America is unique in having set aside many of its most beautiful and unusual places for the enjoyment of the general public. National parks are also usually pretty friendly to bikes; visitors on motorcycles usually pay less than those in cars, bikes often get reserved parking spots close to visitor centers, and we've met a number of rangers who ride. ●

Mount Rainier may often be cloaked in clouds, but nothing beats a ride around it on a beautiful day.

Leaving Paradise, the road zigzags back down the mountain's flanks, offering even more viewpoints and some hairpin turns. Be careful skirting the edge of Stevens Canyon, as it's narrow and has no guardrails. Watch for rocks on the surface as well as dips (usually signed), grates, buckles, and bumps. One of the best short hikes in the park is the Grove of the Patriarchs, a pleasant, flat, shady mile through old growth, near the park's southeastern corner. WA 706 connects with Washington Highway 123 at the park's southeastern (Stevens Canyon) entrance. Just south of that entrance is the Ohanapecosh visitor center and campground. If you need a place to spend the night, or other services, Packwood is the closest option. It's about 13 miles south of the Stevens Canyon entrance via WA 123, which connects with US 12.

To complete the Rainier Loop, turn left on WA 123 and go north to the junction with WA 410. If you have time, do yourself a favor and ride a couple of miles east on WA 410 to Chinook Pass and Tipsoo Lake for a particularly lovely view of Rainier from the east.

After the junction of WA 123 and WA 410, head north on WA 410 along Rainier's eastern flanks. By this time, if you've come around from the south, it's afternoon. While Sunrise is best at sunrise, it's never bad. Don't miss the not-well-marked turnoff to Sunrise Point from the south, which is also the turnoff for White River Campground (the turn is about 3 miles north of the intersection of WA 123 and WA 410).

The 16-mile ride out and back to Sunrise is mostly a series of giant zigzags up the mountainside. The road hugs cliffs with no guardrails and feels more exposed than the road to Paradise. This part of the park is less crowded, but it still sees its fair share of slow, gawking drivers paying more attention to the sights than to their driving. Though the road is in a bit better condition here than on the south side, it still sometimes bucks and dips. Relax, enjoy panoramic views of the expansive scenery, and take advantage of the frequent pullouts to get eyefuls of the mountains from various vantages.

Sunrise offers no lodging, just a visitor center and cafeteria serving typically bland national-park cafeteria food. Hold out if you can for one of the restaurants along the way home, or bring a picnic.

The views from Sunrise—Mount Rainier surrounded by an impressive array of craggy pinnacles fanning out in all directions—are some of the most spectacular in the park. Many hikes lead from Sunrise to various points on the mountain. Most are too long to be comfortably done in riding boots, but if you're interested, inquire at the visitor center about which ones give you the best views closer in.

Watch your speed coming back down from Sunrise; if you don't pay attention, you could be zooming along and hit some gravel on a guardrail-free hairpin turn. With nothing between you and oblivion, it could be a long time before anything stopped your forward momentum.

Impressive close-up views of Mount Rainier's snowy peak are only a short hike from Sunrise Point.

On its way out of the park, WA 410 passes Crystal Mountain Ski Resort, and travels through dense forest that obscures views until it clears out as civilization reappears. Your next chance for food or fuel is Greenwater, with several possibilities for grub.

WA 410 ends at Enumclaw, and so does this ride. Enumclaw has all services, including fast and slow food (including many biker-friendly places) and distant views of Mount Rainier. We like to go home via Washington Highway 169 through small, pleasant towns like Black Diamond. The Red Dog Saloon in Maple Valley will have bikes lined up outside and, quite possibly, rollicking live music inside.

Restaurants

Elbe
Elbe Bar & Grill
54312 182 Ave. Ct. E (on WA 7)
(360) 569-2545

Maple Valley
Red Dog Saloon
18606 Maple Valley Hwy. SE (WA 169)
(425) 413-8600

RIDE
23

East Cascades Loop

Directions:
east on US 12 from Packwood to Naches
west on WA 410 from Naches to junction with WA 123

Distance:
total distance: 134 miles (160 including Yakima)
Packwood to Naches: 59 miles
Naches to junction with WA 123: 51 miles
Junction with WA 123 to Packwood: 24 miles

Time:
half a day

Services:
Packwood, Naches, Yakima

Best Time of Year:
spring through fall, with colorful trees in the fall

Highlights:
views of Mount Rainier from its less-crowded side; fun
roads with sweeping curves and impressive vistas; the
Yakima Valley's fruit and vegetable bounty

If the slow, tight rides around Rainier make you long for more-
open scenery, never fear: The two highways east of the national
park are some of Washington's best roads for motorcycles. We

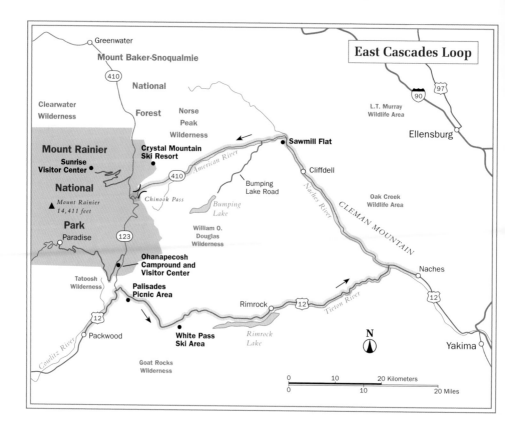

recommend this loop in combination with the Mount Rainier Loop (ride 22), which together would take a day and a half to two full days, with a night spent somewhere along the way. You could also ride either the northern or southern section of Rainier, make half the loop, and stay the night in Yakima, then pick up the second half of the Rainier ride the next day. If you had two or three days, you could do this loop, Rainier, and Mount St. Helens for the full Cascades experience.

This ride begins in Packwood, a convenient base for the region. Reverse these directions if you're heading from Yakima. You could also ride Washington Highway 410 (the northern portion of this route) first and return on U.S. Highway 12, in which case you'd end up at the southeastern edge of the national park. With few services along this route except for Packwood and the Yakima area, start off with a full complement of supplies.

Packwood is a short but pleasant detour south from Mount Rainier National Park on US 12. Situated conveniently between

Riding US 12 means leaving the forested slopes of Mount Rainier and heading toward the Cascades' dry side.

Mount St. Helens and Rainier, it caters to tourists and recreationalists with plenty of food and lodging options. It might be your only option for premium fuel between Ashford at the west entrance to Rainier and Naches in the Yakima valley. (If you'd like to plan ahead and make reservations, www.whitepass byway.com/lodgingandservices.html is one place to start.) If you're headed to Packwood from the west and have already seen enough of Mount Rainier, or if it's cloudy and the Paradise area holds no interest for you, you can skip the national park's superslow roads by dropping down from Elbe on Washington Highway 7 and picking up US 12 eastbound in Morton.

Take US 12 out of Packwood and stay right at the junction with Washington Highway 123 (a left leads to the national park; the Ohanapecosh Visitor Center and Campground are just up WA 123). US 12 makes a big right-hand turn and scales a ridge. Several lovely pullouts offer beautiful views just off the roadway, making

This ride will give you a chance to see larches, coniferous trees that turn bright yellow and lose their needles in the fall. You might see them (and many varieties of other deciduous trees) turning color if you get weather good enough to ride in the fall, usually late September through mid-October. Unlike pine trees, the larches shed their needles to conserve energy through the winter. Seeing what appears to be groups of golden pine trees in the midst of true evergreens is an enchanting experience. ●

it a nice mix of potential stops and good riding on a road that's mostly in great shape. The first stop, the Palisades viewpoint and picnic area, comes soon after the junction and overlooks vertical lava walls that formed when ancient volcanic lava flows hit and backed up behind a barrier, possibly a glacier or a cliff.

The road here is a lot more open than it is in the national park, with many passing lanes and much bigger, more sweeping curves. It's generally in excellent condition, with a few rough spots, notably where landslides have occurred. Partly because it's a fairly new road (it wasn't completed until 1951) and partly because most of the surrounding landscape is national forest, it feels wide open and remote.

Just down the road, at the Lava Creek Falls overlook, water has carved a channel out of volcanic cliffs. A short interpretive hike leads to even better views.

The highway passes just north of the Goat Rocks Wilderness, named for the mountain goats that climb around in these volcanic mountains—as do human climbers. If you get lucky, you may see mountain goats in this area, as well as elk, which are plentiful here. About 6 miles east of the Palisades viewpoint, there's a nice pullout at Goat Rocks Overlook, also signed as a Rainier viewpoint (by now, you've realized most overlooks around here are Mount Rainier overlooks, whatever else they show you). This one offers a particularly nice view of Rainier along with informational panels about the Goat Rocks area, where thousands of years ago, a massive volcano stood more than 12,000 feet high. Erosion has whittled it down to the spiky peaks before you, now a mere 8,000 or so feet.

The road continues through high-alpine forest and over White Pass at an elevation of 4,500 feet (this highway is also called the White Pass Scenic Byway), past the small White Pass ski area. Since most people simply drive the 50 miles from Yakima to ski here in the winter, it offers none of the services you'd see at a typical resort.

Naches orchards are heavy with fruit in late summer.

After White Pass, the road undulates along the cliff face in a surprisingly regular rhythm. You'll notice barriers against—and signs warning about—rock slides. Though the barriers seem to work pretty well, rocks occasionally skitter across the pavement. When we were coming through here, a few rocks tumbled down the hillside in a dusty cloud right in front of us, and a few stones made it onto the road. Don't let the beauty of your surroundings lull you into inattention.

The road passes several pretty lakes, including Rimrock Lake and the aptly named Clear Lake, with its bright emerald-colored water. Rimrock State Park is popular with boaters, hikers, campers, and fishermen. Unless you're looking for a campsite, it doesn't have services.

After this, the landscape is noticeably drier, with the kind of yellow hills you know and love in this part of the world. As you leave the pines of the national forest, you'll see lots of orchards, fruit stands, and "u-pick" places. You might want to leave room in a saddlebag for some super-cheap freshly picked berries, fruits, and vegetables, because the orchards at Naches are famous for their bounty, and they start producing earlier than their counterparts to the north and west. Throughout the summer, Naches serves up an ever-changing harvest of apples, peaches, cherries, beans, onions, garlic, potatoes, zucchini, sweet corn, tomatoes, peppers, watermelons, cantaloupes, apricots, nectarines, pears . . . you get the idea.

If you're planning on making this loop back to the Mount Rainier area and don't have any pressing interest in Yakima, Naches has plenty of restaurants. Grab lunch at the 1885 Bar & Grill (with a big selection of both burgers and beers), the Country Rock Cafe, or the Walkabout Creek Saloon in downtown Naches (a block north of the highway).

Gas up before you hit WA 410 back into the Cascades. Although you'll find intermittent fuel between here and the next major town, it might not be premium and it'll likely be pricey.

WA 410, also known as the Mather Memorial Parkway and the Chinook Scenic Byway, is generally straighter and faster than US 12, usually clipping along at 55 mph. Although there aren't many passing lanes per se, there are a lot of pullouts and signs reminding slow drivers that it's illegal for anyone to let more than five vehicles pile up behind them without pulling over. We're not sure how well the authorities enforce this, but it's not usually

---

About 10 miles west of Naches, you'll notice a section of newer pavement. In October 2009, a massive landslide covered WA 410 as an entire hillside slumped into the Naches River. Fortunately, no one was killed in the slow-moving slide, but it and flooding damaged or destroyed twenty-five homes, and the Naches River was permanently rerouted. The highway was closed as crews worked to keep a local access road open. Within weeks, workers were rebuilding the 0.25-mile section of WA 410 to have it open by the next summer. Although parts of it always close in winter, this highway is too important to close indefinitely. ●

crowded enough to be an aggravation unless it's the beginning or end of a weekend or other busy time.

As the road reenters the hills, gradually but steadily climbing, the surroundings become more forested with ponderosa pine (about 20 miles from Naches, the Sawmill Flat Interpretive Trail is an easy 0.25-mile walk with information about the forest). The road follows the Naches River through a shallow canyon that's a magnet for hikers, anglers, and other urban refugees. Campgrounds and hiking trails line the road most of the way through here. There's also camping and lots of fishing at Bumping Lake, down a paved road to the south off WA 410, about 12 miles east of the intersection with WA 123.

On this northern side of the loop, there are more privately owned campgrounds, RV parks, motels, vacation homes, and attendant general stores than on the southern side. Some have fuel, but not always. The recreational hamlet of Cliffdell, for example, is home to Whistlin' Jack Lodge & Restaurant. After that, the next services are 52 miles down the road. This part of WA 410 is closed in winter.

Tipsoo Lake, right off WA 410, is a favorite spot for photographers. Flat, easy walking trails surround the lake.

The valley gets deeper as the road rises, becoming a yawning glacial valley, and the road hugs the mountainside high above the valley floor. Near the summit, WA 410 crosses the Pacific Crest Trail, which runs from northern California to northern Washington. Stop at the parking lot near the summit to look back at the road. Near Chinook Pass (at 5,342 feet), the road passes under a massive stone and log arch and into the national park, but there's no fee station on this side. Just past the summit, Mount Rainier is reflected in Tipsoo Lake. Paths through here are a nice break and the view of Rainier from here is one of the best anywhere.

On its way toward Rainier and the intersection with WA 123 (on the park's east side), the road is carved out of the rock in a series of hairpin twists through craggy peaks and steep canyons.

Hang a right to stay on WA 410 toward Sunrise Point and the Puget Sound area. Turn left to return to Packwood or the Paradise side of the park on WA 123.

Restaurants

Naches
1885 Bar & Grill
208 Naches Ave.
(509) 653-2257

Country Rock Cafe
206 Naches Ave.
(509) 653-2112

Walkabout Creek Saloon
9990 US 12
(509) 653-1314

WA 410
Whistlin' Jack Lodge & Restaurant
20800 WA 410
Chinook Pass
(509) 658-2433

RIDE
24

Mount St. Helens' Approachable Side

Directions:
east on WA 504 to Johnston Ridge Observatory and back

Distance:
total distance (round-trip from Portland): 216 miles
Portland to Castle Rock (junction with WA 504): 57 miles
Castle Rock to Kid Valley: 18 miles
Kid Valley to Hoffstadt Bluffs: 15 miles
Hoffstadt Bluffs to Johnston Ridge Observatory: 18 miles

Time:
half a day or more depending on time at overlooks and the
Johnston Ridge Observatory

Services:
almost every town along I-5; last services on WA 504 are in
Kid Valley

Best Time of Year:
late spring to early fall; WA 504 is closed in the winter

Highlights:
views of Mount St. Helens from Hoffstadt Bluffs; entering
a blast zone; wide curves and smooth pavement through
countless acres of young forest; history, science, and hikes
at Johnston Ridge Observatory

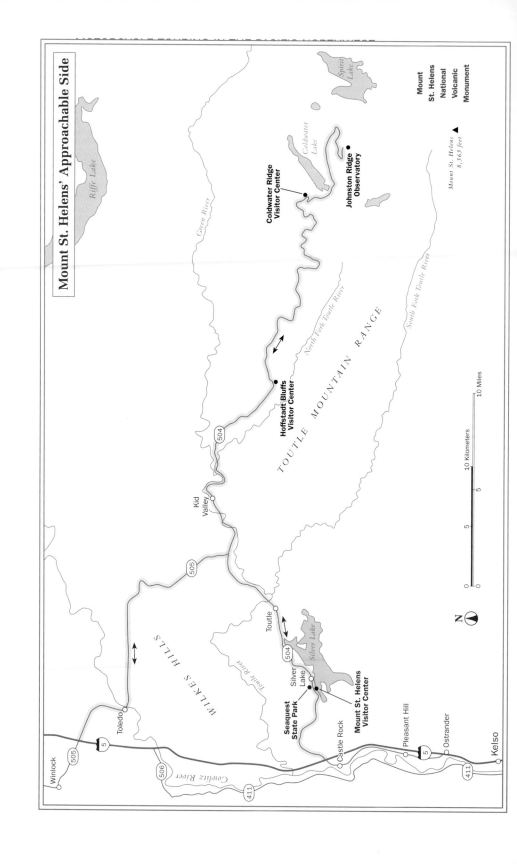

Mount St. Helens' Approachable Side

Riffe Lake

Spirit Lake

Mount St. Helens National Volcanic Monument

▲ Mount St. Helens
8,363 feet

Green River

Coldwater Lake

Coldwater Ridge Visitor Center

Johnston Ridge Observatory

North Fork Toutle River

South Fork Toutle River

T O U T L E   M O U N T A I N   R A N G E

504

Hoffstadt Bluffs Visitor Center

Kid Valley

505

W I L K E S   H I L L S

Toutle

504

Toutle River

Silver Lake

Seaquest State Park

Silver Lake

Mount St. Helens Visitor Center

Castle Rock

Pleasant Hill

Ostrander

Kelso

411

Cowlitz River

411

506

5

Toledo

505

Winlock

906

5

411

N

0   5   10 Kilometers
0   5   10 Miles

Mount St. Helens rises in the distance above the North Fork of the Toutle River.

Mount St. Helens is most famous for May 18, 1980, the day she suddenly reawakened and shattered the serenity of a spring morning by blowing her top in the deadliest and most economically destructive volcanic eruption in United States history.

The blast's effects killed 57 people and destroyed 250 homes, 47 bridges, 185 miles of highway, and 15 miles of railway. More than 150,000 acres of private, state, and federal forest were devastated. The eruption caused a massive avalanche with enough momentum to flow over ridges more than 1,100 feet high and filled some river valleys with more than 150 feet of volcanic debris. It reduced Mount St. Helens' summit from 9,677 feet to 8,363 feet, replacing its symmetrical, cone-shaped peak with a mile-wide horseshoe-shaped crater.

Although St. Helens was active again from October 2004 to late January 2008, scientists say the eruptions are over for now. If there's any hesitation about riding to the top of a recently active volcano, go to http://volcano.wr.usgs.gov/cvo/current_updates .php for weekly status updates for all Cascade volcanoes, including Mount St. Helens.

The most direct route to start this ride is Interstate 5 to Castle Rock and the junction with Washington Highway 504. Castle Rock

239

is about halfway between Portland and Olympia, Washington, so it makes an easy out-and-back day trip from either direction. Depending on where you start, the ride is a mix of urban navigation, 70-mph interstate, and moderate speeds on wide country roads that wander across rural southwestern Washington.

An alternate route from the north follows Washington Highway 505 to its junction with WA 504 about 10 miles east of the Mount St. Helens Visitor Center in Silver Lake. Take I-5 for about 43 miles south of Olympia to exit 63. Head east on WA 505 through Toledo to the junction with WA 504. Entering Toledo from the north, WA 505 makes a sharp left on Cowlitz Street a few blocks before crossing the Cowlitz River.

WA 505 runs straight east for about 5 miles through a patchwork of residential development, farms, and forest. After a 45-degree turn to the right, it moves through low, forested hills for about 7 miles until it joins WA 504, also known as Spirit Lake Highway (it's been called Spirit Lake Highway since it was rebuilt following the eruption).

From Portland, we prefer riding Interstate 205 north through Vancouver, Washington, rather than trying to navigate through the city. I-205 joins I-5 about 15 miles north of downtown Portland near the town of Salmon Creek. Follow I-5 north about 60 miles to Castle Rock and the junction with WA 504.

It's 52 miles and about 4,200 feet in elevation gain to the Johnston Ridge Observatory at the end of WA 504, so we recommend fueling up in Castle Rock. Your last option for fuel is in Kid Valley, about 3 miles east of the junction of WA 504 and WA 505.

The Mount St. Helens Visitor Center is 5 miles east of Castle Rock in Seaquest State Park. With interpretive exhibits, a theater, a nature trail to the shores of Silver Lake, and a bookstore, it's a great place to stop and learn about the mountain. Admission for adults is $3, $1 for kids ages 7 to 17.

If you'd rather head straight for the top, the Johnston Ridge Observatory has interpretive displays, a theater, ranger programs, and a bookstore as well.

Past the visitor center, WA 504 runs parallel to the shoreline

The observatory is named for volcanologist David Johnston, who was camped at an observation post on a ridge
about 6 miles from the volcano's center when Mount St.
Helens erupted. His final words, called in to the temporary
U.S. Geological Survey base in Vancouver, were "Vancouver, Vancouver, this is it!" He and his camp were swept
away when the volcano's side collapsed and a massive
avalanche of debris slid downhill.

Based on his research, which showed a bulge form-
ing on the mountainside, Johnston had disputed previ-
ous USGS forecasts that said the volcano's next eruption
would shoot straight up. He said the volcano would explode
sideways—which means he was, ironically, the only USGS
geologist to accurately predict the blast that killed him.
Johnston's body has never been found.

Johnston knew his work was dangerous. He and other
geologists observed warning signs, including small earthquakes, during the months leading up to the explosion.
But he felt the possibility of learning more about the way
volcanoes work—and coming up with ways to predict eruptions and thus save lives—was worth the risk.

When it appeared that Mount St. Helens might erupt,
Johnston was also one of the geologists who insisted the
area be evacuated, even though some people wanted the
evacuation order lifted. Many more lives, possibly thousands, would have been lost if most people hadn't gotten
out. It's no wonder Johnston is considered a hero. ●

of Silver Lake through dense forest of lowlands largely unaf-
fected by the 1980 eruption. The road crosses the Toutle River
and the North Fork of the Toutle River, climbing steadily toward
the summit.

About 27 miles east of I-5, Mount St. Helens comes into view
at the Hoffstadt Bluffs Visitor Center, which overlooks the North

At 2,340 feet long, Hoffstadt Creek Bridge is the biggest of the fourteen bridges built along WA 504 after the explosion.

Fork of the Toutle River with Mount St. Helens in the background. The debris avalanche triggered by the eruption traveled more than 13 miles down-valley, devastating the Toutle River Valley and filling it with a mix of volcanic debris, glacial ice, and probably water. In some places the debris was more than 150 feet deep.

As captivating as the view is from the Hoffstadt Bluffs, the many viewpoints and overlooks that follow get progressively better as you near the peak. If riding your bike up the side of a volcano isn't thrilling enough, or you want to get to the top faster than your bike will carry you, helicopter tours leave from the Hoffstadt Bluffs Visitor Center every half-hour between 11 a.m. and 6 p.m. The visitor center gift shop sells tickets.

About 3 miles east of Hoffstadt Bluffs, WA 504 reaches the western edge of the blast zone before crossing Hoffstadt Creek via the Hoffstadt Creek Bridge, one of fourteen spans built after the eruption. In the pullout on the north side of the road, interpretive signs overlook the bridge and explain the blast zone and the different levels of destruction within it.

East of the bridge, WA 504 continues climbing and twisting deeper into the blast zone. The farther into the blast zone, the less rapid the ecosystem's recovery. Some of the ridges and hillsides close to the Johnston Ridge Observatory are barren and scarred and look like they may never fully recover.

On the other hand, WA 504 itself is in great shape. As it continues to rise, the turns are big and wide and easy, with a few gently rolling hills thrown in now and then to keep things interesting. The last 7 miles get progressively steeper and the turns a little tighter, but unlike the ride up the mountain's east side to Spirit Lake and Windy Ridge, this is not a difficult or technical ride. Just pull back on the throttle and roll through the turns until

---

Steve: While I was standing at the rock wall lining the back deck of the Johnston Ridge Observatory, I heard the unmistakable *fwop-fwop-fwop* of a helicopter in the distance.

On the ride up I'd seen outfits offering helicopter tours of the peak, so I wasn't surprised to hear the sound, but I was disappointed. My first thought was, Great—all we need to ruin our view is a helicopter buzzing a couple hundred feet from where we're standing. When I tried to find the helicopter against the backdrop of the mountain, the massive scale of what I was looking at became clear: When I finally located it, the helicopter was just a tiny dark speck moving slowly right and left.

I instinctively reached for my camera, hoping to document the source of my indignation. After a few seconds it was lost from view, having departed the north side of the crater for the south. I don't condone invading our national monuments' airspace, but I quickly realized how absurd it would be to show anyone that photo. It would be equivalent to pointing out the housefly in an aerial photo of a football field. I replaced the lens cover and went back to appreciating the view. ●

Visitors congregate at the observatory for up-close views of the crater.

you reach the Johnston Ridge Observatory and the end of Spirit Lake Highway.

A monument pass (wristband) is required of all visitors and is sold inside the observatory for $8. If there's room in the saddlebags, pack a snack or a picnic, because there are no food services up top.

The view of Mount St. Helens from the back deck of the Johnston Ridge Observatory is impressive and expansive. The rangers offer programs that are entertaining and educational and also lead informative hikes. Numerous trails of all difficulty levels start at the observatory. If you're pressed for time, take the 0.5-mile walk on the Eruption Trail that begins near the viewing deck. Interpretive signs describe the fragility of slowly returning life as well as dramatic evidence of the incomprehensible shock this area endured during the 1980 blast.

Wander through the observatory and take a short hike, or eavesdrop on one or two ranger programs. After you've tried to comprehend the magnitude of the forces that created this massive crater and learned about the destruction that followed, it's understandable if your mood is a bit more somber on the ride home. Shake a bit of that feeling off, get back in the saddle, and point the bike west for a fun and relaxing downhill rewind of the ride up.

RIDE 25

Mount St. Helens—Windy Ridge

Directions:
north on I-5 to exit 21 toward WA 503 for Cougar and
Woodland
east on WA 503; becomes FR 90 east of Cougar
east on FR 90 to FR 25
north on FR 25 to intersection with FR 99
west on FR 99 to Windy Ridge

Total Distance:
about 250 miles round-trip

Time:
most of a day, depending on stops

Services:
Portland and surrounding suburbs of Woodland, Yale,
Cougar

Best Time of Year:
late spring to early fall (FR 99 is closed in winter)

Highlights:
serene country surroundings; challenging forest-service
roads through rugged terrain and the blast zone's forests of
dead timber; close-up views of the Mount St. Helens crater
from Windy Ridge

Mount St. Helens–Windy Ridge

504

Silver Lake

504

North Fork Toutle River

TOUTLE MOUNTAIN RANGE

South Fork Toutle River

Kalama River

503

Lake Merwin

GREEN MOUNTAIN

Ariel

Columbia River

5

Lewis River

Woodland

503

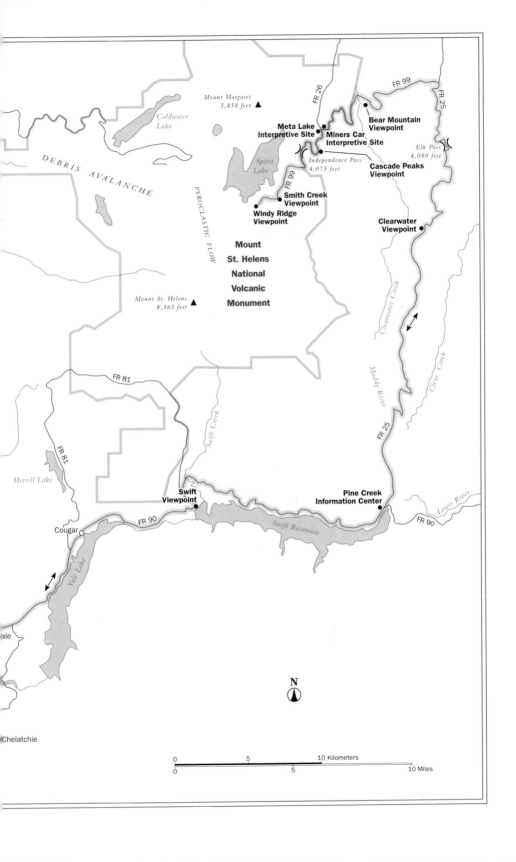

Coldwater
Lake

Mount Margaret
5,858 feet ▲

Meta Lake
Interpretive Site ●
FR 26
FR 99
● **Bear Mountain**
Viewpoint
FR 25

Miners Car
Interpretive Site

Elk Pass
4,080 feet

DEBRIS AVALANCHE

Spirit
Lake

Independence Pass
4,075 feet
Cascade Peaks
Viewpoint

PYROCLASTIC FLOW

FR 99
Smith Creek
Viewpoint ●

Windy Ridge
Viewpoint ●

Clearwater ●
Viewpoint

Mount
St. Helens
National
Volcanic
Monument

Mount St. Helens
8,363 feet ▲

Clearwater Creek

Muddy River

Clear Creek

FR 81

Swift Creek

FR 25

FR 81

Merrill Lake

Swift
Viewpoint ●

Pine Creek
Information Center ●

Lewis River

Cougar ○
FR 90
Swift Reservoir
FR 90

Yale Lake

ale

N
⬆

Chelatchie

0   5   10 Kilometers
0   5   10 Miles

Most people see the devastation caused by Mount St. Helens' 1980 eruption from the volcano's western side, which is easily accessible from Interstate 5. But Windy Ridge's views of eerie Spirit Lake, set amid miles of desolation on the remote eastern side, and far away from tourist amenities, give a better sense of just how much damage the explosion did and how long recovery takes.

Many roads scale Mount St. Helens' eastern slopes, but only one road goes to the top—or as close to the top as you can get on two wheels. This route rambles through gently rolling hills and lake-filled countryside, then trades well-maintained state highways for less civilized national forest roads as it tackles a ridge east of the crater and corkscrews through the blast zone to Windy Ridge.

If you've ridden Spirit Lake Highway to Johnston Ridge on the volcano's west flank and imagine the ride to Windy Ridge is similar, you're in for a surprise. Windy Ridge is accessible via Forest Road 25, which tracks north to south through mountainous terrain east of the crater, and Forest Road 99, which branches off from FR 25 into the blast zone and twists through exposed hillsides that took a direct hit from the eruptions. Allow us a few words of caution: Road conditions and debris-littered pavement testify to the instability of the underlying terrain, and the forest service's lack of funding only makes things worse. The result is that road conditions range from okay to poor to potentially hazardous. Cell reception is spotty, so this is a ride best done with a competent partner—at least let someone know where you're going and when you expect to return.

We don't mean to scare you; it's just that this ride may be challenging depending on your experience and skill level. Certain risks come with every adventure, and it's best to be aware of those and to plan for them before heading out.

This ride really begins once you get off I-5 and onto eastbound Washington Highway 503 at the little town of Woodland, about half an hour north of Portland and beyond the immediate reach of Vancouver's northern suburbs. WA 503 (also known as Lewis River Road) bounces into the hills, curves around the north shore of Lake Merwin, and rolls into the tiny hamlet of Yale.

Clearwater Viewpoint on FR 25 offers the first look at the crater and forests recovering since the eruption.

Near the center of Yale, a green-and-white road sign shows that one leg of WA 503 continues straight to the east while another turns right and heads south. Keep going straight. If you're up for a little detour on your return trip, WA 503 south from Yale is a decent alternative to I-5. It's a narrow, twisty lane, reminiscent of New England country roads, that eventually connects with Interstate 205 in the northeastern suburbs of Vancouver.

East of Yale, WA 503 runs along the shore of Yale Lake and into Cougar, the last option for fuel until you return this way or hit U.S. Highway 12 to the north (if you head that direction from Windy Ridge). It also has a couple mom-and-pop restaurants and a gas station with a well-stocked general store. There isn't a visitor center or cantina at Windy Ridge, and snacks and a drink are welcome treats at the top before you saddle up for the ride back down.

Becoming Forest Road 90 about 3 miles east of Cougar, the road wanders under a canopy of healthy trees beside Swift Reservoir as glistening sunlight occasionally flashes off the water and through the trees. Enjoy these roads east of Woodland: They're clean and smooth and fast, and they're as good as roads on this ride are going to get. It's tempting to push the limits, but watch the speedometer—there's a state patrol office near Cougar.

Just before FR 25 and FR 90 split, the Pine Creek Information Center—a valuable resource for anyone heading into Gifford Pinchot National Forest or Mount St. Helens National Volcanic Monument—sits in a clearing on the north side of the road. It's worth a stop if only to pick up a free copy of the *Volcano Review,* an informative guide to the monument with an overview map of the vicinity and a more-detailed map of the national monument. Less than a mile past the information center, FR 90 makes a right turn toward Troutlake and Carson, while we follow a sweeping bend to the left and head north on FR 25 through one of the area's longest stretches of continuous curves and climbs.

FR 25's first 5 miles wind through a broad, flat basin engulfed in dense, deep green forest. After the road crosses Muddy Creek, the forest opens up, and the pavement ascends through a string of steep S curves and switchbacks, knifing through the lower reaches of a rocky ridge in a quick introduction to what lies ahead. In the 15 miles from the base of the ridge to Elk Pass, the road throws down a gauntlet of randomly mixed twists; smooth linked S curves; and tight, steep switchbacks as it gains about 2,800 feet of elevation. The road implores you to ride hard, and there are segments that allow a little extra juice. But for the most part, it's a good idea to ride from Muddy Creek to Windy Ridge with a certain degree of restraint.

Short segments of high-quality asphalt may encourage you to lower your guard, but prepare to encounter gravel spit from the shoulder, rocks that tumbled from the cliffs above, sections of slumped asphalt, humps, heaves, patches of all shapes and sizes, and potholes big enough to eat your wheels. As if that weren't enough, a sizable elk population lives in the forest covering the ridge's foothills, so keep one eye on the road and another on the trees. This doesn't mean it's a horrible stretch; it's merely a challenge requiring a little more focus and discipline than most rides.

On the left at the far end of a few open curves about 10 miles past Muddy Creek, the Clearwater Viewpoint is the first of many chances to view the crater from various perspectives. About 10 miles from the crater as the crow flies, the viewpoint overlooks Clearwater Valley, which took a devastating blow in the Mount St. Helens explosion. With 24 twisty miles of riding ahead, it's an excellent place to take a break from manhandling the bike through the curves below and recharge for those above.

This ride's curves make it a hit with most bikers, even though the pavement has its challenges.

Young forests, recovering nicely since the 1980 eruption, blanket much of the valley and surrounding ridges here. In other sections, much taller, older trees appear to have escaped the blast's direct impact.

Leave the viewpoint and dive back into the trees, hills, and curves. The crater disappears from view; before long the road crests 4,080-foot Elk Pass, then descends slightly to the intersection with FR 99, the turn for Windy Ridge.

Sixteen miles of asphalt are coiled into the 10 miles between this intersection and Windy Ridge. The road climbs powerfully and zips through a satisfying sequence of linked S turns up the back side of a ridge and through older trees that must have still been standing after the eruption.

There are ten viewpoints along FR 99, including Windy Ridge. Bear Meadows is the first, and it's the only one surrounded by anything resembling normal forest. About a mile farther, the road makes a sharp right-hand turn and enters the blast zone at

Dead standing trees blanket the hills just past Blast Edge Viewpoint.

the Blast Edge Viewpoint. The Mount St. Helens eruption obliterated everything within 8 miles of the crater, as evidenced by the barren hills below the parking area, which is ringed by a line of still-standing dead trees. That contrasts with the hillside behind, which is covered in a mix of blast-affected old growth and new forest. It's a clear demonstration of how narrow the line was between complete annihilation and possible survival.

Heading deeper into the blast zone, the road passes below hillsides full of weathered but standing dead trees with new forest sprouting at their feet. On many of the hillsides below, trees lie tossed about like huge matchsticks, while others are more orderly, with all the trees lying parallel to each other, blown uphill in the direction of the blast.

Across the valley, the road traces a clearly visible path through dead trees and low vegetation along the barren hillsides. In some sections where you can see the apexes of multiple curves ahead, a part of your brain is telling you to ride hard, but the more-sensible part warns you not to take this road in haste. Successful navigation here requires extra focus, quick reflexes, good bike handling, and obstacle avoidance. Many of the tightest curves are not well marked and come up fast. Debris—ranging

Steve: As I rounded a tight right-hand curve on my way to Windy Ridge, I almost ran into a boulder, about half the size of a small car, sitting on the edge of my lane surrounded by cones and temporary barricades and wrapped in bright pink tape. Luckily, I swerved to avoid it and there wasn't any traffic in the oncoming lane. It's not something you see every day, so I stopped to take a couple photos and went on my way.

As I passed that spot on my return, the barricades were gone, and so was the boulder—replaced by a flagger, a front-end loader, and a deep divot where the big rock had landed and stuck. Scratches and gouges led to the outside edge of the pavement. I must have just missed the front-end loader as it pushed the boulder to a less-hazardous resting place below the road. ●

from dust and pebbles to massive boulders—tumbles from the hillsides above, often lying in the blind parts of curves. Sections of pavement have sunk, were patched, then sank again. Most of the road lacks guardrails—heightening the sense of exposure on the ride down—and error by an operator traveling in either direction could result in a speedy and unfortunate encounter with rocks and logs below.

Windy Ridge has a parking lot, a restroom, and a small seating area with a wind block, facing the crater to the west. A set of wooden stairs leaves the parking lot near the restrooms, zigzagging to the top of the ridge immediately to the east. With 428 steps by our count, the climb requires considerable effort; if you choose to make it, take your time. Your reward: sweeping views of the crater and a magnificent panoramic vista of Spirit Lake, which still has thousands of dead trees floating on its surface, ripped from the surrounding hillsides when the 600-mph explosion turned the lake into one giant wave of water. If you're a photography buff, you'll get the best images of the crater early in the

From the top of the stairs at Windy Ridge, you can see thousands of dead trees still floating on the surface of Spirit Lake.

day before the sun is too far overhead or after it dips below the rim. Spirit Lake and the raft of logs are spectacular with the sun hanging in the western sky.

Take your time, enjoy the views, and rest on the railing. On a clear day, you may see Mount Rainier, Mount Adams, and even Mount Hood in the distance. The 428 steps down are much easier than the climb up, but the journey is only half over, and the second half of the ride is no less challenging than the first. Return the way you came, possibly taking the other leg of WA 503 to the Vancouver suburbs, or go north on FR 25 as it meanders to US 12. Once you're on US 12, either I-5 or the Mount Rainier area is not far away.

EASTERN WASHINGTON

We like eastern Washington; we really do. But when there's so much great riding to do in all directions, much of this region feels like a place to ride through to get someplace more interesting.

The big problem is the terrain: hundreds of square miles of landscape that's remarkable mostly for its sheer monotony. It goes on and on in an apparently endless sweep of yellow vegetation, farmland, and occasional vineyard. This means the roads are straight, flat, and deadly boring. We mean that literally—we're afraid of falling asleep on the bike. This part of Washington is also very hot in summer (reaching 100 degrees or higher), windy, and cold with blowing snow in winter.

There are exceptions, of course—really satisfying riding on good twisty roads through alpine terrain. The most interesting rides are to the north and south, along the Columbia River or in the mountain ranges that straddle the Canadian border. The riding in northeastern Washington is similar to northeastern Oregon, but it covers a smaller geographic area and is harder to reach. And unless you're prepared to cross the Canada border, many of the rides are out-and-back.

Many riders head along the eastern edge of the Cascades, along the Columbia River valley, all the way from the Canadian border to northern Oregon. Washington Highway 821, Yakima Canyon Road, is a scenic and efficient alternative to the interstate between Yakima and Ellensburg. U.S. Highway 97 is a well-traveled route from Chelan or Yakima to the Klickitat/Mount Adams area (which we cover as a Portland-area day ride).

Like Yakima, Walla Walla is an increasingly popular destination for wine lovers and those who just want to dry out and warm up. It's easy to connect with if you're already in northeastern Oregon, which we prefer to crossing the prairie from Western Washington.

We've recommended our favorite eastern Washington rides here. Beyond that, when you're scanning a map for possible routes, look for bendy roads, often along rivers or ridges. A jaunt on them can relieve the tedium of a long ride across the high plains.

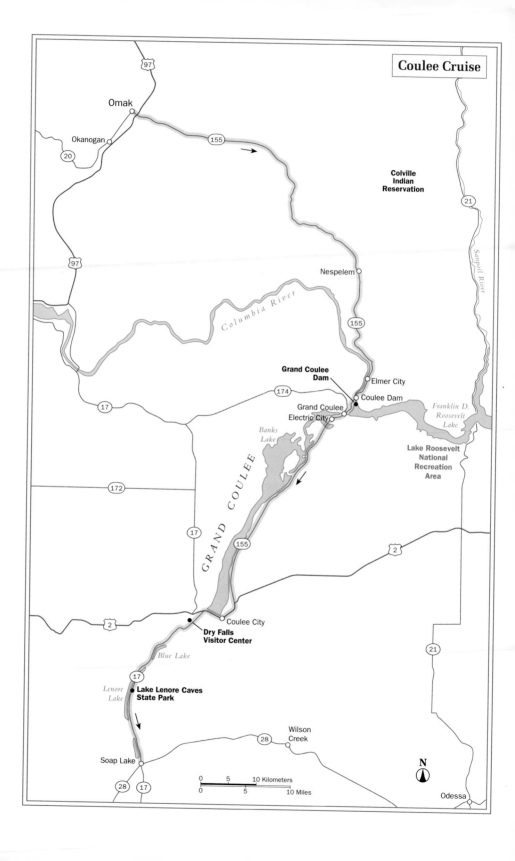

RIDE
26

Coulee Cruise

Directions:
from Omak:
south on WA 155 through Grand Coulee Dam and Electric City to Coulee City
west on US 2 across Dry Falls Dam
south on WA 17 to Soap Lake

Distance:
total distance from Omak to Soap Lake: 107 miles
Omak to Grand Coulee Dam: 55 miles
Grand Coulee Dam to Coulee City (intersection with WA 17): 29 miles
Coulee City to Soap Lake: 23 miles
(option) Soap Lake to Davenport via WA 28: about 80 miles
Davenport to Kettle Falls: 82 miles

Time:
half a day, perhaps a little more depending on time spent at Grand Coulee Dam and Dry Falls

Services:
Omak, Nespelem, Electric City, Coulee City, Soap Lake

Highlights:
varied terrain of central Washington; the mighty and ubiquitous Columbia River; a grand dam; lakes, caves, and waterfalls

This ride is more off the beaten track than many others in this book. It runs through north-central Washington, east of the Cascade Mountains—which for a lot of us is not really on the way to or from anywhere. This unique ride begins in the rain shadow of the Cascades, where vegetation is sparse and the terrain shows evidence of ancient volcanic activity. We climb through pine forest, descending to the barren banks of the region's mightiest river and that river's biggest dam, and glide along the shores of Banks Lake, a 27-mile-long reservoir with earthen dams on each end. The water in Banks Lake fills the northern portion of the Grand Coulee, an ancient glacial drainage. South of Banks Lake, it drops into a landscape scoured by massive, catastrophic floods from the end of the last ice age and passes the skeletal remnants of an ancient waterfall that was ten times the size of Niagara Falls.

We start in the interesting little town of Omak, about 44 miles south of the U.S.-Canada border at the intersection of U.S. Highway 97/20, Washington Highway 215, and Washington Highway 155. Omak hosts the Omak Stampede rodeo and "The World-Famous Omak Suicide Race." The race, held the second weekend of August every year, consists of riders on horseback careening at full gallop off the crest of "Suicide Hill," running and plunging 210 feet downhill into the Okanogan River. Horse and rider swim across the river, then make a short but spirited uphill sprint to the finish. If you can't make it to the stampede, a mural on the south side of the Main Street Market, on the northwest corner of Main Street and Central Avenue West in downtown Omak, provides one artist's representation of the event. Suicide Hill sits directly across the Okanogan River from the rodeo grounds, which are nestled east of Main Street in a sweeping bend in the river.

Omak is also interesting for the unusual diversity of businesses you'll find on or near Main Street (WA 215). In the span of a few blocks, you could get a tattoo or piercing, have your boots and tack repaired, or outfit your kid with a skateboard and hip attire to match. You could finish the day with a nice dinner at one of the finer restaurants that offer more than the usual pub food

Omak's annual "Suicide Race" is memorialized in this roadside mural.

one would expect to find in a town of this size in north-central Washington.

The Okanogan River makes a big sweeping turn to the west just as it reaches Omak. It separates the older part of town (including downtown) to the west from blooming suburbs to the east. US 97/20, the main north-south corridor, runs east of downtown; WA 215 intersects it a little northeast of downtown. Taking a right at this intersection will take you into downtown Omak. You're looking for WA 155, which cuts off to the southeast about a mile to the south.

Shortly after turning onto WA 155, you'll enter the Colville (pronounced Call-ville) Indian Reservation, more accurately the Confederated Tribes of the Colville Reservation. You are a guest traveling across the lands of a sovereign nation, so do your best to be respectful and courteous. If you have questions or would like to camp, fish, or hunt on tribal land, contact the Colville Reservation at (509) 634-3145, or via the Web at www.colvilletribes.com.

WA 155 immediately begins to climb its way southeast in nice, big sweepers interspersed with 1- or 2-mile-long stretches

Steve: On one trip to Canada, I was motoring northbound on US 97 when I heard what I thought was the sound of sticky tar-covered pebbles hitting the inside of my rear fender. The pavement didn't look new, so I stopped several times to investigate the sound's origins. I eventually realized that I was hearing the ball bearings popping out of a badly damaged rear wheel bearing.

I limped into Omak, found a hotel room, and grabbed a phone book. The list of motorcycle repair shops in Omak is short. It was late in the day on a Tuesday and technically after shop hours for Go Moto, but I called anyway. To my pleasant surprise, Dennis Ayiko, the owner and head mechanic, answered. He said he'd worked on a couple of Buells and would be willing to take a look at mine but wouldn't make any promises. We agreed that I would find a source for parts and meet him at his shop in the morning. The next morning, I slowly rode my disabled Buell the agonizing couple blocks to Go Moto.

By midday the next day, I had ordered the necessary parts from American Sport Bike (www.americansportbike.com). The company shipped them next-day delivery from southern California, but because of my remote location, they wouldn't guarantee Thursday delivery. When I called Dennis Thursday morning to let

of straight pavement. The map says you're riding through French Valley, but from the looks of the terrain and vegetation—dry grass and sagebrush—we'd swear we were somewhere in New Mexico.

About 9 miles southeast of Omak, the dry grass and sagebrush gives way to lodgepole pine, and the road begins a series of nice S curves and sweepers. This is a fun road, and the pavement is in good condition. Your tendency may be to push the speed limit, but we recommend that you sit back and enjoy the sights and smells of this alpine forest because it doesn't last long.

You climb to Disautel Summit at 3,252 feet, then descend through more curves and lodgepole forest until the little town of Nespelem, 37 miles from Omak.

him know I'd ordered parts, he surprised me again: They had already arrived.

Dennis had a tough time removing the bearing. The outer bearing race had cracked along the circumference and the inside half had welded itself to the wheel. By midday Thursday, he'd used every trick in the book to dislodge it, with no success—yet. I told him I'd wait to hear from him, hoping against hope he'd have me back on the road by Friday. By Friday noon, I couldn't wait any longer and called Go Moto. Dennis had the new bearings installed, had reassembled the wheel, and was about to take the bike for a test ride. I was back on the road by Friday afternoon.

Long story short: If you find yourself needing repairs near Omak, give Dennis a call. He has experience working on all kinds of bikes and will do whatever it takes to get you back on the road as quickly as possible.

The same goes for American Sport Bike. The owners, Al and Joanne Lighton, are motorcycle enthusiasts who know their stuff and will do what they can to get you the parts you need when you need them. Al is a mechanical engineer with a wealth of knowledge and a passion for Buells that dates back to the early tube-frame days, and Joanne rides dirt bikes and a Buell XB9S. ●

The terrain and the vegetation south of Nespelem couldn't be more different from that to the north. As soon as the road leaves town, the trees disappear, and so do the nicely linked turns. If you've studied your map, you know that, as the crow flies, you're about 15 miles north of Grand Coulee Dam. You also know that the Columbia River is making a huge, but as yet unseen, sweeping turn at the base of the rolling hills off to your right. From Nespelem, the road takes a shortcut high above the river and across rolling hills. Closer to the dam you get expansive views of the river below. WA 155 drops toward the river, then climbs away from it. At the crest of this short climb, there's a rugged gravel pullout at the base of a large gap in a rock outcropping. If

The Columbia River runs through yellow rolling hills below Grand Coulee Dam.

you stop, you'll see the waters of the Columbia gently flowing as it grinds its way to the Pacific Ocean.

Head south about 2.5 miles from the outcropping, through Elmer City, and down a quiet, tree-lined neighborhood street through the town of Coulee Dam. The road drops and crosses the Columbia River before climbing quickly to the parking lot for the Grand Coulee Dam Visitor Center. It seems strange that the roads leading to a dam of this size and significance are not set up to handle hordes of traffic. Unlike Nevada's massive Hoover Dam, the road does not pass across the top of this dam, which may explain the absence of security checkpoints.

From the parking lot, walk the grounds and view the dam from below. Another parking lot farther south offers views of the dam from above. Despite its size and reputation, Grand Coulee Dam is, visually, not exceptionally impressive. The Lake Roosevelt National Recreation Area encompasses the 130-mile-long reservoir behind the dam and Franklin D. Roosevelt Lake, which offers fishing, boating, and camping.

From Grand Coulee Dam, WA 155 climbs up and away from the Columbia River and tops out at Electric City. Electric City is well past its prime, consisting mostly of old run-down motels and restaurants from a bygone era. Riding south on WA 155, you surmise that most visitors are not drawn here to visit the dam but to recreate on Banks Lake. Banks Lake was created in 1951 by damming the north and south ends of an ancient basalt-lined channel of the Columbia River known as the Grand Coulee (the water that fills Banks Lake is pumped from Lake Roosevelt). The 27-mile-long reservoir is renowned for its epic large- and small-mouth bass fishing.

Follow the eastern shores of Banks Lake, with basalt cliffs and talus slopes towering above to the left. The road skims along the lake's edge, sometimes not more than 6 or 8 feet above the water-line. At Coulee City, the road crosses Dry Falls Dam at the southern end of Banks Lake. Within a few hundred feet of the crossing,

On your way through Electric City, be sure to stop and take a look at Emil Gehrke's windmill garden, just off WA 155 about 0.5 mile south of town. As a hobby, Gehrke made more than 100 colorful, whimsical windmills and whirligigs from scrap metal and used them to decorate his yard. When Gehrke offered to give the city his art as decorations for a public park, the city, which long fought to get him to clean up what it saw as junk, said "Absolutely not." But Gehrke got the last laugh. After the old man died, some of his neighbors donated land to display the windmills, now set up inside a fence. Still spinning on their posts, Gehrke's windmills just go to prove one man's eyesore is another's art. ●

Just south of Electric City, Emil Gehrke's colorful windmills rotate in the breeze.

Dry Falls, seen from the Dry Falls Overlook, was once the world's largest waterfall.

take a left onto Washington Highway 17. About 2 miles south of the turn watch for the Dry Falls viewpoint and visitor center.

This is one of the most interesting parts of this entire ride. Dry Falls is the remnant of what was once the largest waterfall in the world. The signs at the interpretive center overlooking the falls provide a complete explanation of what Dry Falls is, how it was created, and its significance. You need to see it and read about it at the same time to fully understand and appreciate the scale of what you are seeing.

WA 17 passes a series of lakes created as Dry Falls worked its way from Soap Lake to its present location. If you'd like to get off the bike and do a little exploring, watch for signs for the Lake Lenore caves, a series of naturally occurring caves that show evidence of use by prehistoric Native peoples. The caves are scattered about the park, but several are an easy 0.75-mile hike from the parking area. Others require hiking steep sandy trails and climbing across rock ledges. Lake Lenore Caves State Park is about 4 miles north of Sun Lakes State Park; you'll see signs for the caves once you pass Blue Lake.

Lake Lenore Caves is a short distance from the town of Soap Lake and the official end of the Coulee Corridor Scenic Byway.

The natural and man-made structures that helped shape the landscape north of here disappear and the dramatic scenery ends abruptly as the countryside opens into the vast rolling hills and agricultural lands that make up this part of Washington.

If you peeled off the Cascades Loop to ride the Coulee Corridor, you can pick up Washington Highway 28 in Soap Lake, head west toward Wenatchee, and rejoin the loop.

If you're headed to northeastern Washington, you could take WA 28 eastbound about 80 miles to its intersection with U.S. Highway 2 and Washington Highway 25 in the little town of Davenport. Take WA 25 north as it crosses the Spokane River at Fort Spokane, then follows the eastern contours of the 130-mile-long Lake Roosevelt all the way to the Canadian border. It's a pleasant ride on a good road with an endless array of recreational opportunities. For those who enjoy motorcycle camping, there are plenty of well-appointed campgrounds on the eastern shore of Lake Roosevelt. Most have boat launches and fish-cleaning stations, and some have showers. Because the National Park Service administers the Lake Roosevelt National Recreation Area, the symbols for them don't appear on most state road maps.

Restaurants

Omak
The Corner Bistro
19 East Apple Ave.
(509) 826-4188

Breadline Cafe
102 South Ash St.
(509) 826-5836

For motorcycle repairs:
Go Moto LLC
204 Omak Ave.
(509) 826-3930

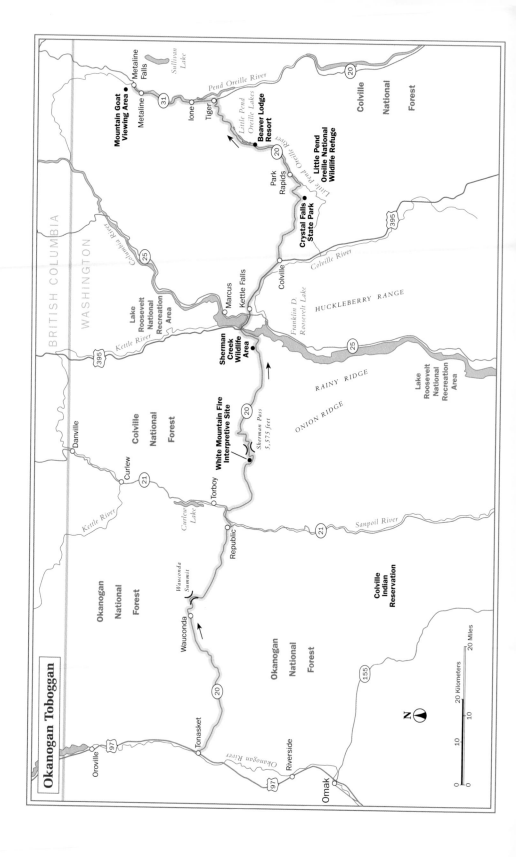

Okanogan Toboggan

RIDE

27

Okanogan Toboggan

Directions:
east on WA 20 from Tonasket to Tiger
north on WA 31 to Metaline Falls

Distance:
total distance: 143 miles
Tonasket to Republic: 40 miles
Republic to Kettle Falls: 44 miles
Kettle Falls to Colville: 9 miles
Colville to Metaline Falls: 50 miles

Time:
half a day or more, depending on stops

Best Time of Year:
summer, since the road hits high mountain passes

Highlights:
miles of twisty mountain roads; rustic little towns; Lake
Roosevelt National Recreation Area; easy access to
Canada

This ride offers a chance to experience a part of Washington many people never see: its sometimes dry, sometimes wooded northeastern corner. It starts in the arid Okanogan region that straddles the Canadian border, passes through national forests

Flanked by dry, barren hills, the Okanogan River nourishes the Okanogan Basin.

and small towns, crosses Lake Roosevelt, and ends on the banks of the Pend Oreille River near the border. Not all of this route is forested, but almost all of it is curves and hills, so it dispels the myth that all of Washington east of the Cascades is flat.

Tonasket, at the intersection of U.S. Highway 97 and Washington Highway 20, is about 22 miles from the Canadian border. Tonasket lies in the Okanogan Basin carved by glaciers during the last ice age; "the Okanogan," as it's commonly called, is an arid region that spans both sides of the border (it's spelled Okanagan in Canada and Okanogan in the United States). Its barren, rocky cliffs and sage-stippled foothills invoke images of southern Arizona. With a history and economy based on ranching, mining, orchards, and vineyards, it includes Oroville to the north and Omak, Okanogan, and Chelan to the south.

Heading slightly southeast, WA 20 begins to climb and enters a dry, narrow canyon, then runs through a series of S curves before making a sweeping left-hand turn and rounding the base of Barker Mountain. The terrain is so desiccated and rocky, and the turns come so fast, that you probably won't even notice Bonaparte Creek off to the right. Just past Barker Mountain, the road enters a broad agricultural valley, running through a couple of huge, wide-open sweepers before turning northeast. The smooth pavement in the valley and beyond makes for a fast ride toward Wauconda Summit.

The terrain and vegetation change as the road heads northeast. Gone are the parched and barren cliffs surrounding Tonasket. The road has gained significant elevation, and while the hills' southern faces remain sun-baked, the northern flanks are flush with healthy forest. Just past the ghost town of Wauconda, the road whips through a couple of fast, well-banked curves, climbing sharply and gaining about 800 feet before cresting Wauconda Summit.

At about 4,200 feet and in the trees, the summit can be refreshing when the valleys are hot, but downright cold when the lowlands are cool. The pavement is surprisingly clean, for the mountains, and in generally good shape. From the summit, it's 13 eastbound miles of well-marked and well-banked S curves through the Okanogan National Forest, then a steady descent into Republic.

Visit the Stonerose Interpretive Center and Eocene Fossil Site—a short walk from the center of town in Republic—to see the remains of ancient plants, fish, and insects. Why are the Stonerose fossils important? The volcanic and tectonic forces at play in the region 50 million years ago created warm, temperate uplands, a unique environment setting the stage for habitats in which plant and animal species rapidly appeared and diversified. The earliest existing fossil records of the rose and maple families, for example, were found in shale fossil beds at Stonerose.

For a small fee and with the correct tools (a hammer and cold chisel work best), visitors may look for fossils on the hillside near the interpretive center. If you didn't pack tools suitable for archaeological exploration, you can rent them at the center. You may keep three fossils per day—after you show your haul to the center's staff. The center has first dibs on anything you find and will keep any fossils that may be important to paleontology or its collection. ●

Built on the side of a hill, Republic has retained the look and feel of the Old West. It's very biker-friendly and popular with American and Canadian bikers alike. WA 20 makes a big S curve just west of town, then becomes West 6th Street for about a block before intersecting with Clark Avenue, the main north-south road through the heart of town.

Follow Clark Avenue / WA 20 south out of town and make the soft left at the junction of WA 20 and Washington Highway 21. About 2 miles east of town, WA 21 splits from WA 20 and heads north to Canada, crossing the border into Grand Forks (ride 32 in this book's British Columbia section describes the ride from Republic to Nakusp, BC).

WA 20 bears southeast into Colville National Forest before beginning its ascent to Sherman Pass. This stretch of road is similar to WA 20 east of Wauconda Summit: The pavement is in good condition with surprisingly well-marked and well-banked curves as it climbs deeper into the forest.

Almost within view of Sherman Pass, WA 20 enters the aftermath of the White Mountain fire. On August 24, 1988, lightning strikes ignited six fires in this area. Fanned by hot winds, they quickly became one fast-moving inferno that leaped from ridge to ridge, overwhelmed fire crews, and destroyed nearly 21,000 acres of Colville National Forest.

Hillsides scarred by the massive 1988 White Mountain fire are visible from one of the pullouts along WA 20.

Shortly after the road enters the burn area, pullouts allow you to view the recovering forest as well as the dead trees left standing—monuments to nature's powerful force. An interpretive site provides more views of the burn area as well as information about the fire's impact on the ecosystem, the recovery process, and the U.S. Forest Service's involvement in managing fires.

The road begins climbing in earnest just past the interpretive site, tossing in a few tight turns and big sweepers before reaching the summit. At 5,575 feet, Sherman Pass is Washington's highest maintained pass (this section of WA 20 is also called the Sherman Pass Scenic Byway). A rest-area overlook just past the summit's crest comes complete with a short, paved interpretive hike into the forest. Scars from the fire are visible on ridgelines to the west.

Leaving the pass, WA 20 continues winding through the national forest, slowly but perceptibly descending through a long series of gentle curves and rolling hills toward Kettle Falls, 26 miles to the east.

Don't bother asking around Kettle Falls for the town's namesake waterfalls. If you do, you'll probably be directed to Meyers Falls, south of town. The only connection is that the town of Kettle Falls was relocated to its present location north of Meyers Falls when the original town, the waterfall, and more than 21,000 acres were submerged in 1940 under Columbia River water impounded behind the Grand Coulee Dam.

Before then, Kettle Falls was a historically rich and important salmon and steelhead fishing site for Native American tribes. Tribes traveled from the coast and the plains to fish, trade, and socialize here. Some tribes relied on the fish to supply up to six months' worth of food for the coming year. The dam blocked the fish migration, ending a traditional way of life for the many Native cultures that revolved around it. ●

Even the street signs celebrate Colville's Western heritage.

WA 20 joins U.S. Highway 395 before it crosses Lake Roosevelt, and they join Washington Highway 25 about a mile west of Kettle Falls.

WA 20/US 395 continues east to Colville, where it makes a right onto Main Street, heads south 2 blocks, then leaves Colville eastbound via a left on 3rd Avenue. The downtown turn onto WA 20 is easy to miss. If you see the sidewalks and brick buildings at the north end of Main give way to wider streets and newer buildings set back from the street, you've missed it.

After Colville, the road climbs and twists through the rural outskirts of Colville toward the Selkirk Mountains. Homesteads are set back from the road, so stay alert to cross traffic and vehicles turning quickly on and off the pavement. By about 5 miles east of town, with the suburbs in the rearview mirror, you'll find the road in fine shape as it rises into the Selkirk Mountains and enters a long series of linked S curves and big sweepers.

Farther southeast, the Colville National Forest boundary flanks the road to the north, and the Little Pend Oreille National Wildlife Refuge lies to the south. (Pend Oreille, French for "hanging from the ears," was the name French explorers gave the local Native Americans because of the earrings they wore. It's pronounced something like pond-e-RAY.) The vehicular sorts of obstacles are behind you, but the vast tracts of public land here serve as forest habitat for a variety of wildlife, and you'll have plenty of opportunities to encounter it.

The pullout for Crystal Falls is about twenty minutes east of Colville, and the overlook is a 50-yard walk from the road. This isn't a spectacular waterfall, at least not in the middle of summer, but it's a pleasant place to take a break.

Steve: I decided to camp in Little Pend Oreille Lakes on one of my trips through here. I chose my site, surprised to find one unclaimed in the middle of summer. I set up camp and walked back to the entry kiosk to pay my fee, slipping the envelope into the ubiquitous steel collection tube slot.

Only then did I notice the warning that an "unruly" bear had been prowling the campground. The notice advised storing all food in coolers and all coolers inside locked cars. Since I was on a bike, I had neither a cooler nor a vehicle in which to store it. But it was too late to pull up camp and head elsewhere. With a little trepidation, I made dinner, thoroughly cleaned my dish, and tossed my soup can deep in the trash.

When I heard loud laughter coming from at least one big family at a nearby campsite, I considered the situation and tried to think like an unruly bear. After a little thought, I rationalized that any bear, even (or maybe especially) an unruly one, would surely head straight for the site with the greatest chance of yielding an easy food bonanza. Kids drop chips and popcorn and cheese curls on the ground; I don't. Besides, which of us would a bear consider the more tender, tasty morsel? I drifted off to sleep, confident I would not be visited by an unruly bear in the middle of the night—and I wasn't. ●

The forest grows noticeably denser as the road gains elevation and bends to the northeast. WA 20 enters the national forest near Little Pend Oreille Lakes, a recreation area enveloping a chain of small mountain lakes that offers fishing, camping, boating, off-road-vehicle trails, and horseback riding, as well as snowmobiling and cross-country skiing in winter. The Beaver Lodge Resort, a log inn set back from the road and decorated with a big wooden beaver, is the area's most memorable landmark.

Get early-morning scenery like this by camping at one of the Little Pend Oreille Lakes.

A couple miles past the lakes, the road begins descending through a series of tight curves and switchbacks to the junction with Washington Highway 31 and the remnants of Tiger. The only building left standing—the Tiger Store and Post Office, built in 1912—serves as a regional visitor center, museum, and gallery for local artists.

WA 31 heads north along the languid Pend Oreille River as both make their way toward Canada. The short stretch is an easy and pleasant ride with smooth, wide curves following the contours of the river.

Ione is about 3 miles up the road, and Metaline Falls—the last town before the Canadian border—is about 10 miles past that. There isn't much going on in either; they are small, quiet, remote communities and appear to like it that way. Ione is the smaller of the two and feels a bit more weathered. The historic buildings in Metaline Falls, built during its mining and lumber eras, help flesh it out. Both have a full range of services and offer easy access to all the pleasures the mountains and river provide. Either makes a reasonable base for riding farther north into

Canada (if that's your plan, see ride 32). Note that gas prices can be as much as 50 percent higher in Canada, so fill up in Ione or Metaline Falls.

If you prefer a larger town, backtrack to Colville.

Restaurants

Republic
The Klondike Motel
150 Clark St.
(509) 775-3555
Reasonable rates and biker-friendly (owned by a husband-and-wife team; he rides)

Tonasket
Okanogan River Co-op Deli
21 W. 4th St.
(509) 486-4188

Tonasket Pizza Company
15 W. 4th St.
(509) 486-4808

Raft of logs at east end of Duffey Lake attests to the strong winds that blow through the valley.

BRITISH COLUMBIA

Americans, grab your passports! One of the best things about riding in the Northwest is easy access to a whole different country. Canada has a lot to offer, including roads through rugged territory, old mining towns that have redefined themselves for tourism, and riding that ranges from fast and easy to tight and technical.

Vancouver is a thriving and diverse economic and cultural powerhouse. Victoria, on the southern tip of Vancouver Island, is an appropriately genteel reminder of Victorian times. Aside from those two cities and their suburbs, most of British Columbia is populated by a number of small, picturesque towns with roots in mining or timber.

Most cities and towns are surrounded in some way by mountains. They're located in river valleys or along lakeshores, at a

Known as the Crowsnest Highway or simply "the Crowsnest," British Columbia Highway 3 (BC 3) is the main thoroughfare across southwestern British Columbia, snaking from its western terminus in Hope, near Vancouver, to Medicine Hat in Alberta. It follows an old gold-rush trail through the mountains, connecting a series of historic towns and recreation spots. It's named for Crowsnest Pass on the continental divide on the BC–Alberta border. We've met some bikers who also call it "the Raven," which has a nice ring to it but isn't technically correct.

Even though it's the quickest land route from the west coast to Medicine Hat, its undulating path across a map is a good indicator of the mountainous terrain it encounters. From beginning to end, the Crowsnest's roller-coaster curves and climbs are popular with motorcyclists. Five of the seven rides in this section hit one segment or another of the Crowsnest Highway. ●

The terrain and the wildlife change as soon as you cross the border into Canada.

significantly lower elevation than the mountains around them. That means roads climb out of towns and through mountains before dropping, sometimes rapidly, through a series of steep and tight turns into the next town.

Because BC means mountains, you'll be riding up or down one valley or another or crossing a ridge or pass from one valley to the other. Every road goes through mountainous terrain, and Canadians are more willing to build roads in places Americans might think twice about. In those places, the condition of the pavement can be unpredictable and in some cases downright sketchy.

Watch for avalanche/slide signs, a good indication that you're entering a stretch of road built into a cliff or through a slide area, which means road conditions may deteriorate and are likely to be a little rough.

Almost without exception, gravel or paved pullouts a few kilometers outside towns have visitor information kiosks. These are valuable resources for getting acquainted with the towns and their road configurations in advance. They usually feature a map, a list of businesses, information about the town and what it's known for, and sometimes a calendar of events. The maps are even more useful because, unlike rural highways in the United States, main roads don't usually lead into town centers. Instead, traffic is routed to junctions at the outlying edges that connect the roads coming in from all directions. If you don't know what you're doing, it's easy to get on the right road but be headed in the wrong direction, or on the wrong road headed to a town you have no intention of visiting.

Road signage in BC can be confusing and challenging until you get the hang of it. For example, British Columbia Highways 3, 3A, and 3B intersect and run together for a while until one splits off. The confusion is magnified by BC's complex geography, which doesn't let roads run straight. Take British Columbia Highway 6: It winds its way southeast from Vernon to the Needles Fauquier ferry, north to Nakusp, south through New Denver and the Slocan Valley, east to Nelson, then south to the border.

For more about the particulars of getting into and riding in British Columbia, see "Riding in Canada" in the Helpful Information section at the front of this book.

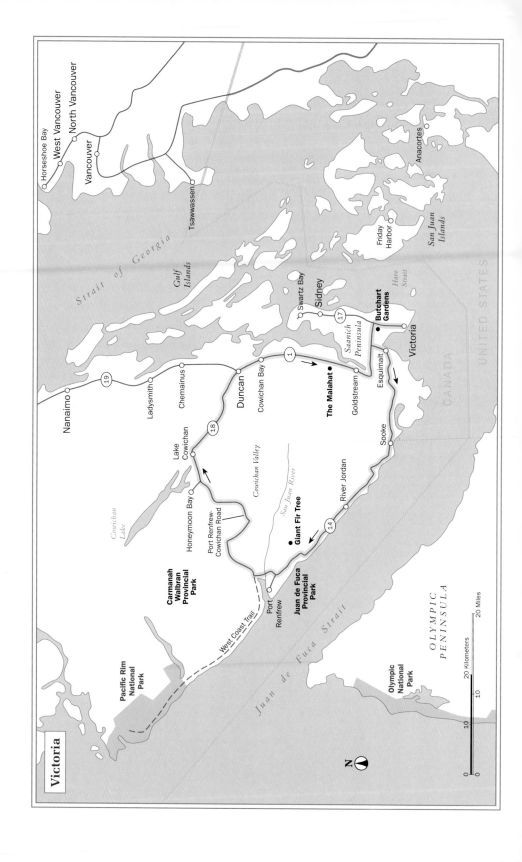

Victoria

RIDE

28

Victoria

Directions:
from Victoria:
west and north on BC 14
east on Port Renfrew-Cowichan Road
southeast on BC 18 from Lake Cowichan to Duncan
south on BC Highway 1 from Duncan to Victoria

Distance:
total distance: 158 miles (255 km) for whole "Marine Circle" loop
Swartz Bay to Victoria: 19 miles (31 km)
Victoria to Sooke: 23 miles (37 km)
Sooke to Port Renfrew: 46 miles (71 km)
Port Renfrew to Lake Cowichan: 32 miles (52 km)
Lake Cowichan to Victoria: 38 miles (61 km)

Time:
full day for the whole loop (short distances are deceptive, since some stretches are slow)

Services:
Victoria and suburbs, Sooke, Port Renfrew, Lake Cowichan, all towns between Duncan and Victoria

Best Time of Year:
late spring to fall

Highlights:

the island's Victorian charm; wild and sometimes woolly coastal and mountain roads; Vancouver Island's sunny side

Vancouver Island is full of contradictions. It's a massive, mountainous, rugged island crawling with wildlife, pounded by ocean waves, and covered in deep, dark forests. But its main city, Victoria, has long been a seat of highbrow culture and still revels in its old-fashioned charm. The island's west coast is wet

You'll have to take a ferry to Vancouver Island. And your ferry experience can be quite different depending on which one you take. Options include:

Coho's Black Ball Ferry Line runs twice a day each way from Port Angeles, Washington, to Victoria. The fare is about $30 each way, a little less than half the car fare. Reservations are highly recommended (there are only six bike spots); a reservation fee of $6 each way applies. The trip takes about ninety minutes. Since the sea can get rough across the Strait of Juan de Fuca, you'll have to secure your bike and you might also get seasick. For those with any kind of weak stomach, it's probably better to just head out from Vancouver. Go to www.cohoferry .com for information.

The Washington State ferry leaves from Anacortes, north of Seattle. It's a beautiful trip—if you like looking at the world from a boat. One way to break up this three-hour journey, if you have time for a multiday tip, is to hit the San Juan Islands (ride 16) and then take the ferry from Friday Harbor to Victoria, which cuts the journey into two pretty equal segments.

Note that you'll have to arrive ninety minutes before departure when you return to the States, since American customs and immigration procedures happen on the Canadian side.

and green, while the east coast is warmer, drier—and still pretty green. Victoria, on the south end, averages only 24 inches of rain a year (less than half of Vancouver's average), while the island's northwest coast can get 250 inches or more.

Its roads are also contradictions. Some run along rocky coastlines and through beautiful mountains, while others slog through suburban traffic. They can be boring (all that forest can seem endless) or too exciting (you're tooling along on a road you think is paved—and then, suddenly, it isn't). Since the 300-mile-long island is as big as some countries and covered with everything from four-lane highways to dirt logging roads, you could spend a

It's much easier if you're already in Canada. You'll spend half as much time on the ferry than you would from Anacortes, you don't have to worry about immigration hassles, and ferries leave about once an hour rather than twice a day. BC Ferries runs from Vancouver to Victoria—actually from the southern Vancouver suburb of Tsawwassen to the Victoria suburb of Swartz Bay. You can also take the Horseshoe Bay ferry from just northwest of Vancouver to Nanaimo, north of Victoria on the island's east coast. The motorcycle fare is about $25 each way for either route, half the car fare.

Motorcycles on oceangoing BC ferries are directed to their own waiting area and usually boarded first, as with many Washington State ferries. You don't need reservations unless it's a busy time (summer weekends are worst) or you're with a group (groups of six or more get a discount). It's best to arrive about twenty to thirty minutes early to ensure you're there at boarding time. When you're on the boat, you'll be given blocks to help stabilize the bike, but you shouldn't have trouble with the waves. These are big boats on a relatively protected crossing.

Go to www.bcferries.com for more information; the site is easy to use and, in true Canadian style, full of helpful tips. ●

lifetime getting to know it, and it could easily be the subject of its own book. We'll check out the island's scenic southern coasts; the west, which is rugged and remote; and the east, which has more amenities and faster roads but can at times feel like any suburb in the Pacific Northwest.

We'll start near Victoria. We prefer to stay outside the pricey city center, and most of the tourist-oriented towns along the east coast offer lodging. You could also make a day trip to Victoria from Vancouver on a long summer day.

Ferries from Tsawwassen land in Swartz Bay, near Sydney on the north end of the Saanich Peninsula, which has Victoria on its south end. It's about a half-hour from Victoria via the boring British Columbia Highway 17 (17A is a more curvy and scenic alternative that ends up in the same place). You'll pass Butchart Gardens, one of the island's most famous attractions. If you're a gardener, stop by for a tour of the splendid surroundings.

Victoria is a beautiful city full of things to do and see, most of them within walking distance of its famous waterfront promenade. Douglas Street is its major thoroughfare—and the start of BC Highway 1, the first leg of the Trans-Canada Highway. Always a political and economic center, Victoria's economy now thrives on tourism. Like any old city, its downtown is full of narrow streets and ways to get lost, so bring a map.

We're more interested in riding outside the city, so we head for the island's west coast. Much of it is so rugged that few roads even go there. British Columbia Highway 14, along the relatively dry south coast, is an exception. Like Victoria, this safe stretch is protected by the Olympic Peninsula's storm-blocking "rain shadow." You can do it as an out-and-back, turning back whenever you like. Or, if you're feeling adventurous and want to get away from civilization, make a loop via the newly paved forest road from Port Renfrew through the Lake Cowichan area to the east coast. That option will take a full day. While these roads are scenic, they are rarely fast.

Get onto BC 1, heading north for about 4 miles (7 km) to the intersection with BC 14. Following signs for Sooke and Port

Sooke's clear waters and relatively dry weather make it an attractive vacation spot.

Renfrew, go west on BC 14 as it leaves the Victoria suburbs and goes through increasingly forested territory, throwing in a few easy curves before it hits the coast at the small town of Sooke, 23 miles (37 km) later. Sooke is a very popular day trip from Victoria, which is good to keep in mind; the route can be crowded on a Saturday morning.

Sooke is a charming little town on its own little bay. Stop in at the Sooke Region Museum, which houses the regional visitor information center. Some people stop here and spend an afternoon before heading back to Victoria, maybe dipping their toes into the water at Sooke Potholes Provincial Park, a popular swimming spot, or exploring the rural roads around town.

After Sooke, everything becomes wilder. The next town with all services, Port Renfrew, is about 46 miles (71 km) away, which doesn't seem like much until you remember that the speed limit is 60 kph at best. The trip usually takes about two hours, not including stops. The road is a pretty typical two-lane coastal highway, with a few rough spots, a few curves, cliffs, sandy beaches, and bounteous forests. There aren't many passing lanes, which means possible torture by the line of traffic in front of you.

Starting about 23 miles (35 km) from Sooke at River Jordan, the road heads away from the beach and cuts through what feels like endless forest. Juan de Fuca Provincial Park stretches along the coast from here to Port Renfrew. The park's southern end features many critter-filled tide pools and some gorgeous beaches, most notably China Beach, 23 miles (37 km) from Sooke, a nice picnic spot and a good place to turn around if you don't feel like tackling the sometimes-rough roads ahead. While much of the island has been logged, the parkland on the road's east side preserves old-growth forest. That includes Canada's largest and oldest Douglas fir tree, thought to be up to 1,000 years old, with a 41-inch circumference.

Unfortunately, the next stretch of BC 14 doesn't live up to the surroundings. The surface is increasingly beat up, rutted, and rough. Now leaving the "rain shadow," it's more susceptible to storms; Port Renfrew gets 145 inches of rain a year, six times as much as Victoria. The highway climbs and falls with the pace of the coastal hills, but the shore isn't visible from the road, which

Christy: My list of animals to see in the wild before I die includes bald eagles, wolves, whales, and bears—especially bears. I went camping in Alaska bear country, but I never got closer than a warm pile of berry-filled scat. I'd about given up on ever seeing one of the elusive creatures, but I got my chance with a friend while driving on BC 14 north of Sooke. A black bear ambled right out in front of us, forcing us to slam on the brakes. I scrambled to get my camera out while the bear took its time crossing a mere 3 feet away.

By the time I'd located my camera, the bear had disappeared in the roadside brush. I suggested going after it to get a picture, but my friend would have none of it. "We are not molesting the bear," he said, and we continued down the road—a bit more slowly, and with our eyes peeled. ●

Secluded beaches south of Port Renfrew are prime picnic spots. The Olympic Peninsula is visible across the water.

means the roadside scenery gets pretty monotonous (trees, trees, and more trees). If you're lucky, you'll see some of the wildlife that's rampant through here—but be sure to spot it before you run over it.

If you get to Port Renfrew with time to spare and brought walking shoes, Botanical Beach is internationally renowned for its variety of intertidal sea creatures, from anemones to seals. It's a short walk from a gravel parking area just beyond Port Renfrew.

Port Renfrew is a very small town with a few food and lodging options (reservations are advised). From here, you can either return the way you came or tackle the next leg of the "Pacific Marine Circle Route." The local tourism Web site, www.crd .bc.ca/jdf/tourism, gives a blow-by-blow account of the route. Get to it by turning left at the BC Ambulance Building in Port Renfrew. About 0.5 mile down the road, as it traces Port San Juan Beach, make a right (going left will take you into the Pacheed-aht First Nations Reserve). In a bid to draw tourists by offering them an alternative to retracing BC 14, the last remaining gravel section of this 32-mile (52-km) logging road over the Vancouver

Island Range was finally paved in the summer of 2009. Before then, it was known for gobbling up tires and throwing any kind of vehicle off the road.

Even with constant improvements that have moved much of the road into 60-kph-plus territory, some sections are still slow-going, with climbs, drops, very tight turns, washboards, potholes, narrow bridges, and no services until Lake Cowichan. Those are the exact things some riders love about it and others hate. The payoffs are breathtaking scenery (including gigantic trees, atmospheric steep hillsides, and lush valleys) and not having to return to Victoria the way you came.

Since the latest improvements came just after our last research trip to Vancouver Island, we have not seen this incarnation in person. It was designed to accommodate passenger cars, but we recommend it with the usual caveats: Don't attempt it if weather is bad or you're not confident on twisty mountain roads. Stop in at the visitor center in Port Renfrew, conveniently located right at the turnoff for the road to Lake Cowichan, for up-to-date information.

You can relax again when the road drops and joins British Columbia Highway 18 in Cowichan Valley, home of Cowichan

The small and attractive Gulf Islands lie in the waters off Vancouver Island's southeastern coast.

Lake and many tourist resorts and campgrounds. At the valley's southeastern end, Duncan, "City of Totems," is its biggest town. Hand-carved totem poles decorate the attractive business district.

If you decide not to tackle the high road, Cowichan Lake is still worth visiting from the east via BC 1 and makes a relaxing day trip from Vancouver. On the Vancouver Island Range's dry side, this peaceful valley is one of the warmest places in all of Canada. The valley is also home to the Quw'utsun' tribe, the largest in BC (check out the cultural center just off BC 1 in Duncan to learn more about them). The Cowichan region is famous for its wine and hard cider, which might sound good right about now if you've just descended from the mountains.

From Duncan, make a right and go south on BC 1 toward Victoria; if you have time to explore it, the coast north of here is gorgeous. South of Duncan, the picturesque town of Cowichan Bay offers good dining options, especially if you like ice cream or cheese. The colorful wooden houses are built along a bay surrounded by forest, and sometimes on pilings right over the water.

Returning to Victoria, you'll find one of the island's most famously entertaining (if heavily used) stretches of road—the Malahat Highway section of BC 1. It's 16 miles (25 km) of climbs, drops, and scenic curves, but unlike other island roads, this one is fast; you'll probably hear complaints about how much speeding goes on along "the Malahat." It climbs to the top of 1,155-foot (352-meter) Malahat Summit, giving lots of great views of mountains, inlets, bays, islands, peninsulas, and, on a good day, the mainland. Several pullouts, including one right near the summit, allow you to enjoy the view without getting run over.

Restaurant

Port Renfrew
Coastal Kitchen Cafe
Parkinson Rd.
(250) 647-5545

RIDE

29

The Sea-to-Sky Highway

Directions:
north on BC 99 from Horseshoe Bay to Pemberton
northeast on BC 99 (the Duffey Lake Road) to Lillooet

Distance:
total distance: 174 miles (368 km)
Surrey to Horseshoe Bay: 28 miles (45 km)
Horseshoe Bay to Squamish: 27 miles (43 km)
Squamish to Whistler: 37 miles (60 km)
Whistler to Pemberton: 20 miles (32 km)
Pemberton to Lillooet: 62 miles (100 km)

Time:
one long day

Services:
Vancouver, Squamish, Whistler, Pemberton, Lillooet

Best Time of Year:
late spring to early fall

Highlights:
views from the edge of majestic Howe Sound; Whistler's
Olympic-caliber appeal; great riding along freshly paved
mountain highways

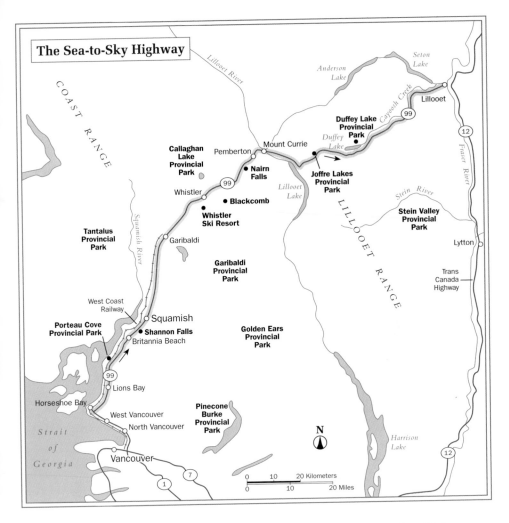

The Sea-to-Sky Highway

British Columbia Highway 99, known as the Sea-to-Sky Highway, meanders from coastal rain forest north of Vancouver into the Coast Mountains, arriving at Whistler—home to Whistler Blackcomb, a host resort for the Vancouver 2010 Winter Olympic and Paralympic Games. The highway charges northeast as the Duffey Lake Road, then leaves the mountains behind as it drops precipitously into historic Lillooet.

The suburbs of Vancouver make a great starting point. Lodging is considerably less expensive outside the downtown area, but the city center is easily accessible via the Sky Train, the metropolitan area's automated mass-transit system. Getting through Vancouver from the south is surprisingly easy: Follow signs for Maple Leaf Highway 1 and westbound BC 99. Highway 1 passes east of

The Gastown Steam Clock is a landmark in one of downtown Vancouver's oldest neighborhoods.

downtown into North Vancouver, then west through West Vancouver before the junction with BC 99's southern terminus on Horseshoe Bay, at the mouth of Howe Sound.

Built on the cliffs overlooking Howe Sound, Canada's southernmost fjord, BC 99 has a notorious history. For years it was a two-lane undivided highway with no outside barrier where motorists lost their lives due to bad weather, speeding, poor visibility, unsafe passing, and drunk driving. This led to nicknames such as "Killer Highway," "Highway of Death," and our personal favorite, the "Drive-to-Die-Highway." We wouldn't make light of tragedy, but we can only imagine that back in the day, riding a motorcycle on this paved death trap must have been an exciting but nerve-wracking affair.

Because BC 99 is the main artery from Vancouver to Whistler, British Columbia authorized major upgrades to accommodate increased traffic loads the 2010 Olympics would bring. That included widening stretches, adding a concrete divider, and, of course, installing fresh asphalt. The new pavement is in great shape with a lot of nice, smooth curves, expanded passing lanes, and barriers to divide traffic.

Squamish, at the head of Howe Sound, calls itself the "Outdoor Recreation Capital of Canada." Larger than Whistler, smaller than Vancouver, and equidistant from both, it affords easy access to the amenities of each. It's renowned for world-class rock climbing, windsurfing, and mountain biking. Heading north from

Steve: I was looking for a place to take some photos and pulled into Porteau Cove Provincial Park, on the west side of the road about midway between Horseshoe Bay and Squamish. An elderly couple pointed me to an area nearby with great views of the park and the sound. The gentleman explained that a couple of sunken vessels and artificial reefs in the park's waters provide habitat for a variety of marine life, making it a popular dive spot. He said he had dived here many times, especially in winter when the visibility in the cold water is much better than in summer.

When we parted company, they gave me a stern warning to be extra careful on BC 99. It's not as dangerous as it used to be, they said, but accidents are still common since, post-construction, "People drive like mad." ●

Squamish, the road leaves the coastal lowlands behind and begins climbing into the Coast Mountains. The terrain quickly grows steep, rugged, and beautiful. After giving you just enough time to adjust to the elevation change, the road rounds a big, fast curve, providing expansive and dramatic views of the glacier-encrusted granite peaks in Tantalus Provincial Park to the northwest. The view of the peaks from the road is fleeting, so it's worth spending a little time at the overlook here on the right. It's not well marked, but it's obvious enough, allowing plenty of time to stop.

Continuing north from Squamish, the road climbs sharply for the first 5 or 6 miles, then essentially levels off, ascending and descending gently through a series of narrow valleys filled with lush forest. The road is decent in places and a little beat-up in others—in other words, inconsistent, like most mountain roads in British Columbia. The road makes a slight turn to the northeast just past Garibaldi Lake and begins climbing with a little more energy toward Whistler.

You'll see evidence of Olympics-related road construction for about a 6-mile radius around Whistler. Since we lived in Utah before and during the 2002 Winter Olympic games held there, riding through Whistler brought back memories of what Utah endured to ensure it was ready for the crowds and, most important, the anticipated Olympics-related traffic. At least there, as in British Columbia, all that work resulted in some nice pavement to ride on afterward.

After Whistler, the road snakes its way deeper into the rugged mountains. Between Whistler and Pemberton, the hills grow a little steeper, the turns get a little tighter, and the pavement

With two interesting features—Nairn Falls and the Rubber Boa—Nairn Falls Provincial Park, about twenty minutes north of Whistler, makes for an interesting stop.

Tumbling from Green Lake near Whistler, the broad and fast-flowing Green River meets a fracture in the bedrock that constricts its flow. Rather than letting the water drop a full 197 feet in one steady stream, the fracture transforms it into a roaring cauldron of boiling white water. Silt, sand, and gravel carried by the current scour the rock, creating bowls and potholes. The action ends abruptly below two fenced lookout platforms on a rock outcropping.

As if the waterfall wasn't interesting enough, the park is also home to the only species of boa constrictor snake found in Canada. About 18 to 30 inches long, its thick body, loose skin, and soft scales give the snake its rubbery appearance. Adults are dark olive-green to brown in color, and their bellies are pale yellow to orangish. Also known as the "two-headed snake," it has practically no neck and tiny eyes, so it can be difficult to tell its head from its tail. The snake adds to the confusion when attacked by curling into a ball and hiding its head beneath its body. Chances of seeing one of these nocturnal, sluggish, secretive snakes is slim, since they are happiest when hiding beneath a damp log or in a pile of leaf litter. ●

deteriorates. Traffic drops off noticeably, with the terrain allowing for only the occasional passing lane.

Pemberton, a few miles up the road from Nairn Falls, has a
rustic, Old West character that seems a little contrived, like the
set of a Western movie. Locals enhance the look—a legacy of
the area's ranching and mining heritage—to attract tourism, but
the area is rightfully famous for its rich agriculture. Pemberton's
small airstrip serves Whistler, whose valley doesn't have room
for an airport of its own.

About 10 miles east of Pemberton, at the northwest corner of
Lillooet Lake, BC 99 becomes known as the Duffey Lake Road.
The entire look and feel of the ride changes rapidly and dramatically as it enters a series of steep switchbacks and climbs quickly
above the valley floor. As the road tops the first series of switchbacks, it's strikingly clear why this is called the Sea-to-Sky Highway. Surrounded by the rocky, snowcapped peaks of the Lillooet
Range to the south and the Cayoosh Range to the north, we're
definitely in the Sky portion.

Duffey Lake Road (also known as "the Duffey") from Pemberton to Lillooet is sometimes called British Columbia's most famous
motorcycle road. There are stretches where the asphalt is excellent, others where it is mediocre, and still others where it's missing
completely. But few roads can match its curves and climbs, sparse
traffic, rugged and remote surroundings, and unique scenery.

Until the early 1990s, "the Duffey" was an unpaved logging
road suitable only for the 4x4 crowd. Now, it seems custom-built
for sport bikes. Significant sections comprise steep, tight curves
followed by pavement that almost straightens out before it enters
another series of tight curves. This pattern repeats itself on the
climb to Cayoosh Pass as well as the descent to Lillooet. Sport
bikes are ideally suited for this sort of road, but it can be annoy-
ing if you're not on a sport bike or if you're riding two up or your
bike is heavy with touring gear.

About 10 miles past the first series of switchbacks, with the
road climbing hard and fast, Joffre Lakes Provincial Park comes
up quickly on the right. Glacier-packed peaks rising dramatically

The glacier-laden peaks of Joffre Lakes Provincial Park are visible from the road above the parking lot.

above dark green forest might hold your gaze long enough that you zip by the turn for the parking area. If you miss the turn, we strongly advise against trying to make a U-turn before the gravel parking lot about a mile east. A better view of the peaks is about 0.5 mile down a trail from the parking lot; beyond the viewpoint, the trail becomes rough and steep.

East of Joffre Lakes, the curves and climb continue. The highway crests Cayoosh Pass at 4,138 feet before turning to the northeast and descending almost imperceptibly to the shore of Duffey Lake, the road's namesake. The road traces the shore to the lake's northeastern end, where a rest area with a gravel boat ramp is the only safe place to stop for views of the lake and glacier-capped Mount Rohr looming in the background. The raft of logs clogging the lake's eastern end is testament to the strong winds that occasionally blast through the valley.

East of Duffey Lake, road conditions deteriorate as the pavement slips into a narrow valley between the Cayoosh and Lillooet ranges. Be prepared for bumps and heaves, slides, gravel, rocks, missing chunks of asphalt—in short, any of the worst conditions you might expect to encounter in a remote alpine environment. The road weaves back and forth across the ever-narrowing valley, crossing Cayoosh Creek on one-lane wood-planked bridges.

In Cayoosh Canyon, conditions get slightly worse before they get better. The road hugs steep rock walls, with ridges of the Cayoosh Range rising thousands of feet above the highway and the narrow canyon below, carved progressively deeper by the creek's rapidly descending waters. The final stretch to Lillooet descends through steep, tight switchbacks; 13 percent grades; highway that can turn to gravel without warning; 180-degree turns; and extreme drops, all of which leave little

Cayoosh Canyon makes a steep and somewhat treacherous snaking descent toward Lillooet.

room for operator error. It's not that technical, just a lot packed into a pretty short distance—a bit of a white-knuckler, but exciting.

As the highway descends toward Lillooet, the rapid and dramatic change in terrain and vegetation in a matter of a few miles is almost startling. Obviously in the rain shadow of the Coast Mountains, Lillooet only gets about 16 inches of precipitation annually. Some local microclimates receive less than 2 inches. With hot, dry summers and temperatures in the shade frequently topping 104 degrees, Lillooet fights for the title of "Canada's Hot Spot," vying with Lytton, about 38 miles to the southeast at the confluence of the Fraser and Thompson Rivers.

The historic town sits on the banks of the Fraser River (British Columbia's longest), which carves out the steep, deep walls of Fraser Canyon. These days, Lillooet takes advantage of its location and is a hub for recreation as well as agriculture on the arid plateau above. It's a good place to stay the night before picking up ride 30, which heads south from here into neighboring Thompson canyon.

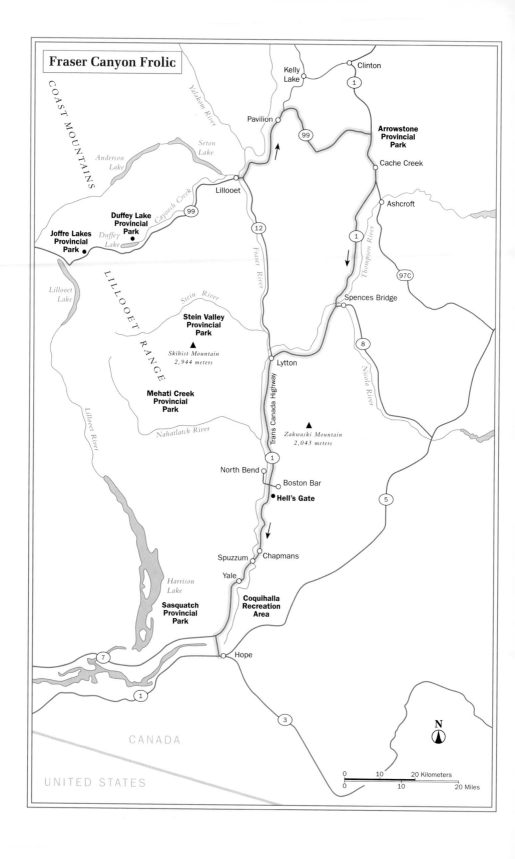

RIDE
30

Fraser Canyon Frolic

Directions:
east on BC 99 from Lillooet to BC 97
south on BC 97 to Cache Creek and junction with BC 1
south on Trans-Canada Highway 1 to Hope

Distance:
total distance: 168 miles
Lillooet to Cache Creek: 52 miles (86 km)
Cache Creek to Lytton: 50 miles (84 km)
Lytton to Boston Bar (Hell's Gate Canyon): 26 miles
(44 km)
Boston Bar to Hope: 40 miles (66 km)

Time:
four to five hours

Services:
Lillooet, Cache Creek, Lytton, Hope

Best Time of Year:
late spring to early fall (summer can be very hot)

Highlights:
basking in Canada's "hot spots"; historic, dramatic canyons; a visit to Hell's Gate; trains, trams, and tunnels

Beginning in Lillooet, one of Canada's warmest towns, this ride heads through varied terrain, leaving and rejoining Fraser Canyon, which divides the Coastal Range and the Canadian Cascades. En route, it takes the Trans-Canada Highway through the steep, dry slopes of Thompson Canyon, past where the Thompson and mighty Fraser Rivers meet before their waters rumble and grind through Fraser Canyon's south end. After riding high above the river, we drop into Hope, where the river turns west toward the Pacific.

Just south of Lillooet, British Columbia Highway 99 strikes out eastbound, crossing the Fraser River via the 23 Camels Bridge, then peels off to the north. It wends along a bench on Fraser Canyon's east side, as the river powers south hundreds of feet below.

It may not look that way now, but during the gold-rush days, prospectors flocked here to try their luck in the surrounding steep, sun-baked mountains.

Lillooet is "Mile 0" on the Cariboo Pavilion Road, built in 1858 by miners with picks and shovels, which linked the Cariboo gold fields and the rest of the world. For the first few years, the road's main traffic consisted of mules and other traditional pack animals delivering goods for the 16,000 prospectors who came through here. Then, someone had the bright idea—perhaps inspired by the dry surroundings—to import twenty-three camels from overseas. They didn't know that camels' feet are too soft for rocky roads, their tempers are notoriously short, and they smell terrible. If the miners had wanted pack animals with those qualifications, they would have hired each other and saved themselves considerable trouble.

The camels were soon abandoned—a couple ended up being eaten. A few were taken in by locals as very strange pets; the last one lived until 1896. Some local landmarks are named for this ill-fated camel brigade. ●

Leaving the canyon, the road climbs high into the sagebrush- and bunchgrass-covered hills to the east.

High above Fraser Canyon, views of the lightly forested Camelsfoot Range to the north are stunning but short-lived as the road sweeps through the rural community of Fountain Valley and a series of huge curves before it intersects with British Columbia Highway 97 about 6 miles north of Cache Creek. The descent from the plateau brings a welcome improvement in the pavement, with the road gods providing 25 to 30 miles of much-appreciated good, clean asphalt and even the occasional well-banked turn.

At Clinton, head south on British Columbia Highway 1, through the gold-rush town of Cache Creek. The place lost a lot of traffic with the completion of shorter and faster British Columbia Highway 5, which bypasses Fraser and Thompson Canyons. Despite that, it has plenty of lodging options, though prices are high given its out-of-the-way location and lack of activity. Dining options are severely limited; we've eaten at several places and can't in good conscience recommend any of them.

Heading south, BC 1 passes through about 6 miles of rolling, sage-covered hills before descending into Thompson Canyon,

A train chugs through Thompson Canyon near Cache Creek.

following the contours of the canyon wall as it drops closer to the fast-flowing, broad and clear Thompson River. The Canadian Pacific and Canadian National railway tracks run parallel to the river between the water and the road. Gravel pullouts give multidirectional views of the tracks and the occasional train directly below the cliffs.

The wide canyon gives the road plenty of room, and nice pavement snakes through a mix of big sweepers and the occasional short series of tighter turns to keep things interesting. After the road crosses to the east side of the river at Spences Bridge, the canyon narrows, and turns are a little tighter and come a little faster. A few miles later, the road whips through a short series of S curves, passes beneath a couple of old bridges, climbs a little higher up the canyon wall, and enters Fraser Canyon a few miles downstream.

At the confluence of the Fraser and Thompson Rivers (which together become the Fraser), Lytton vies with Lillooet, 38 miles up Fraser Canyon, for the title of Canada's Hot Spot. The rocky peaks of the Lillooet Range rise in the distance as forested slopes drop sharply to the river's edge.

Both rivers are known for high-quality, varied rafting, and river-rafting outfitters line the banks of both rivers on all sides of the confluence. More people raft Thompson River between Spences Bridge and Lytton—with its combination of hot summer weather and huge roller-coaster waves—than any other rafting trip in British Columbia.

Heading south, BC 1 climbs out of Lytton, clinging to a narrow strip of land high above the river. As the road weaves its way deeper into the canyon, the air grows cooler and the forest on both sides is noticeably thicker. It's obvious that the most arid section of the canyon is behind you.

About 10 miles south of Lytton, the road reaches Jackass Mountain Summit. It's 1,184 feet above sea level—and the Fraser River is about 600 feet straight down. A pullout gives views of the canyon in both directions, and a short walk from the overlook reveals the remnants of a highway barrier with a date stamp of 1951.

Hell's Gate Airtram departs every ten to fifteen minutes, descending more than 500 feet to the bottom of Fraser Canyon.

Explorer Simon Fraser (the namesake for the river and canyon) penned the first written description of Hell's Gate Canyon in his journal, describing the narrow passage as an "awesome gorge," and proclaiming, "Surely, this is the gate of hell."

Hell's Gate may not be the devil's doorstep, but it is the deepest and narrowest point in the canyon. At its highest volume, the river flows at about 25 miles per hour as more than 200 million gallons of water per minute—twice the volume of Niagara Falls—rushes between sheer rock walls a mere 110 feet apart.

If you'd like to watch rafters navigate the Hell's Gate rapids or want to know what 200 million gallons of water per minute looks like, take a ride on the Hell's Gate Airtram. One of few gondolas in the world that go down from their starting points, not up, it descends into the canyon and across to the other side. At the bottom, viewing platforms and a suspension bridge let visitors stand directly over the gates of hell. ●

Hollywood rolled into Hope in the fall of 1981 with a few dozen crew members who raised an American flag and put up American signs and newspaper stands, transforming the town to represent a place somewhere near Portland. They stayed for almost six weeks filming *First Blood* (also known as *Rambo*) starring Sylvester Stallone and Brian Dennehy. They also built a sheriff's office, a false front on an old gas station, and a gun shop—all of which would be sites of destruction in the film.

Movie madness struck even before filming began. When the filmmakers called for extras, 550 residents showed up to vie for 100 spots. Star-gazing was a new local pastime as Stallone and Dennehy strolled through town and frequented local businesses.

First Blood is perhaps the most famous movie filmed around Hope, but it was far from the last. Thanks to its small-town look and proximity to rugged canyons and majestic mountains, Hope is part of a collection of British Columbia locations referred to as "Hollywood North." Since the province is generally cheaper than the States, offers incentives to filmmakers, and features such a wide variety of terrain, it's been a stand-in for places ranging from Alaska to England to Southeast Asia. *Shoot to Kill,* starring Sidney Poitier, and much of *K2* were filmed in Fraser Canyon. In 2000, Jack Nicholson and Sean Penn arrived to film *The Pledge,* and in 2006, *Underworld: Evolution,* starring Kate Beckinsale, was shot 14 miles away in Yale.

For the most part, the pavement is decent, considering the environment in which it lies. This is not a fast highway with well-banked curves (though some are), and it isn't meant to be. The road closely follows the mountainside's indented contours with a speed limit high enough to make riding enjoyable while allowing an occasional glance at the spectacular scenery on all sides. The good conditions and scenery continue as the road stretches on to the south, making a gradual but steady descent and passing above Hell's Gate Canyon 26 miles south of Lytton.

Hope is part of a collection of British Columbia locations referred to as "Hollywood North."

First Blood spawned *Rambo II* through *IV,* as well countless parodies, and Hope grew into a fan mecca of sorts. In 2007, townspeople celebrated the twenty-fifth anniversary of *First Blood* with events including a screening of the film, a Rambo look-alike contest, a guided tour of filming sites, an exhibit of photos and memorabilia, and a pig roast.

The Hope visitor center at 919 Water Ave. has maps for walking and driving tours, and movie posters and stills are on display at the Hope Museum. ●

Between Boston Bar and Yale, BC 1 passes through a series of seven tunnels; the shortest is less than 200 feet long, while the longest is one of North America's longest at about 2,000 feet. Before it reaches the last tunnel, the road crosses to the west side of the canyon near Chapmans. As it descends, it snakes through a long series of big, smooth turns, sometimes nicely banked and in generally good condition. Mother Nature throws in a couple steep sections for your entertainment before you cruise past the gold-rush town of Yale and into a place called Hope.

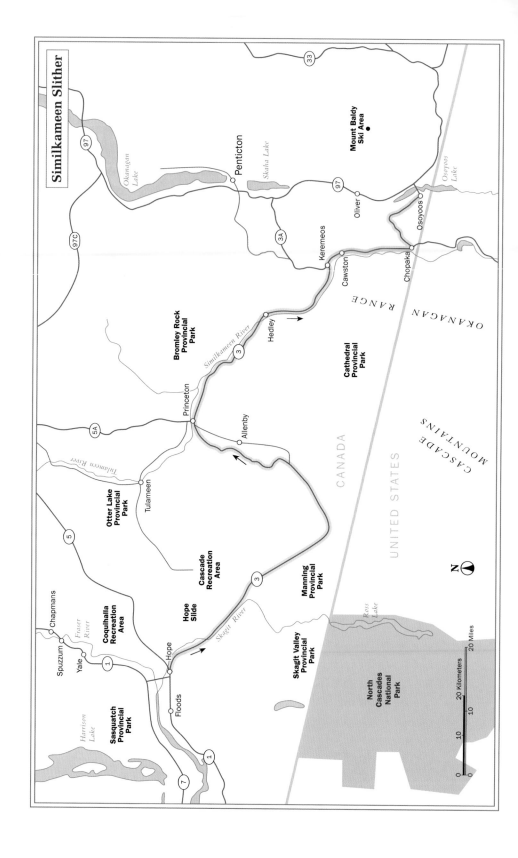

Similkameen Slither

RIDE

31

Similkameen Slither (Hope to Osoyoos)

Directions:
east on BC 3 from Hope through Princeton to Osoyoos

Distance:
total distance: 151 miles (242 km)
Hope to Allison Pass: 34 miles (54 km)
Allison Pass to Sunday Summit: 27 miles (11 km)
Sunday Summit to Princeton: 21 miles (32 km)
Princeton to Keremeos: 40 miles (67 km)
Keremeos to Osoyoos: 29 miles (48 km)

Time:
half a day, depending on stops

Services:
Hope, Hope Slide, Princeton, Keremeos, Osoyoos

Best Time of Year:
late spring to fall

Highlights:
the monumental Hope Slide; historic Hedley and the
Similkameen River Valley; handsome agricultural and resort
communities of Keremeos and Osoyoos; spotting a strange
and colorful lake

Hope is an attractive and appealing base for rides through mountains and valleys in any direction. At the southern end of Fraser Canyon, it has plenty of scenery, history, amenities, and personality. Heading east from Hope, British Columbia Highway 3 (the Crowsnest Highway) rises and falls as it snakes its way through southern British Columbia just north of the international border with the United States.

This route takes the Crowsnest through E. C. Manning Provincial Park, over Allison Pass, and into the Canadian Cascades' eastern reaches. From Princeton, it's a gentle, winding cruise through the Similkameen Valley and the rich agricultural town of Keremeos. This is a relatively short ride that allows plenty of time for dallying along the way and enjoying the funky little resort town of Osoyoos at the end.

This intricately carved face is one of many carvings adorning the sidewalks of Hope.

Whether you're riding or walking around Hope, you can't help but notice the wood carvings that adorn just about every street corner and populate Memorial Park in the center of town. In the early '90s, many trees in the park were afflicted with wood rot and were about to be cut down. That's when local chain-saw carver Pete Ryan proposed carving one of the stumps for the city to display. The resulting 12-foot-tall eagle was a hit with locals and tourists, and Ryan eventually agreed to carve another twenty-seven dead trees around town, a project that has since made Hope a "chain-saw carving capital."

Early each September, as part of the Hope Brigade Days, the town hosts an International Chain-saw Carving Competition where saw-wielding artists bring blocks of cedar to life. Carvings around town by Ryan and others include a massive grizzly bear guarding the Memorial Park entrance, a tribute to a loyal police dog, and intricate human faces. A walking- and driving-tour map showing carvings' locations is available at the Hope Visitor Center.

BC 3 starts out wide and fast as it leaves the southeastern edge of Hope and heads into the Canadian Cascades. It briefly joins British Columbia Highway 5, the closest thing British Columbia

In the early-morning hours of January 9, 1965, a small avalanche blocked BC 3 about 12 miles southeast of Hope, forcing four motorists to stop below Johnson Peak. At about 7 a.m., while the motorists waited for plows to clear the road, an earthquake beneath Johnson Peak caused the southwest slope of the mountain to let loose. One of the largest landslides ever recorded in Canada came rumbling to the valley floor, burying the motorists and their vehicles beneath 63 million cubic yards of debris.

The enormous mass displaced the entire volume of mud and water from Outram Lake, which lay directly below the peak, throwing it against the opposite side of the valley with such force that it wiped the valley wall down to bare rock before sloshing back up Johnson Peak's barren slope. Rocks, trees, mud, and enormous boulders settled into a pile almost 2 miles wide and more than 200 feet deep. Only two of the victims' bodies were found; the others have remained entombed with their cars since 1965.

The debris field was too large to move, so the highway was rerouted around it. But the scars left by the slide and the debris field—reminders of the incredible devastation they caused—are still clearly visible. You can get good views from a viewpoint a short distance from the highway. ●

has to an interstate, for which Hope is the southern terminus. The two roads split, with BC 5 heading north while this route stays on BC 3 toward the southeast, climbing toward Hope Slide.

Past the Hope Slide, the road continues climbing toward Allison Pass, reaching the summit in the middle of E. C. Manning Provincial Park. At 4,403 feet (1,342 meters), it's the highest point on the Crowsnest Highway between Hope and Princeton. Climbing toward the summit, the road is wide and fast, with plenty of big sweeping turns and passing lanes when you need them.

Near the west entrance to E. C. Manning Provincial Park, the road picks up the Skagit River on the right. Rather than running parallel, the road and the river bump up against each other, then separate when the road can't run low in the valley. When the highway must occasionally climb into the mountains, the grade steepens, turns tighten, and road conditions tend to deteriorate.

A mere three hours from Vancouver, Manning Park is a beloved getaway spot for urbanites who flock to its abundant full-service and undeveloped campsites (Lightning Lake has showers, but it's popular and fills up in summer; call 800-689-9025 to make reservations). Its terrain is mountainous but warmer and drier than many areas farther north, and some campgrounds are open year-round. Look for the marmot carving at the west entrance and the bear carving at the east.

Shortly after exiting the park's east gate, the road curves left, climbing out of the bottomland and snaking north up a narrow valley, topping out at Sunday Summit on the eastern edge of the Cascade Range. The highway scrambles over a succession of hills and ridgelines, gradually finding a level course. The road ahead is clearly visible on the ridges in the distance as it traces the contours of the increasingly dry, sparsely forested terrain it cuts through. The road eventually plunges into Princeton through a typical sequence of steep, sharp BC mountain curves.

Heading slightly southeast from Princeton, BC 3 follows the Similkameen River through a broad, semi-arid valley. In the summer, when the water level is lowest, the river's descent is almost imperceptible as the road courses over one gently rolling hill after another. Road conditions are excellent between Princeton and Keremeos, and your urge to pull back and throttle through the easy turns is tempered by an inclination to kick back and relax.

If it's summer and the pavement is radiating heat, the Similkameen is a great place to cool off. About fifteen minutes from Princeton, keep an eye out for Bromley Rock, a steep-faced stone rising about 50 feet above the river. It's a popular swimming hole and cliff-jumping spot. If cliff-jumping with a flock of teenagers isn't to your liking, sandy beaches offer easy access to the chilly water.

About 22 miles past Princeton, the road bends through the former gold-mining town of Hedley, where rusty remnants of old Mascot Mine buildings still cling to the rocky cliffs of Nickel Plate Mountain above town. Run by the Upper Similkameen Indian Band, the mine is open for tours (note that the tour involves taking 589 stairs into the mine). For more information, check at the Snaza'ist Discovery Centre—Snaza'ist (pronounced Sna-za-eest) is the Similkameen people's name for this valley. The name, appropriately, means "striped rock."

Continuing east, the road slides into Keremeos, where it makes a left on 7th Street and winds around east of downtown.

The Lower Similkameen Valley is dominated by farms, ranches, orchards, and vineyards.

It's no wonder that the heart of the Lower Similkameen Valley—a landscape dominated by farms, ranches, orchards, and vineyards—is called the "Fruit Stand Capital of Canada." The valley is famous for its more than 200 varieties of pepper and the sweet-tart taste of its tomatoes. Heading east out of town toward arid, sparsely forested mountains, the road makes a 90-degree turn and heads south, climbing to the bench lands overlooking the valley.

The healing mud and water of Spotted Lake are sacred to the Okanagan Valley's First Nations people.

Dropping in to Osoyoos, you may notice signs for something called Spotted Lake. The lake contains one of the world's highest concentrations of minerals, including magnesium sulfate (Epsom salts), calcium, and other trace minerals including silver and titanium. The healing mud and waters are sacred to the First Nations people of the Okanagan Valley and have long been used to alleviate aches and pains, including arthritis. In the summer, most of the water evaporates, leaving the minerals behind. This produces round, white-rimmed spots whose varying colors depend on their mineral composition. The lake is considered sacred and access is restricted, but you can get a good view from the gated entrance a few steps off the highway. ●

As the road extends south and climbs a little higher, orchards and vineyards cede to farms, and farms eventually yield to ranches.

BC 3 comes within a few miles of the U.S.-Canadian border before bending east in a sideways S as it snakes across Richter Pass, the southern tip of the Thompson Plateau that divides the Lower Similkameen Valley from the Okanagan Valley to the east. Beyond the summit, it's a smooth and steady descent to the western edge of Osoyoos and the junction with British Columbia Highway 97.

Osoyoos has a sort of Mediterranean look and feel to it. With a climate and amenities offering something for just about everyone, it's fast becoming a year-round resort community and home to a growing retiree population. It's a destination for sailing, wind-surfing, and waterskiing during the long, hot days of summer. In winter, people ski at Mount Baldy Ski Area to the east. Irrigation makes the desert valley lush and green, vineyards are creeping into every arable acre, and orchards produce a variety of sweet, juicy fruit including cherries, plums, peaches, and even bananas.

From this point near the U.S.-Canadian border and at the junction of the Crowsnest and BC 97, you've got many choices for your next destination. Grab a handful of cherries and a glass of wine and dangle your feet in the lake while you decide where to go next.

Restaurants

Osoyoos
Campo Marina Café
5907 Main St.
(250) 495-7650

The Ridge Brewing Company
9907 BC 3 (corner of BC 97 and BC 3)
(250) 495-7679

Smitty's
8906 Main St.
(250) 495-6333

RIDE 32

Kootenay Holiday (Republic to Nakusp)

Directions:

north on WA 21 from Republic, Washington

cross U.S.-Canada border at Danville into Carson, British Columbia

north on BC 41 (Government Road) to junction with BC 3

east on BC 3 to Castlegar

north on BC 3A to South Slocan, with an out-and-back on BC 3A to Nelson

north on BC 6 to Nakusp

Distance:

total distance from Republic to Nakusp: 215 miles (346 km)

Republic to Grand Forks, British Columbia: 35 miles (56 km)

Grand Forks to Castlegar: 60 miles (97 km)

Castlegar to Slocan: 42 miles (68 km)

Slocan to New Denver: 20 miles (32 km)

New Denver to Nakusp: 29 miles (47 km)

Time:

the better part of a day depending on stops and optional detour to Nelson

Services:

Republic, Grand Forks, Christina Lake, Castlegar, Glade, Nelson, Crescent Valley, Silverton, New Denver, Nakusp

Best Time of Year:
late spring to early fall

Highlights:
British Columbia's sunny Boundary Country; quaint resort towns; mountain, lake, and valley views from good roads

This ride begins in a rustic Western town and travels across the U.S.-Canadian border into British Columbia's arid Boundary Country. It offers a detour to funky Nelson in the West Kootenay Mountains before turning north up the Slocan Valley, along

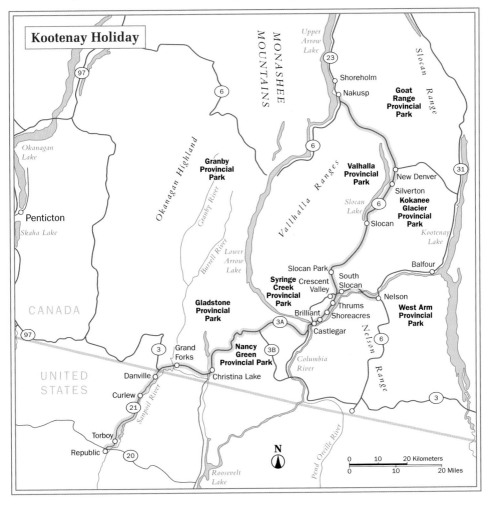

Kootenay Holiday

Slocan Lake. It lands in Nakusp, a welcoming town on the shore of Upper Arrow Lake.

Head north on Washington Highway 21 from Republic, Washington. The highway passes through several small towns that offer few services, then picks up the Kettle River in Curlew before leaving the United States at Danville, Washington. Crossing the border into Carson, British Columbia, WA 21 becomes British Columbia Highway 41—also known as Government Street—a mile-long spur connecting the border crossing with British Columbia Highway 3. Make a right onto BC 3, the Crowsnest Highway, and head east for just under 3 miles (about 4 km) to Grand Forks, whose motto is "Visit Grand Forks, Famous for Sunshine and Borscht."

As BC 3 heads east out of town, the passing lane disappears and two lanes of pavement climb into the mountains. The road crests a hill and then quickly drops to Christina Lake, a beautiful resort town on the southern shore of its namesake lake. Christina Lake lies atop a geothermal fault, which helps raise its average summer water temperatures to 23 degrees Celsius (about 73 degrees Fahrenheit).

BC 3 offers little more than a quick peek at the town before climbing into the hills along the lake's eastern edge and only a few fleeting glimpses of the lake before making a hard right about 5 miles outside of town. After that, the only view of it is in your rearview mirrors.

The road climbs steadily to Bonanza Pass, about 5,000 feet (1,535 meters) in elevation. From the summit, it's a steady descent into Castlegar through a long series of big, wide sweepers in heavily forested mountain terrain. The pavement isn't perfect, but it's better than average. Near Castlegar, BC 3 drops quickly through steep, tight turns to the southwest edge of town.

Castlegar lies at the confluence of the Kootenay and Columbia Rivers, at the southern end of the Arrow Lakes. It is also at the junction of several main highways and alternates, complicating navigation toward British Columbia Highway 3A, the next leg of this ride. To make things a little easier, stop at the visitor center on the hill west of town and familiarize yourself with the road configuration.

Steve: When I think of Canada, sunshine and borscht don't immediately come to mind, so I was puzzled by this apparently random combination in Grand Forks. Grand Forks' hot, dry summers explain the "sunshine" part of the motto. But what about borscht? My only experience with borscht was as a student in a Wisconsin middle school, when one of my classmates brought some as part of a class project. The entire class was required to taste it, and I wasn't impressed.

Borscht exists here courtesy of the Doukhobors, a Christian group of Russian origin. Among other things, they rejected secular government, Russian Orthodox priests, church rituals, and the divinity of Jesus. Near the end of the nineteenth century, their pacifism and desire to avoid government interference led them to flee Russia for Canada (they figured the climates would be similar, and the Canadian government was willing to take them in). They moved to Saskatchewan and then split into factions, one of which relocated its 8,000 believers to the Grand Forks area.

Although they tangled over the years with Canadian authorities over things like compulsory education (sometimes staging nude protests—as pacifists, they didn't have many options for getting attention), most of the Doukhobors eventually integrated into society. An estimated 15,000 to 20,000 descendants of the first Canadian Doukhobors now live in British Columbia, Alberta, and Saskatchewan, though only 3,000 or so still practice the religion. If you're a fan of borscht, you'll find a good bowl of it in Grand Forks. ●

Though they may sound confusing, these directions should help, too: Entering Castlegar on BC 3, downtown is off the left handlebar. Keep it there as you work your way around to the northeast corner of the city. Also, although we're heading toward

New Denver or Nakusp, we're following signs for Nelson. Don't follow any sign or take any exit that goes to the Town Centre or toward Rossland, Warfield, or Trout.

Follow BC 3 over the Columbia River via the Kinnaird Bridge. About a kilometer past the bridge, take the first exit ramp on the right, following signs for BC 3A and Nelson. BC 3 goes straight, heading toward Salmo. The ramp loops around past the airport, and BC 3A curves slightly to your right, or northeast. The road is relatively straight and flat, with the Kootenay River off the right handlebar.

About 12 miles (20 km) past the airport, you encounter a stoplight at an intersection that doesn't seem to need one. Make a left onto British Columbia Highway 6. About a mile later, on a bend in the Slocan River that bumps right up against the road, BC 6 enters Crescent Valley. This energetic little town at the valley's southern end rests on the edge of a beautiful sandy beach that's within walking distance of the road. With the easily accessible river, a natural-foods store, and gas station/convenience store, it's a great place to fuel up, stock up, and strip off the riding gear for a refreshing dip before heading north.

Rather than immediately heading left on BC 6, consider continuing on BC 3A eastbound along the Kootenay River to the funky Victorian town of Nelson, which sits on a hill overlooking the West Arm of Kootenay Lake. Offering a mix of high-end boutiques, restaurants, hemp stores, and head shops, Nelson makes a good lunch detour or a chance to get that hemp hat you've been wanting.

BC 6 is a well-known motorcycle road, and the reasons are obvious. Road conditions are excellent, the scenery is spectacular, and the riding is not as technical as some of the other rides in this part of British Columbia. As you ride north up the Slocan Valley—passing between the Selkirk Mountains to the east and the Monashees to the west—rocky peaks are visible at every turn, poking their foreheads above forested mountainsides. The road parallels the Slocan River, passing through the tiny hamlets of Slocan Park and Winlaw before reaching Slocan on the southern shores of Slocan Lake.

Steve: On my first visit to Nelson, I noticed that the town and surrounding area were full of wide-eyed, dreadlocked twenty-somethings who looked as if they'd just left a Phish concert, as well as a significant number of fifty-something hippies who refuse to give up the lifestyle.

British Columbia is well known for the high-quality marijuana it produces—and a high tolerance for its use. While it is illegal to possess marijuana in Canada, Nelson is known in some circles for easy access to a range of "medicinal" herbs, including the famous "BC Bud."

Back in the States, I did a little research. One Web site I visited claimed that one head shop in Nelson will sell pot to anyone over the age of nineteen who has proper identification. Another asserted that some cops (Royal Canadian Mounted Police, or RCMP as they're called in Canada) will take your weed to smoke it themselves, rather than busting you. Yet another warned that if you're caught with baggies, scales, or other selling paraphernalia, you may be charged with trafficking.

Even if I did indulge, I would be crazy to try bringing even a small quantity across the border. And I understand why the border agent gave me a little extra scrutiny, asking me to open two of my cases when I crossed back into the States. ●

Leaving Slocan, BC 6 climbs into the mountains east of the lake, clinging to a thin strip of highly engineered land just wide enough for two lanes of pavement and a concrete barrier. Despite the stunning scenery between Slocan and Silverton, signs warn motorists not to stop along the road, and there are no scenic overlooks.

After descending from the ridge above Slocan Lake and back to the lake's edge, the road enters Silverton. The village has done an excellent job restoring buildings from its mining-town era,

BC 6 hugs the side of the mountain above Slocan Lake south of Silverton.

but unlike Christina Lake and Crescent Valley, the beach was deserted when we came through, and the town, almost empty, felt forgotten.

Another 3 miles up the road, New Denver also has roots in the silver rush of the late 1880s and the logging boom that followed. Beautiful and sedate, it's nestled on the eastern shore of Slocan Lake at the junction of BC 6 and British Columbia Highway 31A. Surrounded by the Selkirk Mountains' Valhalla peaks, which reach almost 7,000 feet, New Denver has remade itself into a hub for outdoor activities including hiking, biking, fishing, and even scuba diving.

Leaving the enchanting Slocan Valley, BC 6 continues past the tip of the lake and through a gap in the mountains via a series of relatively flat, big, wide, fast turns. The road zips from the Summit Lake Ski Area to the Summit Lake rest area to Summit Lake Provincial Park, then makes an easy descent into Nakusp on the shore of Upper Arrow Lake. Encircled by the Selkirk Mountains to the east, the Valhalla range to the south, and the Monashees to the west, Nakusp is a gem. And with a wide, sandy beach a short walk from both downtown and a municipal campground, as well

The Summit Lake rest area provides a beautiful and peaceful respite from the road.

About 17 miles northwest of New Denver, BC 6 rounds a curve, crests a slight rise, and greets the southern shore of Summit Lake. The best part: the Summit Lake rest area tucked into a little point jutting into the lake. The mountains to the north, which rise above the lake and descend to the water's edge, are a magnificent backdrop for weary travelers. Stroll from the parking area to the shore and soak up the late-afternoon light reflecting the peaks in the water's surface. Nakusp, the end of this day's ride, is a quick 12 miles up the road, so relax and enjoy.

For those who want to stay longer, Summit Lake Provincial Park—about a mile west of the rest area—gives visitors access to canoeing, fishing, or swimming in the lake's clear, crisp mountain water. The park rests on a point almost completely surrounded by water, giving campers the illusion of being on an island, and mountain goats make an occasional appearance on the outcroppings above the lake. ●

The Leland Hotel in Nakusp offers lodging and dining that are obviously biker friendly.

as two hot springs a short drive from town, it's a favorite vacation spot in this part of British Columbia.

The Nakusp Municipal Campground is well used despite being a little rough around the edges, but we can only assume it isn't used to accommodating motorcycle campers. It seems designed for four-wheeled vehicles, which dig telltale ruts in its dirt roads. The parking at some of the sites is a little uneven, making it difficult to get your bike in or out. And $22 for a camp-site is a little steep given the place's general condition; but then, everything north of the border seems to cost half again as much as it does in the States.

The upside: The campground is close to town and within walking distance of the beach, and it has showers, a welcome ame-nity at the end of a long day on the bike. Some things to know before you go: Check in with the manager before choosing your site (his trailer is adjacent to the restrooms); you don't want to set up in a site that someone has already reserved. Credit cards and checks are not accepted, but they do take American cash. If you don't have exact change, you'll get your change in Canadian dollars, which may work in your favor since showers require two loonies (the gold-colored Canadian dollar coins with a loon on one side).

Restaurants and Lodging

Grand Forks
The Borscht Bowl
258 Market Ave.
(250) 442-5977

Nakusp
The Halcyon Hot Springs Resort
20 miles (32 km) north of Nakusp on BC 23, on Upper Arrow Lake
(250) 265-3554

Leland Hotel
96 4th Ave. SW
(250) 265-4221

Nakusp Hot Springs
8500 Hot Springs Rd.
(about a mile off BC 23 down a paved road)
(250) 265-4528

Nakusp Municipal Campground
314 8th Ave. NW
(250) 265-1061
www.nakuspcampground.com

RIDE

33

Monashee Mash (Nakusp to Osoyoos)

Directions:

west on BC 6 from Nakusp to Vernon (via Needles Ferry)
south on BC 97 to Kelowna
east on BC 33 to junction with BC 3 (the Crowsnest)
west on BC 3 to Osoyoos

Distance:

total distance: 258 miles
Nakusp to Needles Ferry at Fauquier: 34 miles (57 km)
Needles to Vernon: 81 miles (135 km)
Vernon to Kelowna: 31 miles (52 km)
Kelowna to Rock Creek: 81 miles (135 km)
Rock Creek to Osoyoos: 31 miles (52km)

Time:

one long day

Services:

Cherryville, Lumby, Coldstream, Vernon, Lake Country,
Kelowna, Rutland, Westbridge, Beaverdell, Rock Creek,
Osoyoos

Best Time of Year:

late spring to early fall

Highlights:
the addictive Mushroom Addition; a cruise on the Needles
Ferry; technical riding on BC 6; the scenic Okanagan Valley
and highlands

After a jaunt south into the Kootenay region and a short ferry
ride across Lower Arrow Lake, this becomes a challenging ride
through the rugged Monashee Mountains toward the resort country of the Okanagan Valley. But rather than slicing through the
resorts' heart, it takes a road less traveled through the Okanagan

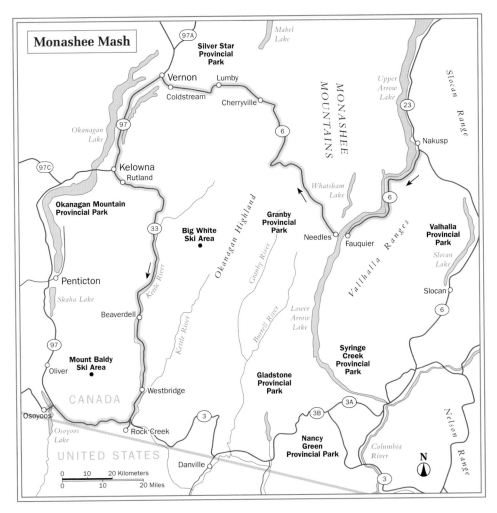

Monashee Mash

Even when air is hazy from forest fires, a refreshing dip in Upper Arrow Lake is a great way to prepare for a day on the road.

Highlands, climbing west into the hills along the border. It drops into the lakeside town of Osoyoos at the southern end of the Okanagan Valley.

Heading south from Nakusp, British Columbia Highway 6 runs through a mix of dense forest and exposed cliffs, tracing the eastern shore of the Arrow Lakes. An occasional opening in the trees or scenic overlook offers glimpses of the lake and the Monashee Mountains that descend to Lower Arrow Lake's western shore. About fifteen minutes south of Nakusp, you may notice what look like big baskets of dead twigs on the cross-timbers of power poles beside the highway. Osprey like to build their nests near the water in which they fish, and the cross-members of the power poles are as good a spot as any.

It's a short ride to Fauquier, where Lower Arrow Lake interrupts BC 6's westward progress. The Needles Cable Ferry picks up where the road leaves off, crossing a narrow section of the lake to Needles on the west side. You may want to do yourself a favor and fuel up before boarding the ferry. Why? One: There is no gas for the next 60 miles of hard riding between Needles and Lumby, and two, the Mushroom Addition.

Stop at the Mushroom Addition restaurant before or after the Needles Ferry.

Steve: Roger and Sandra Stephen, who own Fauquier Gas West and Mushroom Addition, are extremely biker-friendly and rightfully proud of their businesses and the reputation they've built. While you fill up, Roger will give your windshield the best scratch-free cleaning it's seen in a long time. He'll likely ask about your travels, and if you ask about his restaurant, he'll tell you about the specials and brag about being written up in magazines and Web sites. Roger also keeps a running tally of how many bikes have visited so far that season.

Don't miss the chance to grab a meal at the Mushroom Addition. If it isn't full of riders when you arrive, chances are it will be when you leave. It's famous for serving a wide variety of wild mushrooms, all harvested in the Arrow Lakes region, but I also recommend the zucchini pancakes. Zucchini pancakes sounded weird to me at first, but I love zucchini bread and figured what the heck—since they came with eggs, sausage, and toast, I had plenty to eat if I didn't like them. They were delicious, with a texture almost like a thick potato pancake (but better) and real Canadian maple syrup. I'd like to get my hands on that recipe. This is one of those places to circle on your map and ride the roads to get there, even if it's a little out of your way. ●

The Mushroom Addition restaurant and its neighboring convenience store, Fauquier Gas West, are set back off the highway along with a liquor store and a small market on what looks like a short frontage road just before the ferry dock. If you get to the ferry, you just missed it.

Catch the Needles Cable Ferry—with capacity for 30 vehicles and 144 passengers and a crossing time of about five minutes—just down the road from the Mushroom Addition. From Fauquier, it runs every thirty minutes on the hour and half-hour from 5 a.m. to 10 p.m.

As its name implies, the diesel-powered ferry travels back and forth across the lake using a pair of suspended 1-inch-diameter, plastic-coated cables. Not much is left of Needles since the town was flooded in the late 1960s after the Hugh Keenleyside Dam was built at Castlegar. The residents abandoned the town; the ferry landing and a small cemetery are all that remain.

Once the ferry docks, it's a mad dash onto BC 6 as bikes scramble to get in front of cars and cars try to get in front of any vehicle that might impede their progress. The road immediately starts climbing, making a V through a couple of switchbacks before beginning a long climb and tacking back and forth up a relatively wide valley.

As the valley narrows, the road swings to the left, entering one of the most technical sections of riding in the region. The road from Needles to Lumby is a combination of some of the best riding in British Columbia and some of the most unpredictable conditions you're likely to encounter. Some sections are wide open, fast, and fun; and others are more technical. For most riders, it's an exciting and rewarding ride that may at times be more challenging than what they are accustomed to.

The highway is very lightly traveled. Stretches pass through dense forest that comes right to the shoulder, with good pavement and a long procession of gently sweeping turns. Other sections pass through ranchlands where cattle lounge by the roadside, unflinching as you zip by within feet of them.

On the other hand, BC 6 passes through a narrow valley in the rugged Monashee Mountains, with zones you may find exhilarating or challenging, depending on the type of bike you're riding and your experience level. In addition to questionable pavement and the normal range of hazards you'd expect on a remote mountain road, some of these slide zones bring steep climbs with extremely tight curves, limited-visibility hills, narrow S curves or switchbacks on the downside, or some combination of the above. It's a good idea to heed slide-zone signs and check your speed.

About 50 miles from the ferry, the highway enters the former gold-mining town of Cherryville. If your focus is more on the road than the surroundings—and perhaps it should be—you'll be forgiven for zipping past the Gold Pan Café. Biker-friendly and serving hearty home-cooked meals, it's a worthy spot for riders heading in either direction to recharge and regroup.

For about the next 10 miles, the road passes through the Blue Springs Valley before reaching Lumby, where the valley widens, traffic increases significantly, and the pavement becomes downright civilized. If it's a nice weekend, the few gas stations in Lumby will all be crowded. If you filled up in Fauquier and don't want to get in line here, it's only about 20 miles to Vernon.

West of Lumby, the terrain opens up, road quality improves, and riding is easier but less exciting than on BC 6 to the east.

BC 6 intersects with British Columbia Highway 97 in Vernon, at the northern end of the Okanagan Valley. This is big-time resort territory, with dozens of provincial parks, numerous lakes, and all kinds of recreation between one end and the other.

Head south on BC 97 as it traces the western edges of Kalamalka Lake and Wood Lake before reaching Kelowna, the largest and most energetic of the Okanagan cities. For a short time, BC 97 is the closest thing to a U.S. interstate in this part of the province. Speeds increase, the road widens to four sometimes-divided lanes, and the pavement is excellent. There's a lot of traffic heading in both directions, but it flows smoothly.

From Kelowna, two options lead to Osoyoos. BC 97 tracks the west side of Okanagan Lake through a series of resort towns in the center of the Okanagan Valley; the largest are Summerland and Penticton, about 46 km and 64 km south of Kelowna, respectively. Summerland sits on the western shore of Okanagan Lake, while Penticton straddles a narrow strip of land between Okanagan and Skaha Lakes.

When it's 100 degrees Fahrenheit and the pavement is radiating extra heat, we prefer to avoid the towns' restricted speed limits—especially when a beachside getaway isn't in the budget. In Kelowna, British Columbia Highway 33 splits off to the east as BC 97 hooks to the west. Heading through the burg of Rutland, the road makes a slight right and begins climbing a steep ridge overlooking the valley before turning south into the Okanagan Highlands.

After the summit, the road zips past the turnoff for Big White Ski Resort and picks up the West Kettle River on the left. It makes a slow, barely noticeable, sometimes undulating descent through a progression of sweepers and S curves. Most of BC 33's slide-zone signs are found on stretches of pavement cut through outcroppings, with steep rock walls constricting the highway. The road has reached an elevation where the temperature is refreshing. Surrounded by rich, deep green woods, this is an excellent mountain road offering a mix of fast, linked S curves; broad sweepers; and wide-open, straight pavement that invites you to pull back on the throttle and clear the pipes.

Steve: The downside to BC 33 is that just past Rutland, it climbs a long, steep, two-lane ridgeline before leveling out into a series of curves. The combination of the steep ridge and the curves at the top can seriously impede traffic flow. I've climbed this in a pack of twenty or thirty vehicles stuck behind a semi-truck or RV, the entire line of traffic barely chugging along at 10 miles an hour. With no pullouts for slow vehicles and no passing lanes until the road levels off, drivers get edgy and antsy. Eventually, a daredevil will pull into the opposing lane from almost anywhere in the line of traffic, attempt to pass as many vehicles as possible, then sneak back into the uphill lane, forcing others to make space where none existed.

After about 4 miles of climbing, the road levels off slightly and enters a series of intermittently tight and sweeping curves on undulating hills. Now past the narrow ridge's restrictions, it feels as if all rules are off as those who didn't have the nerve to pass on the uphill suddenly begin passing anywhere they please. Watching SUVs driven by Canadian soccer moms and middle-aged couples on holiday cross the double yellow line to pass seven or eight cars at a stretch can be unnerving.

Traffic thins out past the traffic-clogged ridge and subsequent curves, and passing the remaining stragglers becomes easier and safer as the road climbs steadily toward the 4,150-foot (1,265-meter) Rock Creek Summit. ●

BC 33 slips through Beaverdell and Westbridge, meandering south toward Rock Creek and the junction with British Columbia Highway 3, the Crowsnest Highway. There isn't much going on in Rock Creek, but it does have the full range of services.

A left on BC 3 would take you through Boundary Country to border crossings at Midway and, a little farther east, Grand Forks.

The Midway crossing is open from 9 a.m. to 5 p.m., while Grand Forks is open twenty-four hours.

Take a right on BC 3, and the road immediately snakes through a set of switchbacks, pulling you quickly into the hills overlooking Rock Creek and the Kettle Valley. The road rolls high into sun-drenched, south-facing hills and rounds the southern end of the Okanagan Highlands, with views of a narrow valley and dense forest to the south. This fast stretch of pavement rises and falls over big, rolling hills, the road conditions are good, and the turns wide and sweeping. The road dips close to the U.S. border, rounding the southern flank of Anarchist Mountain before twisting through a 9-mile string of steep switchbacks to the valley floor. About halfway down, a paved overlook on the right affords views of Osoyoos Lake and the sparsely vegetated knobby hills that frame the Okanagan Valley.

Osoyoos lies on the shores of Osoyoos Lake at the southern end of the arid Okanagan Valley. It's a popular vacation destination for residents from the rest of British Columbia and Alberta, and it's easy to see why. The mild climate and the recreation-oriented community offer something for just about everyone.

Restaurants

Cherryville
The Gold Pan Café
423 BC 6
(250) 547-2185

Fauquier
The Mushroom Addition
129 Oak St.
(250) 269-7467

RIDE

34

Slocan Slalom
(Metaline Falls to New Denver)

Directions:

north on WA 31 from Metaline Falls to the Canadian border

north on BC 6 from the border to the junction with BC 3
(the Crowsnest)

east on BC 3 to BC 3A near Creston

north on BC 3A to Kootenay Bay

Kootenay Lake Ferry to Balfour

north on BC 31 to Kaslo

west on BC 31A to New Denver

option: northwest on BC 6 to Nakusp

Distance:

total distance: 185 miles to New Denver, 213 miles to
Nakusp (not including detour to Salmo)

Metaline Falls to Nelway (Canadian border): 14 miles

Nelway to junction with BC 3: 6 miles (4 km)

BC 3 junction to Creston: 42 miles (67 km)

Creston to Kootenay Bay Ferry: 63 miles (101 km)

Balfour to Kaslo: 45 miles (72 km)

Kaslo to New Denver: 27 miles (46 km)

New Denver to Nakusp: 28 miles (47 km)

optional: junction BC 6 and BC 3 to Salmo—9 miles (5.4
km)

Time:
a full day

Services:
Ione, Metaline Falls, Salmo, Creston, Kuskanook, Boswell, Crawford Bay, Balfour, Ainsworth, Kaslo, New Denver, Nakusp

Best Time of Year:
late spring to early fall

Highlights:
scaling the heights of Kootenay Pass; panoramic views of lakes, fertile fields, and Victorian towns; one of the region's best motorcycle roads

This is one of several cross-border jaunts that introduces Americans to a new world of riding: Canada. It leaves relatively low-elevation mountains and towns of northeastern Washington, climbs into the rugged Nelson Range and over Kootenay Pass, then crosses an intensely agricultural landscape before entering the resort-oriented Kootenay Lake area—where a ferry adds a twist.

This ride starts where ride 27 left off, on Washington Highway 31 in Metaline, Washington. This highway is popular with both motorcyclists and bicyclists, and abundant wildlife draws visitors to viewpoints where bald eagles and mountain goats tend to congregate. About 5 miles north of Ione, the Eagles Nest Viewpoint is an ideal spot for searching out the eagles that fish the Pend Oreille River and nest nearby. A good set of binoculars is helpful, since the birds live in cottonwoods on the opposite bank.

North of Metaline Falls, the Pend Oreille hooks to the northwest, crosses the border, and joins the mighty Columbia River, while WA 31 climbs and twists through a series of tight turns.

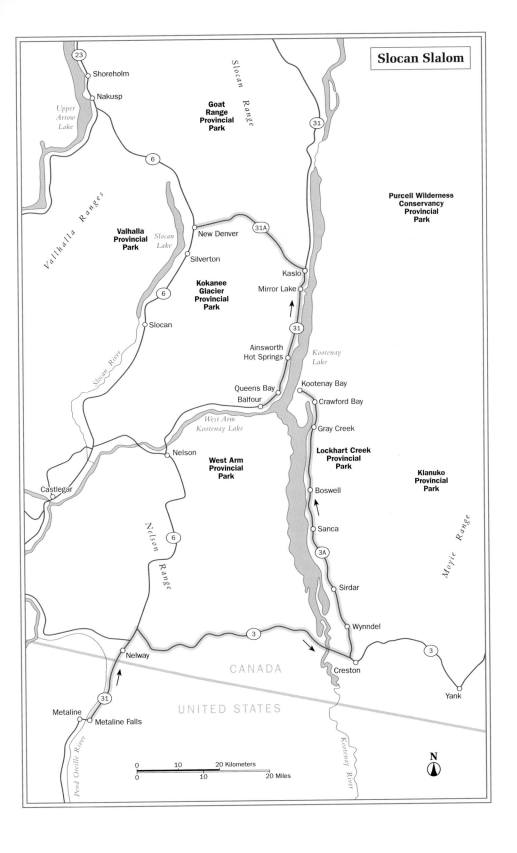

Slocan Slalom

23
Shoreholm
Nakusp

Upper Arrow Lake

Slocan Range

31

Goat Range Provincial Park

Purcell Wilderness Conservancy Provincial Park

6

Valhalla Ranges

Valhalla Provincial Park

Slocan Lake

New Denver

31A

Silverton

Kaslo
Mirror Lake

Kokanee Glacier Provincial Park

6

Slocan

31

Slocan River

Ainsworth Hot Springs

Kootenay Lake

Queens Bay
Balfour

Kootenay Bay
Crawford Bay

Gray Creek

West Arm Kootenay Lake

Nelson

West Arm Provincial Park

Lockhart Creek Provincial Park

Klanuko Provincial Park

Castlegar

Nelson Range

6

Boswell

Sanca

3A

Moyie Range

Sirdar

Wynndel

3

Nelway

3

Yank

CANADA

Creston

31

UNITED STATES

Metaline
Metaline Falls

Pend Oreille River

Kootenay River

0   10   20 Kilometers
0   10   20 Miles

N

Early morning light flatters the Sullivan Creek Powerhouse, an abandoned hydroelectric plant in Metaline Falls.

The road isn't technical; it's simply a good way to say good-bye to the States and hello to Canada.

Across the border, WA 31 becomes British Columbia Highway 6. Follow it north for about 6 miles (10 km) to the junction with British Columbia Highway 3. Remember that in Canada all distances are in kilometers, all speed limits are in kilometers per hour, and all gas prices are in liters.

If you need fuel or food, make a left at the junction of BC 6 and BC 3, following BC 6 north to Salmo. Carved out of the forest, Salmo is a pleasant introduction to southern British Columbia. Historically, its economic base was mining, and then lumber—industries whose serious decline gives the town a slightly depressed feel. For our purposes, it has the Dragonfly Café with great coffee, fresh baked goods, and a very friendly staff. Murals, carved into locally quarried stone by students of Salmo's Kootenay Stone Masonry School, depict the area's history on buildings' exterior walls.

This ride's real fun begins on BC 3, the Crowsnest Highway, east of its intersection with BC 6. After Burns Flat, it climbs and twists toward Kootenay Pass on a stretch known as the Kootenay

Skyway, gaining more than 3,600 feet of elevation in 13 miles. At 5,823 feet (1,775 meters), this is Canada's highest highway pass open year-round—or at least most of the year. In this serious slide-zone area, big steel gates near the summit are visible reminders of how harsh and unpredictable the region's weather can be.

The pavement is in surprisingly good shape for a British Columbia mountain road. From the summit, it descends slightly, then continues for about 20 high-alpine miles through a chain of big, sweeping turns with ever-changing views of the heavily wooded Selkirk Mountains. It drops onto the fertile flats around Creston and comes to a T intersection about 2 miles north of town. Make a left at the T and take British Columbia 3A toward the resorts on Kootenay Lake's eastern shore.

Making a right on BC 3 will take you into Creston. To get to the town center, follow the highway south until it makes a soft left-hand curve at the junction with Canyon Street, which runs through the heart of Creston's main business district. With an array of souvenir and T-shirt shops, gas stations, liquor stores, and restaurants, downtown Creston looks like a lot of rural locales but also feels a bit like a resort town. Tourism is increasingly important here, but agriculture and timber are still the local economy's foundations. From Creston, BC 3 continues east on its journey toward Cranbrook and Crowsnest Pass.

Heading north from the T intersection, BC 3A scales the hills north of town. Secure behind 53 miles of dykes that prevent seasonal flooding by the Kootenay River, more than 25,000 acres of agriculture flourishes on rich floodplain land below. An overlook provides views of the bottomland and explains how settlers reclaimed it.

Nestled between the Selkirk Range to the west and the Purcell Mountains to the east, Kootenay Lake is one of Canada's largest natural lakes. BC 3 traces its eastern shore, winding through a string of resort towns from Sirdar to Kootenay Bay. The road is in excellent condition, with plenty of nicely banked curves and climbs, and offers occasional views of the lake and the Selkirks as they descend to its western edge.

The Kuskanook rest area about 17 miles north of Creston has ample parking, picnic tables, and restrooms, as well as a public boat launch and marina. It's a great place to stop for a little while and appreciate the surroundings.

The landscape is lovely, and with all it has to offer, the stretch of pavement from Creston to Kootenay Bay would be one of the region's premier motorcycle roads were it not for severely restricted speeds through the resorts. When you're limited to a maximum of 36 mph (60 kph) unless otherwise posted, this can be a painfully slow stretch.

Steve: On one of my first trips through BC, I got to the Kootenay Lake Ferry and lined up behind a big pickup truck. As I shut down my engine, I gave a quick nod to the guys on bikes to my left. I've learned that riding up on the Buell, pulling out a map, and playing the tourist card is a good conversation starter, so I did just that. The first question from the guys to my left was, "How do you like the Buell?" The second was, "Where are you headed?"

I didn't want to be rude by not discussing my bike, but I was trying to figure out where to go after I crossed the lake, so I made a quick comment about the Buell and switched to the second question. A rapid exchange ensued: Where've you been? Where do you want to go? They tossed out a couple of suggestions as we fired up the bikes and began to board.

Realizing I'd just met bikers willing to give me travel tips, I went in search of them after the ferry was under way. For the next fifteen minutes, Dirty Dave and Casey were my unofficial tour guides, offering advice on roads, towns, and restaurants from Kootenay Bay west across BC. Some were places I'd planned on visiting, but others weren't. They also cautioned that on BC 31's long climb into the hills north of Balfour, I should use the intermittent passing lanes to get around traffic as quickly as possible if I didn't want to get stuck behind a slow vehicle in the hills or curves.

The pavement ends at Kootenay Bay, and the Kootenay Lake Ferry takes over. Travel time from Kootenay Bay to Balfour is about thirty-five minutes, and boarding time can add another ten or fifteen. (For inland ferry information, go to www.th.gov.bc.ca/marine/ferry_schedules.htm.)

Sadly, motorcycles don't get priority boarding or their own waiting area for inland ferries, so arriving just before departure and riding to the front of the line to board first isn't an option on this boat. On the plus side, waiting gives you a chance to meet fellow riders.

Casey (left) and Dirty Dave were Steve's unofficial tour guides aboard the Kootenay Lake Ferry.

They were headed to Nelson and Osoyoos, and because of their advice I was now off to New Denver and Nakusp. When the ferry docked in Balfour, Dirty Dave and Casey went left, and I went right. I was grateful for their help. That kind of generosity from other riders is one of the best things about touring by bike. ●

From the Balfour ferry terminal, head north on British Columbia Highway 31 along the west shore of Kootenay Lake. The first stop is Ainsworth Hot Springs, about 9 miles (15 km) up the road. British Columbia is peppered with hot springs, and with a forty-three-room resort and ample parking, Ainsworth Hot Springs is an appealing vacation spot for locals and tourists, so you might want to end your day here.

Some bikers like the entertaining series of curves and climbs between Kaslo and New Denver so much that they'll ride laps back and forth.

Steve: I met a group of riders from Canada as I was passing through Republic, Washington. They were on their way to dinner; I was looking at my map, trying to decide how much farther I wanted to ride. I told them I was headed to this part of BC and, as a group, they all pointed to BC 31A, describing the section of road from Kaslo to New Denver as one of the best in southeastern British Columbia. One of the guys said he knew a group of sport-bike riders who did laps back and forth and back again. They warned that a couple stretches are a little technical. After riding it, I now understand why the guys on sport bikes do those laps—and if this is what's considered technical in BC, I'll take technical any day. ●

It's an easy ride from Ainsworth to Kaslo, 12 miles (20 km) to the north. Kaslo's tree-lined streets and Victorian-era buildings overlook Kootenay Lake and stunning views of the Purcell Mountains to the east, so it's no wonder it's been called "British Columbia's Prettiest Town" and the "Switzerland of the Americas." Kaslo is also home to a wood-plank road bridge that caught our attention on a warm, sunny day; we don't want to think about how slick those planks could get during a steady rain.

After making a 90-degree left turn in the heart of Kaslo, BC 31 intersects with British Columbia Highway 31A two blocks to the west. While BC 31 splits off and makes a soft right onto Marine Drive, BC 31A heads straight for a couple of blocks before making a left on Washington Street and ascending toward New Denver.

For the next 27 miles, BC 31A is one of the region's best stretches of pavement. Shaped like a boomerang, the road heads northwest and then drops to the southwest through a narrow valley in the Selkirk Range. It climbs, twists, and dives into curves on its way to New Denver. The pavement is in great shape with posted speed limits higher than any since this route picked up BC 3A outside of Creston.

We can end the day in New Denver. If you're headed to Nakusp, refer to ride 32 for information on BC 6 from New Denver to Nakusp.

Restaurant

Salmo
Dragonfly Café
413 Railway Ave.
(250) 357-2867

APPENDIX:
MOTORCYCLE DEALERSHIPS
(BY MAKE AND STATE)

APRILIA

Oregon

Bend Euro Moto
1064 SE Paiute Way, #1
Bend, OR 97702
(541) 617-9155
www.bendeuromoto.com

Bike Barn Motorcycles
3434 N. Pacific Hwy.
Medford, OR 97501
(541) 282-9772
www.bikebarnmc.com

MotoCorsa
2170 NW Wilson St.
Portland, OR 97210
(503) 292-7488
www.motocorsa.com

Wheelworks LLC
407 W. 11th Ave.
Eugene, OR 97401
(541) 431-7300

Washington

Aprilia Bellingham
960 Harris Ave., Ste. 103
Bellingham WA 98225
(360) 647-1196
www.vespabellingham.com

Aprilia of Olympia
2405 Harrison Ave. NW, #101
Olympia WA 98502
(253) 565-1117
www.nwmotorscooters.com

Aprilia Spokane
2405 N. Division
Spokane, WA 99207
(509) 458-2619

Cliff's Cycle Center
1200 Charleston Beach Rd. W.
Bremerton, WA 98312
(360) 377-5568
www.cliffscyclecenter.com

Cycle Works Powersports
485 Rainier Ave. S.
Renton, WA 98055
(206) 652-5200
www.cycleworkswa.com

Family Powersports Center
1607 W. Broadway Ave.
Moses Lake, WA 98837
(509) 765-4456
www.familypowersportscenter.com

Moto International, Ltd.
7701 Aurora Ave. N.
Seattle, WA 98103
(206) 297-3822
www.motointernational.com

NW Motor Scooters
5428 S. Tacoma Way
Tacoma, WA 98409
(253) 565-1117

Ride Motorsports
19035 Woodinville-Snohomish Rd.
Woodinville, WA 98072
(425) 487-3881
www.ridemotorsports.com

RPM Motorsports of Spokane
3511 N. Market St.
Spokane, WA 99207
(509) 489-9180
www.rpmmotorsportsspokane.com

Shumate Motorsports
3305 W. 19th Ave.
Kennewick, WA 99338
(509) 735-9775
www.shumatemotorsports.com

British Columbia
British Italian Motorcycles
1764 Powell St.
Vancouver, BC V5L 1H7
(604) 253-1117

IRC Cat Shack
4884 N. Access Rd.
Chetwynd, BC V0C 1J0
(250) 788-9558

Kelowna Yamaha Motorcycles
#1-1515 Westgate Rd.
Kelowna, BC V1Z 3X4
(250) 769-1013

Rivercity Cycle
1794 Kelly Douglas Rd.
Kamloops, BC V2C 5S4
(250) 377-4320

SG Power
730 Hillside Ave.
Victoria, BC V8T 1Z4
(250) 382-8291

BMW
Oregon
BMW Motorcycles of Western
    Oregon-Eugene
2891 W. 11th Ave.
Eugene, OR 97402
(541) 338-0269
www.bmwor.com

BMW Motorcycles of Western
    Oregon-Tigard
12010 SW Garden Pl.
Tigard, OR 97223
(503) 597-7097
www.bmwor.com

Hansen's Exclusive BMW Motorcycles
3598 S. Pacific Hwy.
Medford, OR 97501
(541) 535-3342
www.hansensmc.com

Portland Motorcycle Company
10652 NE Holman St.
Portland, OR 97220
(503) 255-5787
www.portlandmotorcycle.com

Salem Honda-BMW
1515 13th St. SE
Salem, OR 97302
(503) 364-6784
www.salemhonda.com

Washington
Mac's Cycle
700 Bridge St.
Clarkston, WA 99403
(509) 758-5343
www.macscycle.com

Ride West BMW
8100 Lake City Way, NE
Seattle, WA 98115
(206) 527-5511
www.ridewest.com

South Sound BMW Motorcycles
3605 20th St.
Fife, WA 98424
(253) 582-1838
www.southsoundbmw.com

British Columbia
Island BMW
2758 Peatt Rd.
Victoria, BC V9B 3V3
(250) 474-2088
www.smcycle.com

John Valk BMW
3061 Grandview Hwy.
Vancouver, BC V5M 2E4
(604) 731-5505
www.johnvalkbmw.ca

Pacific Yamaha BMW
#1000-21000 Westminster Hwy.
Richmond, BC V6V 2S9
(604) 276-2552
www.pacificyamahabmw.com

Southwest Motorrad
3575 Alcan Rd.
Kelowna, BC V1X 7R3
(250) 807-2697
www.southwestmotorrad.com

BUELL

Oregon

Cascade Buell
63028 Sherman Rd.
Bend, OR 97701
(541) 330-6228
www.cascadeharley.com

Latus Motors
870 E. Berkeley
Gladstone, OR 97027
(503) 249-8653
www.latus-hd.com

Paradise Harley Davidson-Buell
10770 SW Cascade Ave.
Tigard, OR 97223
(503) 924-3700
www.paradiseh-d.com

Washington

Buell of Seattle
5711 188th St. SW
Lynnwood, WA 98037
(425) 921-1100
www.harley-davidsonofseattle.com

Destination Buell Shop
18810 Meridian Ave. E.
Puyallup, WA 98375
(253) 693-5700

Destination Harley Davidson-Buell
2302 Pacific Hwy. E.
Fife, WA 98424
(253) 922-3700
www.destinationharley.com

Downtown Buell
3715 E. Valley Rd.
Renton, WA 98057
(425) 988-2100
www.downtownharley.com

Eastside Buell
14408 NE 20th St.
Bellevue, WA 98007
(425) 702-2000
www.eastsideharley.com

Legend Harley Davidson-Buell
9625 Provost Rd. NW
Silverdale, WA 98383
(360) 698-3700
www.legendharleysilverdale.com

Legend Harley Davidson-Buell
Wenatchee
3013 G. S. Center Rd.
Wenatchee, WA 98801
(509) 662-3434
www.legendharleywenatchee.com

Shumate Harley Davidson-Buell
Spokane
6815 E. Trent
Spokane, WA 99212
(509) 928-6811
www.shumateharley.com

Shumate Motorsports
3305 W. 19th Ave
Kennewick, WA 99338
(509) 735-9775
www.shumatemotorsports.com

British Columbia

Barnes Harley-Davidson Buell
8859-201 St.
Langley, BC V2Y 0C8
(604) 534-6044
www.barneshd.com

Buell of the Kootenays
1817 Cranbrook St. N.
Cranbrook, BC V1C 3S9
(250) 426-6606
www.harleydavidsonkootenays.com

House of Buell
1875 Boundary Rd.
Vancouver, BC V5M 3Y7
(604) 291-2453
www.trevdeeley.com

Kamloops Harley Davidson
1465 Ironmask Rd.
Kamloops, BC V2C 5N6
(250) 828-0622
www.kamloopshd.com

Steve Drane Harley-Davidson
2940 Ed Nixon Terrace
Victoria, BC V9B 0B2
(250) 475-1345
www.stevedraneharley.com

DUCATI

Oregon

Bend Euro Moto
1064 SE Paiute Way, #1
Bend, OR 97702
(541) 617-9155
www.bendeuromoto.com

Hansen's BMW/Ducati
3598 South Pacific Hwy.
Medford, OR 97501
(541) 535-3342
www.hansensmc.com

MotoCorsa
2170 NW Wilson St.
Portland, OR 97210
(503) 292-7488
www.motocorsa.com

Washington

The Brothers Powersports
5205 First St.
Bremerton, WA 98312
(360) 479-6943
www.brotherspowersports.com

Ducati Seattle
711 Ninth Ave. N.
Seattle, WA 98109
(206) 298-9995
www.ducatiseattle.com

Eastside Moto Sports
13029 NE 20th St.
Bellevue, WA 98005
(425) 882-4300
www.eastsidemotosports.com

Skagit Powersports, Inc.
1645 Walton Dr.
Burlington, WA 98223
(360) 757-7999
www.skagitpowersports.com

British Columbia

Harbour City Motorsport
1613 Bowen Rd.
Nanaimo, BC V9S 1G5
(250) 754-3345
www.harbourcitymotorsport.com

John Valk Motorsports
3061 Grandview Hwy.
Vancouver, BC V5M 2E4
(604) 731-5505
www.johnvalkducati.ca

Richmond Motorsport
Unit 1100, 21320 Westminster Hwy.
Richmond, BC V6V 2X5
(604) 276-8513
www.richmondmotorsport.com

SouthWest Ducati
3575 Alcan Rd.
Kelowna, BC V1X 7R3
(250) 807-2697
www.southwestmotorrad.com

HARLEY DAVIDSON

Oregon

American M/C Classics H-D
1600 Century Dr. NE
Albany, OR 97322
(541) 928-6234
www.americanmotorcycleclassicshd
.com

Cascade Harley-Davidson
63028 Sherman Rd.
Bend, OR 97701
(541) 330-6228
www.cascadeharley.com

D & S Harley-Davidson, Inc.
3846 S. Pacific Hwy.
Medford, OR 97501
(541) 535-5515
www.dsharley.com

Doyle's Harley-Davidson, Inc.
86441 College View
Eugene, OR 97405
(541) 747-1033
www.doyleshd.com

Hwy. 101 Harley-Davidson
536 S. 2nd St.
Coos Bay, OR 97420
(541) 266-7051
www.highway101hd.com

Latus Motors Harley-Davidson
870 E. Berkeley
Gladstone, OR 97027
(503) 249-8653
www.latus-hd.com

Paradise Harley-Davidson
10770 SW Cascade Ave.
Tigard, OR 97223
(503) 924-3700
www.paradiseh-d.com

Salem Harley-Davidson
3601 Silverton Rd. NE
Salem, OR 97305
(503) 363-0634
www.salemharley.com

Washington
Columbia Motorcycle Harley-Davidson
1314 NE 102nd St.
Vancouver, WA 98686
(360) 695-8831
www.columbiahd.com

Destination Harley-Davidson
2302 Pacific Hwy. E.
Fife, WA 98424
(253) 922-3700
www.destinationharley.com

Destination H-D Shop
18810 Meridian Ave. E.
Puyallup, WA 98375
(253) 693-5700
www.destinationharley.com

Downtown Harley-Davidson
3715 E. Valley Rd.
Renton, WA 98057
(425) 988-2100
www.downtownharley.com

Eastside Harley-Davidson, Inc.
14408 NE 20th St.
Bellevue, WA 98007
(425) 702-2000
www.eastsideharley.com

Harley-Davidson of Bellingham, Inc.
1419 N. State St.
Bellingham, WA 98225
(360) 671-7575
www.harleyofbellingham.com

Harley-Davidson of Seattle
5711 188th St. SW
Lynnwood, WA 98037
(425) 921-1100
www.harley-davidsonofseattle.com

Legend Harley-Davidson
9625 Provost Rd. NW
Silverdale, WA 98383
(360) 698-3700
www.legendharleysilverdale.com

Legend Harley Davidson-Buell
Wenatchee
3013 G. S. Center Rd.
Wenatchee, WA 98801
(509) 662-3434
www.legendharleywenatchee.com

Northwest Harley-Davidson, Inc.
8000 Freedom Lane NE
Lacey, WA 98516
(360) 705-8515
www.nwharley.com

Owens Yamaha, Suzuki,
Harley-Davidson
1707 N. First St.
Yakima, WA 98901
(509) 575-1916
www.owensharley.com

Shumate Harley-Davidson
3305 W. 19th Ave.
Kennewick, WA 99338
(509) 735-9775
www.shumateharley.com

Shumate Harley-Davidson Spokane
6815 E. Trent
Spokane, WA 99212
(509) 928-6811
www.shumateharley.com

Skagit Harley-Davidson
1337 Goldenrod Rd.
Burlington, WA 98233
(360) 757-1515
www.skagitharley.com

Sound Harley-Davidson
16212 Smokey Point Blvd.
Marysville, WA 98271
(360) 454-5000
www.soundharley.com

British Columbia
Barnes Harley-Davidson Buell
8859-201 St.
Langley, BC V2Y 0C8
(604) 534-6044
www.barneshd.com

Harley-Davidson of the Kootenays
1817 Cranbrook St. N.
Cranbrook, BC V1C 3S9
(250) 426-6606
www.harleydavidsonkootenays.com

Harley-Davidson of Prince George
2626 Vance Rd.
Prince George, BC V2N 7A7
(250) 564-6667
www.harleydavidsonpg.bc.ca

Harley-Davidson of Smithers
4320 Hwy. 16
Smithers, BC V0J 2N0
(250) 847-3784
www.hdsmithers.ca

Kamloops H-D
1465 Ironmask Rd.
Kamloops, BC V2C 5N6
(250) 828-0622
www.kamloopshd.com

Kane's Harley-Davidson
888 McCurdy Rd.
Kelowna, BC V1X 8C8
(250) 860-0666
www.kanesharleydavidson.net

Mountainview Harley-Davidson
44768 Yale Rd. W.
Chilliwack, BC V2R 0G5
(604) 792-7820
www.mountainviewhd.com

Steve Drane Harley-Davidson
2940 Ed Nixon Terrace
Victoria, BC V9B 0B2
(250) 475-1345
www.stevedraneharley.com

Trev Deeley Motorcycles
1875 Boundary Rd.
Vancouver, BC V5M 3Y7
(604) 291-2453
www.trevdeeley.com

HONDA
Oregon
Beaverton Honda
10380 SW Cascade Ave.
Portland, OR 97223
(503) 684-6600
www.beavertonmotorcycles.com

Cliffs Saws & Cycles, Inc.
2619 10th St.
Baker City, OR 97814
(541) 523-2412

Columbia River Honda Suzuki
58245 Columbia River Hwy.
Saint Helens, OR 97051
(503) 397-3502
www.columbiarivermoto-sports.com

Cycle Country Honda Suzuki
1230 Broadway St. NE
Salem, OR 97301
(503) 378-0532
www.cyclecountry.net

Cycle Sports of Eugene
555 River Rd.
Eugene, OR 97404
(541) 607-9000
www.cyclesports.net

Cycle Sports-Salem
4764 Portland Rd.
Salem, OR 97305
(503) 390-9000
www.cyclesports.net

Cycletown
2200 N. Hwy. 395
Hermiston, OR 97838
(541) 567-8919
www.hondayamahacycletown.com

Edge Performance Sports
1625 N. Oregon
Ontario, OR 97914
(541) 889-4099
www.edgeperformancesports.com

Forest Grove Honda
3619 Pacific Ave.
Forest Grove, OR 97116
(503) 357-7300

Fun Country Power Sports
1318 W. 2nd St.
The Dalles, OR 97058
(541) 298-1161
www.funcountrypowersports.com

Honda of St. Johns
7741 N. Lombard St.
Portland, OR 97203
(503) 286-8816
www.hondaofstjohns.com

Honda of Tillamook
1000 N. Main St.
Tillamook, OR 97141-9272
(503) 842-5593

Moto Sport Hillsboro
809 NE 28th Ave.
Hillsboro, OR 97124
(503) 648-4555
www.hillsboromotorcycles.com

Pro Caliber Motorsports-Bend
3500 N. Hwy. 97
Bend, OR 97701
(866) 949-8606
www.procaliberbend.com

Roseburg Power Sports
1305 W. Central Ave.
Sutherlin, OR 97479
(541) 672-6065

Salem Honda
1515 13th St. SE
Salem, OR 97302
(503) 364-6784

Taylor Honda Sports
2140 N. Pacific Hwy.
Woodburn, OR 97071
(503) 981-1813

Tread & Track Motorsports
3500 Eberlein Ave.
Klamath Falls, OR 97603
(541) 880-5577

Washington
Allsport Polaris Honda
19505 E. Broadway
Liberty Lake, WA 99016
(509) 891-8217

Al's Honda
2336 James St.
Bellingham, WA 98225
(360) 733-1000

The Brothers Powersports
5205 1st St.
Bremerton, WA 98312
(360) 479-6943
www.brotherspowersports.com

Everett Powersports
215 SW Everett Mall Way
Everett, WA 98204
(425) 347-4545
www.everettpowersports.com

Hinshaw's Motorcycle Store
1611 W. Valley Hwy.
Auburn, WA 98001
(253) 939-7164
www.hinshawsmotorcyclestore.com

I-90 Motorsports
200 NE Gilman Blvd.
Issaquah, WA 98027-2902
(425) 391-4490
www.I-90motorsports.com

Lake City Powersports
12048 Lake City Way NE
Seattle, WA 98125-5332
(206) 364-1372
www.lakecitypowersports.com

Lifestyles Honda
3302 Cedardale Rd.
Mount Vernon, WA 98274-9502
(360) 757-4449

Lynnwood Cycle Barn
5711 188th St. SW
Lynnwood, WA 98037
(425) 774-3538
www.cyclebarn.com

Mac's Cycle
700 Bridge St.
Clarkston, WA 99403-1899
(509) 758-5343
www.macscycle.com

Omak Honda
10 E. Central Ave.
Omak, WA 98841
(509) 826-2050

Outlaw Motor Sports
504 NW 1st St.
Enterprise, OR 97828
(541) 426-3491
www.outlawmotorsportsinc.net

Port Angeles Power Equipment
2624 East Hwy. 101
Port Angeles, WA 98362
(360) 452-4652
www.papowerequipment.com

Poulins Motorcycle
513 S. 1st St.
Yakima, WA 98901
(509) 452-7493
http://poulinsmotorcycle.hondamc
dealers.com

Powersports Northwest
300 S. Tower Ave.
Centralia, WA 98531
(360) 736-0166
www.powersportsnorthwest.com

Pro Caliber's Motorsports-Longview
1020 Industrial Way
Longview, WA 98632
(360) 636-1220
www.procaliberlongview.com

Pullman Honda
245 S. Grand Ave.
Pullman, WA 99163
(866) 568-3575

Rainier Honda Yamaha
16002 Pacific Ave. S.
Spanaway, WA 98387
(253) 537-0831
www.tacomamotorsports.com

Renton Motorcycles RMC
3701 E. Valley Rd.
Renton, WA 98057
(425) 226-4320
www.rentonmotorcycles.com

Ride Motorsports
19035 Woodinville-Snohomish Rd. NE
Woodinville, WA 98072
(425) 487-3881
www.ridemotorsports.com

Shumate Motorsports
3305 W. 19th Ave.
Kennewick, WA 99338
(509) 735-9775
www.shumatemotorsports.com

Smokey Point Cycle Barn
3131 Smokey Point Dr., Ste. A1
Arlington, WA 98223
(360) 530-7800
www.smokeypointcyclebarn.com

South Bound Honda
2724 96th St. S.
Lakewood, WA 98499
(253) 582-2288
www.hondabike.com

South Sound Honda
2115 Carriage Dr. SW
Olympia, WA 98502
(360) 357-9633
www.hondabike.com

Spokane Powersports
6521 N. Division St.
Spokane, WA 99208
(509) 467-8185
www.spokanepowersports.com

Steel Dreams Honda
1851 Bouslog Rd.
Burlington, WA 98233
(360) 757-4449

Tacoma Motorsports
4701 S. Center St.
Tacoma, WA 98409
(253) 564-8678
www.tacomamotorsports.com

U.S.A. Honda
1371 Dalles Military Rd.
Walla Walla, WA 99362
(509) 522-1601

Wenatchee Honda
314 S. Wenatchee Ave.
Wenatchee, WA 98801
(509) 663-0075
www.wenatcheehonda.com

Westside Motorsports
4201 S. Grove Rd.
Spokane, WA 99224
(509) 747-1862
www.westsideracing.com

British Columbia
Action Motorcycles Inc.
1234 Esquimalt Rd.
Victoria, BC V9A 3N8
(250) 386-8364
www.action-motorcycles.com

B & F Sales & Service Ltd.
7466-2nd St.
Grand Forks, BC V0H 1H0
(250) 442-3555

Barrett Boat & Trailer Sales Ltd.
1470 Hwy. 3B
Fruitvale, BC V0G 1L0
(250) 367-6216
www.barrettshondayamaha.com

Big Top Powersports
7869 Enterprise Way
Chilliwack, BC V2R 4H2
(604) 703-0221
www.bigtoppowersports.com

Carter Motorsports
1502 W. 3rd Ave.
Vancouver, BC V6J 1J7
(604) 736-4547
(800) 668-7468
www.cartermotorsports.com

Coast Line Power Sports
1870 Cosyan Way, Box 2217
Sechelt, BC V0N 3A0
(604) 885-4616

Courtenay Motorsports Center
4883 N. Island Hwy.
Courtenay, BC V9N 5Y9
(250) 338-1415
www.courtenay-motorsports.com

C. R. Cycle Ltd.
22674 Dewdney Trunk Rd.
Maple Ridge, BC V2X 3J9
(604) 467-2344
www.crcycle.com

Cycle North
5905 Gauthier Rd.
Prince George, BC V2L 3C5
(250) 964-9091

Ghostrider Motorsports
30 Shadow Rd.
Fernie, BC V0B 1M0
(250) 423-9251
www.ghostridermotorsports.ca

Holeshot Motorsports Ltd.
8867 210st St.
Langley, BC V2Y 0C8
(604) 882-3800
www.holeshotracing.ca

Honda Centre
3766 E. 1st Ave.
Burnaby, BC V5C 3V9
(604) 293-1022
www.hondacentre.com

Kootenay Honda Powerhouse
2108 Cranbrook St. N.
Cranbrook, BC V1C 3T1
(250) 489-5415

Les Koleszar Services Ltd.
4462 Willingdon Ave.
Powell River, BC V8A 2M6
(604) 485-5616

Lino's Sales Ltd.
Hwy. 16
Burns Lake, BC V0J 1E0
(250) 692-7959

Macandale Rentals
8640 Wollason St.
Port Hardy, BC V0N 2P0
(250) 949-8442

Main Jet Motorsports
111 McDonald Dr.
Nelson, BC V1L 6B9
(250) 352-3191
www.mainjet.ca

M & M Performance Motorsports
2890 Hwy. 97 N.
Kelowna, BC V1X 6W7
(250) 491-4800
www.mmperformance.com

Neid Enterprises Ltd.
4921 Keith Ave.
Terrace, BC V8G 1K7
(250) 635-3478

Northern Metalic Sales Ltd.
4804-45 St.
Fort Nelson, BC V0C 1R0
(250) 774-6101

Penticton Honda Centre
100 Industrial Ave. E.
Penticton, BC V2A 3H8
(250) 492-3808
www.hondapenticton.com

Performance All Terrain & Rentals Ltd.
867 Adler Ave.
100 Mile House, BC V0K 2E0
(250) 395-2550
www.performanceallterrain.com

Quesnel Honda
161 Marsh Dr.
Quesnel, BC V2J 1E8
(250) 992-8371
www.quesnelhonda.com

RTR Performance
2051 Trans Canada E.
Kamloops, BC V2C 4A5
(250) 374-3141
www.rtrperformance.com

Salmon Arm Honda Powerhouse
650 Trans Canada Hwy. NE
Salmon Arm, BC V1E 4N7
(250) 832-6107
www.salmonarmhonda.com

SG Power Products Ltd.
#730 Hillside Ave.
Victoria, BC V8T 1Z4
(250) 382-8291

3-D Cycles Ltd.
2121 Clearbrook Rd.
Abbotsford, BC V2T 4H6
(604) 859-4732
www.3-dcyclesltd.shawbiz.ca

Trails North Holdings Ltd.
3334 Frontage Rd. Hwy. 16
Smithers, BC V0J 2N0
(250) 847-2287

Tran-S-Port Honda Powerhouse
8708-100th Ave.
Fort St. John, BC V1J 1X1
(250) 785-1293
(800) 663-8311
www.transporthonda.com

Vernon Motorsports Ltd.
6381 Hwy. 97 N.
Vernon, BC V1B 3R4
(250) 545-5381
www.vernonmotorsports.com

V. I. Honda Powerhouse
1809 Bowen Rd.
Nanaimo, BC V9S 1H1
(250) 754-6638
www.vihonda.ca

Williams Lake Honda
1065 S. Lakeside Dr.
Williams Lake, BC V2G 3A7
(250) 392-2300

KAWASAKI
Oregon
Action Motorsports-Oregon City
1301 Main St.
Oregon City, OR 97045
(503) 657-4654
www.factoryms.com

Baker Valley Marine
3395 10th St.
Baker City, OR 97814
(541) 523-0014

Coos ATV and Cycle Center, Inc.
2273 N. Bayshore Dr.
North Bend, OR 97420
(541) 269-6686
www.coosatvandcycle.net

Cycle Sports of Eugene
555 River Rd.
Eugene, OR 97404
(541) 607-9000
www.cyclesports.net

Cycle Sports-Salem
4764 Portland Rd.
Salem, OR 97305
(503) 390-9000
www.cyclesports.net

Edge Performance Sports
1625 N. Oregon
Ontario, OR 97914
(541) 889-4099
www.edgeperformancesports.com

Factory Motor Sports
1301 Main St.
Oregon City, OR 97045
(503) 607-2200
www.factoryms.com

Fun Country, Inc.
1318 W. 2nd
The Dalles, OR 97058
(503) 298-1161
www.funcountrypowersports.com

Hobi Kawasaki
1810 NE Stephens St.
Roseburg, OR 97470
(541) 673-7567

Kawasaki Honda of Medford
3735 Crater Lake Hwy.
Medford, OR 97504
(541) 772-5550
www.itsyourroad.com

Medford Powersports
6006 Crater Lake Ave.
Central Point, OR 97502
(541) 826-9148
www.medfordpowersports.com

Moto Sport Hillsboro
809 NE 28th Ave.
Hillsboro, OR 97124
(503) 648-4555
www.hillsboromotorcycles.com

Portland Motorcycle Company
10652 NE Holman St.
Portland, OR 97220
(503) 258-8888
www.portlandmotorcycle.com

Power Motorsports
345 SW Sublimity Blvd.
Sublimity, OR 97385
(503) 769-8888
www.poweryamaha.com

Stateline Kawasaki
84853 Hwy. 11
Milton Freewater, OR 97862
(541) 938-0343

Taylor Kawasaki
2140 N. Pacific Hwy.
Woodburn, OR 97071
(503) 981-1813

Tread & Track Motorsports
3500 Eberlein Ave.
Klamath Falls, OR 97603
(541) 880-5577

Washington
Bellevue Kawasaki
14004 NE 20th
Bellevue, WA 98007
(425) 641-5040
www.bellevuekawasakiwa.com

Cliff's Cycle Center
1200 Charleston Beach Rd.
Bremerton, WA 98312
(360) 377-5568
www.cliffscyclecenter.com

Cycle Barn Smokey Point Kawasaki
3131 Smokey Point Dr., # 1
Arlington, WA 98223
(360) 530-7800
www.cyclebarn.com

Enumclaw Kawasaki Suzuki Yamaha
408 Roosevelt Ave.
Enumclaw, WA 98022
(360) 825-4502
www.enumclawsuzuki.com

Experience Powersports
1014 W. Marina Dr.
Moses Lake, WA 98837
(509) 765-1925
www.experiencepowersports.com

Kent Kawasaki
821 Central Ave. S.
Kent, WA 98032
(253) 852-8670
www.valleyscooters.net

Knotts Power Sports Kawasaki
1504 Fruitvale Blvd.
Yakima, WA 98902
(509) 965-9889

Lake City Powersports
12048 Lake City Way NE
Seattle, WA 98125-5332
(206) 364-1372
www.lakecitypowersports.com

Lynnwood Cycle Barn
5711 188th St. SW
Lynnwood, WA 98037
(425) 774-3538
www.cyclebarn.com

Mac's Cycle
700 Bridge St.
Clarkston, WA 99403
(509) 758-5343
www.macscycle.com

Mt. Baker Moto-Sports
3950 Home Rd.
Bellingham, WA 98226
(360) 676-4096
www.mtbakermoto.com

Paulson's Motorsports
4402 6th Ave. SE
Lacey, WA 98503
(360) 456-8444
www.paulsonsmotorsports.com

Port Angeles Power Equipment
2624 E. Hwy. 101
Port Angeles, WA 98362
(360) 452-4652
www.papowerequipment.com

Pro Caliber's Motorsports-Longview
1020 Industrial Way
Longview, WA 98632-1039
(360) 636-1220
www.procaliberlongview.com

Pro Caliber Motorsports-Vancouver
10703 NE 4th Plain Blvd.
Vancouver WA 98662
(866) 796-5020
www.procalibervancouver.com

Puyallup Power Sports Kawasaki
500 River Rd.
Puyallup, WA 98371
(253) 864-0964

Renton Motorcycles RMC
3701 E. Valley Rd.
Renton, WA 98057
(425) 226-4320
www.rentonmotorcycles.com

Roundy Kawasaki
11008 N. Newport Hwy.
Spokane, WA 99218
(509) 467-5128
www.roundyskawasaki.com

Shumate Motorsports
3305 W. 19th Ave.
Kennewick, WA 99338
(509) 735-9775
www.shumatemotorsports.com

Skagit Powersports
1645 Walton Dr.
Burlington, WA 98233
(360) 757-7999
www.skagitpowersports.com

Skagit Valley Kawasaki
2330 Freeway Dr.
Mount Vernon, WA 98273
(360) 848-6384
www.skagitvalleypolaris.com

Waldron Arctic Cat Kawasaki
1470 19th Ave. NW
Issaquah, WA 98027
(425) 391-4627
www.waldronarctic.com

Westside Motorsports
4201 S. Grove Rd.
Spokane, WA 99224
(509) 747-1862
www.westsideracing.com

British Columbia
All Seasons Motor Sports
333 Van Horne St. S.
Cranbrook, BC V1C 1Z6
(250) 426-4009

Banngate Holdings
2903-43rd Ave.
Vernon, BC V1T 3L4
(250) 542-0418

Burnaby Kawasaki
7771 Edmonds St.
Burnaby, BC V3N 1B9
(604) 525-9393
www.burnabykawasaki.com

The Cat Shack
4884 N. Access Rd.
Chetwynd, BC V0C 1J0
(250) 788-9558

Clearbrook Cycles
7869 Enterprise Dr.
Chilliwack, BC V2R 4W2
(604) 703-0221

Cycle Enterprises
5905 Gauthier Rd.
Prince George, BC V2N 5M4
(250) 964-9091
www.cyclenorth.com

Duncan Motorsports
1063 Canada Ave.
Duncan, BC V9L 3R7
(250) 746-7148

Fast Trax Motor Sports
8520 100th St.
Fort St-John, BC V1J 3W8
(250) 787-1930

Four Seasons Motorsports
3-4216 25th Ave.
Vernon, BC V1T 1P4
(250) 549-3730
www.vernonpolaris.com

Full Throttle Motorsport
1415 Hwy. 97 N.
Quesnel, BC V2J 5E7
(250) 991-7933
www.fullthrottle.ca

Holeshot Motorsports
8867-201 St.
Langley, BC V2Y 0C8
(604) 882-3800
www.holeshotracing.ca

Kenco Motorcycle & Salvage
2575 Sooke River Rd.
Sooke, BC V9Z 0X8
(250) 642-3924
www.kencomotorcycle.com

Leading Edge Motorsports
701 Tagish St.
Kamloops, BC V2H 1B6
(250) 372-8534
www.leadingedgeonline.ca

Maple Ridge Motorsports
20430 Lougheed Hwy.
Maple Ridge, BC V2X 2P8
(604) 465-0441
www.mapleridgemotorsports.com

Neid Entreprises
4921-A Keith Ave.
Terrace, BC V8G 1K7
(250) 635-3478
www.neidenterprises.com
No Limits Motorsports
4-38921 Progress Way
Squamish, BC V8B 1K6
(604) 815-4444
www.nolimitsmotorsports.com

Richmond Kawasaki
21320 Westminster Hwy.
Richmond, BC V6V 1B6
(604) 276-8513
www.richmondmotorsport.com

S. G. Power Products
730 Hillside Ave.
Victoria, BC V8T 1Z4
(250) 382-8291
www.sgpower.com

Spectra Power Sport
770 N. Broadway Ave.
Williams Lake, BC V2G 2V7
(250) 392-3201

Spunky's Motorcycle Shop
969 Fairdowne Rd.
Parksville, BC V9P 2G3
(250) 248-8828
www.spunkysmc.com

Valley Moto Sport
100-1195 Industrial Rd.
Kelowna, BC V1Z 1G4
(250) 769-3313

www.valleymotosport.com

Valley Moto Sport Kelowna
1075 McCurdy Rd.
Kelowna, BC V1X 2P9
(250) 765-3400

Xcalibur Enterprises
1200 Trans Canada Hwy.
Salmon Arm, BC V1E 4P4
(250) 803-0111
www.xcaliburent.ca

KTM
Oregon
Bronson Polaris
10508 N. McAlister
Lagrande, OR 97850
(541) 963-9027

Cascade Motorsports
20445 Cady Way
Bend, OR 97701
(541) 389-0088
www.cascademotorsports.net

Edge Performance Sports
1625 N. Oregon
Ontario, OR 97914
(541) 889-4099
www.edgeperformancesports.com

G & G Cycle, LLC
2809 SW Pacific Blvd.
Albany, OR 97321
(541) 926-9320
www.gngktm.com

Husqvarna KTM of Gresham
635 E. Powell Blvd.
Gresham, OR 97030
(503) 667-3970
www.ktmnorthwest.com

KTM Country, Inc.
3825 W. 11th, Ste. A
Eugene, OR 97402
(541) 688-5881

L&D Race Tech, Inc.
1035 SE Marlin Ave.
Warrenton, OR 97146
(503) 861-2636

Moto Sport Hillsboro
809 NE 28th Ave.
Hillsboro, OR 97124
(503) 648-4555
www.hillsboromotorcycles.com

Oregon Motorcycle Adventures KTM
3844 S. Pacific Hwy.
Medford, OR 97501
(541) 773-7433
www.oma-ktm.com

Power Motorsports
345 SW Sublimity Blvd.
Sublimity, OR 97385
(503) 769-8888
www.poweryamaha.com

Washington
Cliff's Cycle Center
1200 Charleston Beach Rd. W.
Bremerton, WA 98312
(360) 377-5568
www.cliffscyclecenter.com

Condotta's Motorsports Central
3013 G. South Center Rd.
Wenatchee, WA 98801
(509) 665-6686
www.condottas.com

Dave Russell's European Motorcycles
12611 E. Sprague, #1
Spokane, WA 99216
(509) 926-6798

Experience Powersports
12268 N. Frontage Rd.
Moses Lake, WA 98837
(509) 765-1925
www.experiencepowersports.com

Hinshaw's Motorcycle Store
1611 W. Valley Hwy. S.
Auburn, WA 98001
(253) 939-7164
www.hinshawsmotorcyclestore.com

I-90 Motorsports
200 NE Gilman Blvd.
Issaquah, WA 98027
(425) 391-4490
www.i-90motorsports.com

Lynnwood Motoplex
17900 Hwy. 99
Lynnwood, WA 98037
(425) 774-0505
www.motoplex.net

Mt. Baker Moto-Sports, LLC
3950 Home Rd.
Bellingham, WA 98226
(360) 676-4096
www.mtbakermoto.com

NW European Cycles
14106 Pacific Ave.
Tacoma, WA 98444
(253) 531-4688

Owen's Cycle
1707 N. 1st St.
Yakima, WA 98901
(509) 575-1916
www.owenscycleinc.com

Port Angeles Power Equipment
2624 E. Hwy. 101
Port Angeles, WA 98362
(360) 452-4652
www.papowerequipment.com

Pro Caliber's Motorsports-Longview
1020 Industrial Way
Longview, WA 98632
(360) 636-1220
www.procaliberlongview.com

Pro Caliber Motorsports-Vancouver
10703 NE 4th Plain Blvd.
Vancouver, WA 98662
(360) 892-3030
www.procalibervancouver.com

Skagit Powersports
1645 Walton Dr.
Burlington, WA 98233
(360) 757-7999
www.skagitpowersports.com

Tri-Cities Cycle Supply
504 E. Columbia Dr.
Kennewick, WA 99336
(509) 582-6718

Webb Powersports, Inc.
907 Hibbs Rd.
Ellensburg, WA 98926
(509) 933-1737
www.webbpowersports.com

Yamaha Motorsports of Olympia
6807 Martin Way E.
Olympia, WA 98516
(360) 438-2997

British Columbia
Action Motorcycles Inc.
1234 Esquimault Rd.
Victoria, BC V9A 3N8
(250) 386-8364
www.action-motorcycles.com

Big Top Powersports
7869 Enterprise Dr.
Chilliwack, BC V2R 4H2
(604) 703-0221
www.bigtoppowersports.com

Forest Power Sports Ltd.
1001 Great St.
Prince George, BC V2N 2K8
(250) 563-1021
www.forestpowersports.com

Holeshot Motor Sports
8867-201 St.
Langley, BC V2Y 0C8
(604) 533-4426
www.holeshotracing.ca

Main Jet Motorsports
111 McDonald Dr.
Nelson, BC V1L 6B9
(250) 352-3191
www.mainjet.ca

Maple Ridge Motorsports Ltd.
20430 Lougheed Hwy.
Maple Ridge, BC V2X 2P8
(604) 465-0441
www.mapleridgemotorsports.com

No Limits Motorsports
4-38921 Progress Way
Squamish, BC V0N 3G0
(604) 815-4444
www.nolimitsmotorsports.com

Performance All Terrain & Rentals Ltd.
867 Adler Ave.
100 Mile House, BC V0K 2E0
(250) 395-2550
www.performanceallterrain.com

RTR Performance
2051 Trans Canada E.
Kamloops, BC V2C 4A5
(250) 374-3141
www.rtrperformance.com

Spunky's Motorcycle Shop, Ltd.
969 Fairdowne Rd.
Parksville, BC V9P 2T4
(250) 248-8828
www.spunkysmc.com

Valley Moto Sport
1195 Industrial Rd.
Kelowna, BC V1Z 1G4
(250) 769-3313
www.valleymotosport.com

Vernon Motorsports Ltd.
6381 Hwy. 97 N.
Vernon, BC V1B 3R4
(250) 545-5381
www.vernonmotorsports.com

SUZUKI
Oregon
AC Power Sports
10701 Walton Rd.
La Grande, OR 97850
(541) 663-1111
www.acpowersports.com

Action Motorsports-Oregon City
1301 Main St.
Oregon City, OR 97045
(503) 657-4654
www.factoryms.com

Beaverton Honda
10380 SW Cascade Ave.
Portland, OR 97223
(503) 684-6600
www.beavertonmotorcycles.com

Columbia River Honda Suzuki
58245 Columbia River Hwy.
Saint Helens, OR 97051
(503) 397-3502
www.columbiarivermoto-sports.com

Coos ATV and Cycle Center, Inc.
2273 N. Bayshore Dr.
North Bend, OR 97420
(541) 269-6686
www.coosatvandcycle.net

Cycle Country Honda Suzuki
1230 Broadway St. NE
Salem, OR 97301
(503) 378-0532
www.cyclecountry.net

Edge Performance Sports
1625 N. Oregon
Ontario, OR 97914
(541) 889-4099
www.edgeperformancesports.com

Factory Motor Sports
1301 Main St.
Oregon City, OR 97045
(503) 607-2200
www.factoryms.com

Fun Country Power Sports
1318 W. 2nd
The Dalles, OR 97058
(541) 298-1161
www.funcountrypowersports.com

Grants Pass Suzuki
1831 Rogue River Hwy.
Grants Pass, OR 97527
(541) 476-3301
www.grantspasssuzuki.com

Medford Power Sports
6006 Crater Lake Ave.
Central Point, OR 97502
(541) 826-9148
www.medfordpowersports.com

Moto Sport Hillsboro
809 NE 28th Ave.
Hillsboro, OR 97124
(503) 648-4555
www.hillsboromotorcycles.com

Oregon Power Sports
2260 SE Court
Pendleton, OR 97801
(541) 278-5123

Oregon Trail Yamaha Suzuki
1905 Auburn Ave.
Baker City, OR 97814
(541) 523-3500

Portland Motorcycle Company
10652 NE Holman St.
Portland, OR 97220-1202
(503) 258-8888
www.portlandmotorcycle.com

Pro Caliber Motorsports of Bend
Oregon
3500 N. Hwy. 97
Bend, OR 97701
(866) 949-8606
www.procaliberbend.com

Ramsey-Waite, Co.
4258 Franklin Blvd.
Eugene, OR 97403
(541) 726-7625
www.ramseywaite.com

Roseburg Power Sports
1305 W. Central Ave.
Sutherlin, OR 97479
(541) 672-6065

Tread & Track Motorsports
3500 Eberlein Ave.
Klamath Falls, OR 97603
(541) 880-5577

Washington
Adventure Motorsports
17321 Tye St. SE, #A
Monroe, WA 98272
(360) 805-5550
www.adventuremotorsports.net

Aurora Suzuki
7409 Aurora Ave. N.
Seattle, WA 98103
(206) 783-2323
www.aurora-suzuki.com

Cliff's Cycle Center
1200 Charleston Beach Rd.
Bremerton, WA 98312
(360) 377-5568
www.cliffscyclecenter.com

D & B Power Sports of Spokane
1521 N. Argonne Rd.
Spokane Valley, WA 99212
(509) 535-4116

Desert Valley Power Sports
325 Merlot Dr.
Prosser, WA 99350
(509) 786-0260
www.desertvalleypowersports.com

Eastside Moto Sports
13029 NE 20th St.
Bellevue, WA 98005
(425) 882-4300
www.eastsidemotosports.com

Enumclaw Kawasaki Suzuki Yamaha
408 Roosevelt Ave.
Enumclaw, WA 98022
(360) 825-4502
www.enumclawsuzuki.com

Everett Powersports
215 SW Everett Mall Way
Everett, WA 98204
(425) 347-4545
www.everettpowersports.com

Experience Powersports
1014 W. Marina Dr.
Moses Lake, WA 98837
(509) 765-1925
www.experiencepowersports.com

Hinshaw's Motorcycle Store
1611 W. Valley Hwy.
Auburn, WA 98001
(253) 939-7164
www.hinshawsmotorcyclestore.com

Lynnwood Cycle Barn
5711 188th St. SW
Lynnwood, WA 98037
(425) 774-3538
www.cyclebarn.com

Mac's Cycle
700 Bridge St.
Clarkston, WA 99403-1899
(509) 758-5343
www.macscycle.com

Mt. Baker Moto-Sports
3950 Home Rd.
Bellingham, WA 98226
(360) 676-4096
www.mtbakermoto.com

Owen's Cycle
1707 N. 1st St.
Yakima, WA 98901-1705
(509) 575-1916
www.owenscycleinc.com

Paulson's Motorsports
4402 6th Ave. SE
Lacey, WA 98503
(360) 456-8444
www.paulsonsmotorsports.com

Port Angeles Power Equipment
2624 E. Hwy. 101
Port Angeles, WA 98362
(360) 452-4652
www.papowerequipment.com

Powersports Northwest
300 S. Tower Ave.
Centralia, WA 98531
(360) 736-0166
www.powersportsnorthwest.com

Pro Caliber's Longview Motorsports
1020 Industrial Way
Longview, WA 98632-1039
(360) 636-1220
www.procaliberlongview.com

Pro Caliber Motorsports-Vancouver
10703 NE 4th Plain Blvd.
Vancouver, WA 98662
(866) 796-5020
www.procalibervancouver.com

Renton Motorcycles RMC
3701 E. Valley Rd.
Renton, WA 98057
(425) 226-4320
www.rentonmotorcycles.com

Shumate Motorsports
3305 W. 19th Ave.
Kennewick, WA 99338
(509) 735-9775
www.shumatemotorsports.com

Skagit Powersports
1645 Walton Dr.
Burlington, WA 98233-4611
(360) 757-7999
www.skagitpowersports.com

Smokey Point Cycle Barn
3131 Smokey Point Dr., Ste. A1
Arlington, WA 98223
(360) 530-7800
www.smokeypointcyclebarn.com

Spokane Powersports
6521 N. Division St.
Spokane, WA 99208-3937
(509) 467-8185
www.spokanepowersports.com

Tacoma Motorsports
4701 S. Center St.
Tacoma, WA 98409
(253) 564-8678
www.tacomamotorsports.com

British Columbia
Action Motorcycles
1234 Esquimalt Rd.
Victoria, BC V9A 3N8
(250) 386-8364
www.actionsuzuki.ca

Bayshore Services Ltd.
2602 Nicola Ave., Box 1729
Merritt, BC V1K 1B8
(250) 378-2234

Big Top Powersports
7869 Enterprise Dr.
Chilliwack, BC V2R 4H2
(604) 703-0221
www.bigtopsuzuki.com

Breaker's Marine Ltd.
3620 3rd Ave.
Port Alberni, BC V9Y 4E8
(250) 724-3346
www.breakerssuzuki.com

Campbell River Boatland
2625 N. Island Hwy.
Campbell River, BC V9W 2H9
(250) 286-0752
www.campbellriverboatland.com

C. R. Cycle Ltd.
22674 Dewdney Trunk Rd.
Maple Ridge, BC V2X 3J9
(604) 467-2344
www.crcycle.com

Four Seasons Motor Sports Ltd.
4216 25th Ave., Unit 3
Vernon, BC V1T 1P4
(250) 549-3730
www.4seasonssuzuki.com

Guy's Cycle Works
4473 Franklin Ave.
Powell River, BC V8A 5B5
(604) 485-8228
www.guyscycleworks.com

Harbour City Motorsport
1613 Bowen Rd.
Nanaimo, BC V9S 1G5
(250) 754-3345
www.harbourcitymotorsport.com

Holeshot Racing Ltd.
8867 210st St.
Langley, BC V2Y 0C8
(604) 882-3800
www.holeshotracing.ca

Innovative Motorsports Ltd.
727 Stremel Rd., Unit 12
Kelowna, BC V1X 5E6
(250) 765-9457
www.innovativemotorsportskelowna
.ca

Jim Pattison Suzuki-Burnaby
5400 Kingsway Ave.
Burnaby, BC V5H 2E9
(604) 437-8511
www.jpsuzuki.com

Mile Zero Motorsports Ltd.
13136 Thomas Rd., Unit 3
Ladysmith, BC V9G 1L9
(250) 245-5414
www.themilezero.com

Modern Motorcycling Ltd.
2816 Commercial Dr.
Vancouver, BC V5N 4C6
(604) 876-0182
www.modernmotorcycling.com

North Shore Suzuki Yamaha
1395 Main St.
North Vancouver, BC V7J1C4
(604) 986-1581
www.northshoresuzukiyamaha.com

NR Motors Ltd.
805 1st Ave.
Prince George, BC V2L 2Y4
(250) 563-8891
www.nrmotors.ca

Orca Bay Suzuki
2850 Shaughessy St., Unit 8100
Port Coquitlam, BC V3C 6K5
(604) 464-3330
www.suzukivancouver.com

Rivercity Cycle Ltd.
1794 Kelly Douglas Rd.
Kamloops, BC V2C 5S4
(250) 377-4320
www.rivercitysuzuki.ca

S & V Motorcycle World
10607 King George Hwy.
Surrey, BC V3T 2X3
(604) 582-9253
www.motorcycleworldsuzuki.ca

Savage Cycles
141-2956 Westshore Pkwy.
Victoria, BC V9B-0B2
(250) 475-8885
www.savagecycles.ca

Shuswap Xtreme Recreation
1100 4th Ave. SW
Salmon Arm, BC V1E 1T1
(250) 832-3883
www.shuswapxtreme.com

Valley Moto Sport Ltd.
1195 Industrial Rd., Unit 100
Kelowna, BC V1Z 1G4
(250) 769-3313
www.vmssuzuki.com

TRIUMPH
Oregon
Cascade Moto Classics
13705 SW Farmington Rd.
Beaverton, OR 97005
(503) 574-3353
www.cascademoto.com

Cycle Parts
1110 Ocean St.
Eugene, OR 97402
(541) 343.8949
www.time-to-ride.com

Hansen's BMW Triumph Ducati
    Motorcycles LLC
3598 S. Pacific Hwy.
Medford, OR 97501
(541) 535-3342
www.hansensmc.com

Portland Motorcycle Co.
10652 NE Holman St.
Portland, OR 97220
(503) 258-8888
www.portlandmotorcycle.com

Washington
Champion Cycle
615 W. Holly St.
Bellingham, WA 98225
(360) 734-1320
www.callatg.com/~cycle

Empire Cycle & Power Sports
7807 E. Sprague Ave.
Spokane Valley, WA 99212
(509) 892-6368
www.empire-cycle.com

I-90 Motorsports
200 NE Gilman Blvd.
Issaquah, WA 98027
(425) 391-4490
www.i-90motorsports.com

Lakewood Motorsports
12007 Pacific Hwy. SW
Lakewood, WA 98499
(253) 581-0812

Lynnwood Cycle Barn
5711 188th St. SW
Lynnwood, WA 98037
(425) 774-3538
www.cyclebarn.com

Thunder Alley Triumph
6200 Clearwater
Kennewick, WA 99336
(509) 783-2325
www.thunderalleyvictory.com

British Columbia
British Italian Motorcycles
1764 Powell St.
Vancouver, BC V5L 1H7
(604) 253-1117
www.motorcyclesource.com

Savage Cycles
141-2956 Westshore Pkwy.
Victoria, BC V9B 0B2
(250) 475-8885
www.savagecycles.ca

Southwest Motorrad
3575 Alcan Rd.
Kelowna, BC V1X 7R3
(250) 807-2697
www.southwestmotorrad.com

Western Powersports
111-20551 #10 Hwy.
Langley, BC V3A 5E8
(604) 530-9788
(888) 819-8188
www.westernpowersports.com

VICTORY
Oregon
Cascade Motorsports
20445 Cady Way
Bend, OR 97701
(541) 389-0088
www.cascademotorsports.net

Mt. Hood Polaris
27850 SE Hwy. 212
Boring, OR 97009
(503) 663-3544

Oregon's Best Motorsports
870 Redwood Hwy.
Grants Pass, OR 97527
(541) 955-6456

Polaris of Portland
815 SE Oak St.
Portland, OR 97214
(503) 872-0000

Stateline Polaris Kawasaki
84853 Hwy. 11
Milton Freewater, OR 97862
(541) 938-5309

Washington
Allsport Polaris Honda
19505 E. Broadway Ave.
Liberty Lake, WA 99016
(509) 926-5044

Hinshaw's Motorcycle Store
1611 W. Valley Hwy. S.
Auburn, WA 98001
(253) 939-7164
www.hinshawsmotorcyclestore.com

Skagit Valley Polaris Kawasaki
2330 Freeway Dr.
Mount Vernon, WA 98273
(360) 848-6384
www.skagitvalleypolaris.com

British Columbia
Cycle North Enterprises Ltd.
780 3rd Ave.
Prince George, BC V2L 3C5
(250) 563-5091
www.cyclenorth.com

Schultz Motorsports Inc.
1455 Iron Mask Rd.
Kamloops, BC V1S 1C8
(250) 828-2200
www.schultzmotorsports.com

Sea to Sky Motorsports Inc.
8860 201 St., Unit #105
Langley, BC V2Y 0C8
(604) 888-1400
www.seatoskymotorsport.com

M & M Performance
2890 Hwy. 97 N.
Kelowna, BC V1X 6W7
(250) 491-4800
www.mmperformance.com

YAMAHA
Oregon
Action Motorsports-Oregon City
1301 Main St.
Oregon City, OR 97045
(503) 657-4654
www.factoryms.com

Bay Area Yamaha
1397 Sherman Ave.
North Bend, OR 97459
(541) 756-1278
www.bayareayamaha.com

Beaverton Honda
10380 SW Cascade Ave.
Portland, OR 97223
(503) 684-6600
www.beavertonmotorcycles.com

Cottage Grove Yamaha
120 Palmer Ave.
Cottage Grove, OR 97424
(541) 942-3335

Cycle Sports-Eugene
555 River Rd.
Eugene, OR 97402
(541) 607-9000
www.cyclesports.net

Cycle Sports-Salem
4764 Portland Rd.
Salem, OR 97305
(503) 390-9000
www.cyclesports.net

Cycletown
2200 N. Hwy 395
Hermiston, OR 97838
(541) 567-8919
www.hondayamahacycletown.com

Factory Motor Sports
1301 Main St.
Oregon City, OR 97045
(503) 607-2200
www.factoryms.com

Florence Yamaha
2130 Hwy. 126
Florence, OR 97439
(541) 997-1157

Medford Power Sports
6006 Crater Lake Ave.
Central Point, OR 97502
(541) 826-9148
www.medfordpowersports.com

Mid-Columbia Marine & Motorsports
3335 W. Cascade Ave.
Hood River, OR 97031
(541) 386-2477
www.mcmyamaha.com

Naumes' Oregon Motorsports
2233 S. Pacific Hwy.
Medford, OR 97501
(541) 772-6223
www.oregonmotorsports.com

Oregon Trail Yamaha Suzuki
1925 Auburn Ave.
Baker City, OR 97814
(541) 523-3500

Power Motorsports
345 SW Sublimity Blvd.
Sublimity, OR 97385
(503) 769-8888
www.poweryamaha.com

Pro Caliber Motorsports-Bend
3500 N. Hwy. 97
Bend, OR 97701
(866) 949-8606
www.procaliberbend.com

Ramsey-Waite, Co.
4258 Franklin Blvd.
Eugene, OR 97403
(541) 726-7625
www.ramseywaite.com

Roseburg Power Sports
1305 W. Central Ave.
Sutherlin, OR 97479
(541) 672-6065

Tread & Track Motorsports
3500 Eberlein Ave.
Klamath Falls, OR 97603
(541) 880-5577

Yamaha Sports Plaza
22455 NE Halsey St.
Fairview, OR 97024
(503) 669-2000
www.yamahasportsplaza.com

Washington
Adventure Motorsports
17321 Tye St. SE, #A
Monroe, WA 98272
(360) 805-5550
www.adventuremotorsports.net

Bellevue Kawasaki
14004 NE 20th St.
Bellevue, WA 98007
(425) 641-5040
www.bellevuekawasakiwa.com

The Brothers Powersports
5205 1st St.
Bremerton, WA 98312
(360) 479-6943
www.brotherspowersports.com

Colville Motor Sports Inc.
165 W. Birch Ave.
Colville, WA 99114
(509) 684-5540
www.colvillemotorsports.com

Condotta's Motorsports Central
3013 GS Center Rd.
Wenatchee, WA 98801
(509) 665-6686
www.condottas.com

Desert Valley Power Sports
325 Merlot Dr.
Prosser, WA 99350
(509) 786-0260
www.desertvalleypowersports.com

Eastside Moto Sports
13029 NE 20th St.
Bellevue, WA 98005
(425) 882-4300
www.eastsidemotosports.com

Experience Powersports
1014 W. Marina Dr.
Moses Lake, WA 98837
(509) 765-1925
www.experiencepowersports.com

I-90 Motorsports
200 NE Gilman Blvd.
Issaquah, WA 98027-2902
(425) 391-4490
www.i-90motorsports.com

Lakewood Motorsports
12007 Pacific Hwy. SW
Lakewood, WA 98499
(253) 581-0812
www.lakewoodmotorsports.com

Lynnwood Motoplex
17900 Hwy. 99
Lynnwood, WA 98037
(425) 774-0505
www.motoplex.net

Owen's Cycle
1707 N. 1st St.
Yakima, WA 98901-1705
(509) 575-1916
www.owenscycleinc.com

Pacific Marine & Powersports
2730 Simpson Ave.
Hoquiam, WA 98550
(360) 532-0464

Port Angeles Power Equipment
2624 E. Hwy. 101
Port Angeles, WA 98362
(360) 452-4652
www.papowerequipment.com

Powersports Northwest
300 S. Tower Ave.
Centralia, WA 98531
(360) 736-0166
www.powersportsnorthwest.com

Pro Caliber's Motorsports-Longview
1020 Industrial Way
Longview, WA 98632-1039
(360) 636-1220
www.procaliberlongview.com

Pro Caliber Motorsports-Vancouver
10703 NE 4th Plain Blvd.
Vancouver, WA 98662
(866) 796-5020
www.procalibervancouver.com

Rainier Honda Yamaha
16002 Pacific Ave. S.
Spanaway, WA 98387
(253) 537-0831
www.tacomamotorsports.com

Renton Motorcycles RMC
3701 E. Valley Rd.
Renton, WA 98057
(425) 226-4320
www.rentonmotorcycles.com

Ride Motorsports
19035 Woodinville-Snohomish Rd. NE
Woodinville, WA 98072
(425) 487-3881
www.ridemotorsports.com

Skagit Powersports
1645 Walton Dr.
Burlington, WA 98233-4611
(360) 757-7999
www.skagitpowersports.com

Smokey Point Cycle Barn
3131 Smokey Point Dr., Ste. A1
Arlington, WA 98223
(360) 530-7800
www.smokeypointcyclebarn.com

South Seattle Yamaha Sports Plaza
33003 Pacific Hwy. S.
Federal Way, WA 98003
(253) 838-3290

SportLand Yamaha Inc.
4402 Bullfrog Rd.
Cle Elum, WA 98922
(509) 649-2259
www.sportlandyamaha.com

Tacoma Motorsports
4701 S. Center St.
Tacoma, WA 98409
(253) 564-8678
www.tacomamotorsports.com

Westside Motorsports
4201 S. Grove Rd.
Spokane, WA 99224
(509) 747-1862
www.westsideracing.com

Yamaha Country Inc.
428 E. Columbia Dr.
Kennewick, WA 90336
(509) 586-4191

Yamaha Motorsports of Olympia
6807 Martin Way E.
Olympia, WA 98516
(360) 438-2997
www.motorsportsofolympia.com

British Columbia
Action Motorcycles
1234 Esquimalt Rd.
Victoria, BC V9A 3N8
(250) 386-8364
www.action-motorcycles.com

Alpine Motorsport
2750-10th Ave. SW
Salmon Arm, BC V1E 4N3
(250) 804-4334
www.alpinemotorsport.ca

Barrett Boat & Trailer Sales Ltd.
1470 Hwy. 3B
Fruitvale, BC V0G 1L0
(250) 367-6216
www.barrettshondayamaha.com

Clearbrook Yamaha
101-31324 Peardonville Rd.
Abbotsford, BC V2T 6K8
(604) 854-3440

Coast Line Power Sports
1870 Cosyan Way, Box 2217
Sechelt, BC V0N 3A0
(604) 885-4616

Courtenay Motorsports Center
4883 N. Island Hwy.
Courtenay, BC V9N 5Y9
(250) 338-1415
www.courtenay-motorsports.com

Daytona Motorsports
13479 King George Hwy.
Surrey, BC V3T 2T8
(604) 588-4988

Daytona Motorsports
1768 E. Hastings St.
Vancouver, BC V5L 1S9
(604) 251-1212

Diamond Head Yamaha
147-39002 Discovery Way
Squamish, BC V8B 0E5
(604) 892-9700
www.diamondheadyamaha.com

Duncan Motorcycle Sales Ltd.
1063 Canada Ave.
Duncan, BC V9L 1V2
(250) 746-7148
www.duncanmotorcycles.com

Eldorado Recreation Ltd.
1805 Cariboo Hwy. N.
Quesnel, BC V2J 3P2
(250) 992-5602
www.eldoradorec.ca

Fast Trax Motor Sports Ltd.
8520 100 St.
Fort St. John, BC V1J 3W8
(250) 787-1930

G. A. Checkpoint
3034 St. John's St.
Port Moody, BC V3H 2C5
(604) 461-3434
www.gacheckpoint.com

Ghostrider Motorsports
30 Shadow Rd.
Fernie, BC V0B 1M5
(250) 423-9251
www.ghostridermotorsports.ca

Harbour City Motorsport
1613 Bowen Rd.
Nanaimo, BC V9S 1G5
(250) 754-3345
www.harbourcitymotorsport.com

Kelowna Yamaha (Downtown)
2331a Enterprise Way
Kelowna, BC V1X 7E1
(250) 763-1010
www.kelownayamaha.ca

Kelowna Yamaha (Westside)
1-1515 Westgate Rd.
Kelowna, BC V1Z 3X4
(250) 769-1013
www.kelownayamaha.ca

Ken's Marine
4946 Greig Ave.
Terrace, BC V8G 1N4
(250) 635-2909
www.kensmarine.ca

North Shore Suzuki Yamaha
1395 Main St.
North Vancouver, BC V7J 1C4
(604) 986-1581
www.northshoresuzukiyamaha.com

Outdoor Adventures
121 Francois Lake Dr.
Burns Lake, BC V0J 1E0
(250) 692-3777

Pacific Yamaha BMW
21000 Westminster Hwy., Unit 1000
Richmond, BC V6V 2S9
(604) 276-2552
www.pacificyamahabmw.com

Peak Performance Motorsports
2001 Kootenay St. N.
Cranbrook, BC V1C 5M2
(250) 417-3310

Penticton Yamaha and Marine
124 South Beach Dr.
Penticton, BC V2A 3W3
(250) 492-8300

Playmor Power Products Ltd.
1043 Playmor Rd., Box 11
Crescent Valley, BC V0G 1H0
(250) 359-7111
www.playmorpower.com

Prince George Yamaha
1001 20th Ave.
Prince George, BC V2L 5K2
(250) 562-4151
www.princegeorgeyamaha.com

Rosk Yamaha
Lot 140 N. Mackenzie Ave.
Williams Lake, BC V2G 1N6
(250) 392-2528

Schultz Motorsports Inc.
1455 Iron Mask Rd.
Kamloops, BC V1S 1C8
(250) 828-2200
www.schultzmotorsports.com

South Cariboo Motor Sports Ltd.
752 Alpine Way
100 Mile House, BC V0K 2E0
(250) 395-2366

Spunky's Motorcycle Shop
969 Fairdowne Rd.
Parksville, BC V9P 2G3
(250) 248-8828
www.spunkysmc.com

Valley Yamaha
Unit 2, 44310 Yale Rd. W.
Chilliwack, BC V2R 4H1
(604) 795-4403
www.valleyyamaha.ca

Vernon Motorsports
6381 Hwy. 97 N.
Vernon, BC V1B 3R4
(250) 545-5381
www.vernonmotorsports.com

Western Powersports
Unit 111-20551, #10 Hwy.
Langley, BC V3A 5E8
(604) 530-9788
www.westernpowersports.com

INDEX

ABOUT THE AUTHORS

Christy Karras is the author or co-author of four books, including *More than Petticoats: Remarkable Utah Women* and *Scenic Driving: Utah.* She has written for a wide range of print and online publications and is a regular contributor to the *Seattle Times.* She has also been associate editor at *Wasatch Journal* magazine, an arts critic for the *Salt Lake Tribune,* and a general-assignment reporter for the Associated Press in Portland, Oregon, and Salt Lake City.

She lives in Seattle but would always rather be on the road. She hasn't followed through on her threat to buy a pink helmet and matching fringed suede chaps—yet.

Having a bit of the vagabond spirit, **Stephen Zusy** has lived in a long list of places including New York City, Denver, San Francisco, Tucson, and Salt Lake City. With a degree in business and a passion for photography, he has worked in real estate in New York, commercial photography in northern California, and as a photojournalist at the *Park Record* and the *Salt Lake Tribune* in Utah. He has done work for a diverse range of publications and news outlets including Getty Images, *Wasatch Journal* magazine, *Park City Magazine*, and *Entertainment Weekly*.

A motorcycle enthusiast since he was a child, he has ridden all manner of bikes over the years. There is no place he'd rather be than on a motorcycle, twisting back the throttle, searching for an endless series of perfectly banked curves. For now, home is Park City, Utah, but he's considering a move to a place where he can ride year-round.

Christy and Steve are also the authors of *Motorcycle Touring in the Southwest.* Contact them and learn more about their travels at www.roadwriters.com.

Travel Like a Pro

The Cheap Bastard's Guide® to
NEW YORK CITY
MORE THAN 1,000 **FREE** LISTINGS

100 BEST
Resorts of the Caribbean

OFF THE BEATEN PATH
VIRGINIA A GUIDE TO UNIQUE PLACES →

The Luxury Guide to
Walt Disney World® Resort
Second Edition
How to Get the Most Out of the
Best Disney Has to Offer

shifra stein's
day trips®
from kansas city
fifteenth edition

JOHN HOWELL S
NINTH EDITION
CHOOSE COSTA RIC
FOR **RETIREMENT**

FUN WITH THE FAMILY
Hundreds of Ideas for Day Trips WITH THE Kids
Connecticut

INSIDERS' GUIDE®
Florida Keys
and Key West

SCENIC DRIVING
COLORADO
STEWART M. GREEN
THIRD EDITION